☆ What Kind of Europe?

What Kind of Europe?

LOUKAS TSOUKALIS

OXFORD
UNIVERSITY PRESS

OXFORD

UNIVERSITY PRESS

Great Clarendon Street, Oxford OX2 6DP

Oxford University Press is a department of the University of Oxford.
It furthers the University's objective of excellence in research, scholarship,
and education by publishing worldwide in

Oxford New York

Auckland Bangkok Buenos Aires Cape Town Chennai
Dar es Salaam Delhi Hong Kong Istanbul Karachi Kolkata
Kuala Lumpur Madrid Melbourne Mexico City Mumbai Nairobi
São Paulo Shanghai Taipei Tokyo Toronto

Oxford is a registered trade mark of Oxford University Press
in the UK and in certain other countries

Published in the United States
by Oxford University Press Inc., New York

British Library Cataloguing in Publication Data
Data available

Library of Congress Cataloging in Publication Data
Data available

ISBN 0-19-926666-2

10 9 8 7 6 5 4 3 2 1

Typeset by Newgen Imaging Systems (P) Ltd., Chennai, India
Printed in Great Britain
on acid-free paper by
Biddles Ltd., Guildford & King's Lynn

For Maria

Contents

CONTENTS

☆ PART III. Conclusions

Preface

Starting from an analytical base, this book tries to explain and highlight some of the fundamental issues at stake in the further development of Europe as a regional economic and political entity, and the key choices associated with those issues. It goes beyond the narrow confines of a strictly academic work, seeking to engage the generally informed reader and thus contribute to the ongoing debate on the future of Europe. It is, perhaps, ambitious, but also consistent with its main premise that issues pertaining to the integration of Europe need to become more political.

It has taken more than a year to write this book, and many more years to distil the ideas contained in it. Ideas have been borrowed from different sources, and some of them may now be difficult to trace or recognize in their original form. I have drawn from long experience as academic and researcher in different countries, as well as from those shorter periods that I have spent in the private sector and in public policy-making, and indeed from the continuing and constantly enriching experience of trying to be an active citizen of Europe in the making.

The ideas contained in this book have been tested before many different audiences, ranging from students to practitioners, all over Europe and elsewhere. This book would have been impossible to write without the inspiration, information, and rich feedback I have received from a wide variety of people. Even in a peripatetic existence, some stopovers last longer than others. Athens, Oxford, London, Bruges, and Florence have been places where I have spent a good part of my life so far. I am grateful to all friends and colleagues for the privilege of learning from them.

I am especially grateful to Helen Wallace and William Wallace for their detailed comments and valuable advice on earlier drafts, and to Chris Hill, Nikos Koutsiaras, George Pagoulatos, and Xavier Prats for their critical comments and suggestions. I should like to thank Susan Woodward, André Sapir, and Panos Tsakloglou for their help on individual chapters, and Marta Arpio for her advice on legal matters. Dimitris Bourikos has provided valuable assistance in the collection of statistical data and the preparation of figures and tables, while Vivian Politou has done an excellent job in helping to keep many loose threads together.

PREFACE

I have had a long and fruitful collaboration with Oxford University Press. This time, Tim Barton, Dominic Byatt, and many others pulled out all the stops to combine high quality with remarkable speed of publication. They have done an excellent job and I should like to thank them for their efforts. Thanks are also due to Michael James for his highly efficient copy-editing.

The book is dedicated to Maria Logotheti, who has contributed in many more ways than one to the writing of it. I continue to owe a huge debt of gratitude to my parents, a small part of which I am now trying to repay through Christos and Panos. This is, I suppose, the good side of the inter-generational redistribution that social scientists often refer to.

March 2003   *Loukas Tsoukalis*

1

☆☆☆☆☆

What Kind of Europe?

Europe is changing fast, and if anything the pace of change is accelerating. Many things that would have been unthinkable ten or fifteen years ago are indeed happening, and the everyday lives of citizens are being directly affected. Since 1 January 2002 twelve countries of Europe have replaced their national currencies with the euro, also abandoning in the process any semblance of monetary sovereignty. Several others are considering doing the same, while some of their less fortunate fellow Europeans are simply reconciling themselves to the idea of a de facto euro standard for their domestic economies. Meanwhile, former communist countries of central and eastern Europe, a good number of them currently led by former communists born again as social democrats and now elected under the rules of 'bourgeois democracy', have been agitating to join the club in which their counterparts in western Europe have been slowly and painfully learning ways and means of sharing sovereignty and jointly managing their capitalist economies: a club officially known as the European Union (EU).

Societies that had been long accustomed to sending many of their young and dynamic members abroad in search of jobs and a better future, a tradition which has marked their literature and popular music, have in recent years been trying to adjust to waves of immigrants, often from faraway countries. Other societies with long histories of immigration and valiant efforts at multiculturalism are now experiencing a backlash from sizeable sections of their population which believe that the number of foreigners in their country has risen beyond the threshold of tolerance—and this has become a major political issue. Meanwhile, as the internal aspects of national security increasingly merge with the external, police officers and home ministry officials, representing the inner sanctum of the old sovereign state, are beginning to learn the rules of mutual recognition and burden sharing; a common European force of border guards may not be that far away.

Some changes are more palpable than others; some affect large numbers of people while others relate only to specific groups. A steadily growing number of Europeans make their living out of transnational cooperation/integration; in other words, Europe has become a profession, and usually a lucrative one. Many more benefit as consumers, producers, or citizens. But there are also those who simply do not understand or, worse, feel threatened by rapid change, the source of which appears to be located in distant places in Europe or further away. Being so distant, the precise location hardly matters, so the European merges with the global in the minds of those who consider themselves as powerless objects (and victims) of changes beyond their influence and comprehension. The number of losers, or imaginary losers, appears to be growing, and this is in turn translated into protest movements that challenge the established truth of European integration—and globalization.

Frontiers have come down, although the boundaries between societies remain significant. Having invented the nation-state, and the concept of sovereignty that goes with it, Europeans have been experimenting for more than 50 years with a new political and economic order for their continent in which sovereignty is no longer treated as an absolute concept, while transnational cooperation/integration has reached levels unknown in other parts of the world. This is being gradually extended to the whole of Europe, especially since the fall of the Soviet empire. Many aspects of the everyday life of European citizens now depend on decisions taken beyond their national borders.

The EU has served as the main instrument and catalyst for the establishment of this new European order. Surely, there are many other regional organizations: the spectrum from simple cooperation to full integration is densely populated by all kinds of organizations, governmental as well as non-governmental, with universal or limited membership, covering a very wide range of activities. They have all contributed in different degrees to the so-called process of Europeanization marked by intense cooperation and close interpenetration of societies, markets, and governments: a process also characterized by mutual influence between European and national institutions. At the same time, they have contributed to the slow emergence of a regional European identity, albeit apparently still limited to representatives of national elites. Yet, in this complex web of transnational interaction, the EU clearly stands out in terms of its institutional structure, the functions it performs, and its political ambitions enshrined in the holy texts of European integration. In fact, it bears little resemblance to any other regional organization in Europe or elsewhere.

The European Union is in the process of transforming itself, and this transformation is bound to have a major impact on Europe as a whole. Two important agents of transformation are the new single currency and the imminent accession of many new members. Both have been on the European political agenda for some time. Others may prove equally, if not more, important in the future. Developments in the world economy, changing relations with the United States, the only remaining superpower, not to mention new crises, especially if they were to erupt in Europe's immediate neighbourhood, are bound to influence the shape of the European construction. And, of course, this European construction requires a combination of active support and passive acquiescence from large sections of our societies, which increasingly show signs of indigestion of things European. It is possible that regional integration has taken a step too far. We shall find out as it goes through successive popular tests. All in all, the official agenda could be completely overthrown by developments on the external or the internal front. Events have this nasty habit of hijacking even the best designed policies.

This book is about what kind of Europe we want to build and the main issues at stake. It is about the regulation of markets, economic efficiency and solidarity, winners and losers. It is also about the management of globalization as well as the management of the new single currency, about Europeanization and modernization in the new democratic states. Last but not least, it is about the export of common values to the inner and outer periphery. There are political choices to be made on all those issues, including the choice about what Europeans want to do together and what separately, how, and for what purpose. The trade-off between closer cooperation and integration on the one hand, and greater autonomy and diversity on the other, needs to be made more explicit. There is broad agreement that common European institutions are no longer up to the tasks assigned to them. The democratic process is also weak; as a consequence, public debate is distorted by the lack of an appropriate forum for issues that cross national boundaries. Nobody has yet come up with a clear answer as to the question of how democracy can function properly at a level higher than the nation-state.

This has been the starting point for the ongoing debate on the future of Europe, a debate which has been steadily gathering momentum and which focuses on the future of the enlarged European Union. Admittedly, there is a kind of EU imperialism which appropriates to itself the name of Europe and thus follows the earlier example of the United States, which also tends to monopolize the name of the entire continent of America. The debate has been directly linked to the workings of the European Convention which, with the participation of representatives from 28 European countries and the EU institutions, is preparing the ground for a new revision of the European treaties; this could be completed before the end of 2003 at the earliest, although the ratification process would extend well into 2004. At the time of writing, the final outcome of this long and complicated exercise in constitutional reform at the European level is unknown, but is likely to be a European constitution, or a constitutional treaty (a typical European compromise), accompanied by important institutional reforms. Inevitably, given the nature of the exercise, the debate has so far been very much about EU institutions and the division of powers between different levels of authority; hence the repeated use of those long words, such as 'sovereignty' and 'subsidiarity', which sometimes serve as mere substitutes for substantive arguments or as a cloak behind which specific interests try to hide.

'How much Europe?' is, of course, a relevant question, although inadequate and potentially misleading when asked out of any context. The number of those who argue for a further transfer of powers to European institutions for its own sake has been diminishing. They are the old breed of European federalists, usually old and not particularly relevant. The opposite camp may still count more supporters: those who cling to the nation-state without bothering to make the crucial distinction between formal and real autonomy in a world where markets and the international environment impose increasing constraints on independent action by elected governments. The large majority of people are to be found somewhere in between: generally supportive of European cooperation/integration, difficult to mobilize, and at least vaguely aware of a reality which is much more complex and varied than either of the two opposing camps at the extremes of the spectrum is prepared to recognize.

'How much Europe?' is one question, and 'What kind of Europe?' is another, although the two are closely related. Let us consider a few examples. The lack of a political institution responsible for European macroeconomic policy may have negative consequences for financial stability, growth, and the credibility of the new single currency: do we all accept that recessions are an act of God not to be interfered with by sinful governments, or even that money is neutral and should be taken completely out of the political sphere? Market liberalization without effective regulatory powers often implies choices in the trade-offs between efficiency, stability, and equity; are such choices not an integral part of contemporary politics, and, if so, who will make them and how in the European single market? A strong social Europe may provide a protective shield for the more advanced economies; is that the purpose of harmonizing standards, and, if not, does competition among national systems automatically lead to harmonization down to zero? Competition among different models of capitalism within Europe needs rules; which model should they favour, and what is the price of diversity? In the Union, we have reversed the traditional sequence from taxation to representation: we already have the latter without the former; are we now ready for a European tax? With further enlargement, economic disparities will be very wide; what will this mean for the cohesion of the Union, and should convergence be left only to markets to take care of? Defending common values and interests abroad requires money and, as a last resort, troops as well; if we assume we are prepared to pay that price, can a common foreign policy function without a strong European executive or, alternatively, can a concert of big powers substitute for it?

This is just an indicative list of real questions facing today's Europe. The European Convention is not expected to provide the answers, although decisions relating to institutional reform and general constitutional provisions are bound to influence future policy outcomes. All the above questions refer to policy dilemmas as well as to different interests and ideologies. Reducing them to a simple choice between European supranationality (another long word) and national sovereignty would be a complete misrepresentation of what is really at stake. Everyday politics in the European Union is very much about providing answers to the above questions—and many more. Admittedly, they are not always presented as such in European councils; the official EU vocabulary tends to be politically sterilized, thus making it difficult for public debate to take off. As we begin to debate such questions seriously, having finally cast off the straightjacket of old clichés about sovereignty and the European superstate, we may also gradually discover that being British or German, Swedish or Greek is not necessarily the only determining factor in the kind of preferences we express; left or right, new or old, green or black (is black the opposite of green in politics?) will then acquire an increasingly important role in the kind of Europe we opt for. We are still at the beginning, and this promises to be a slow process. Perception lags behind a rapidly changing reality, while institutions set the framework for the public debate.

The above questions form the core of the book, which is about what kind of Europe we want to build and the goods it should deliver; it thus has a strong policy orientation. The emphasis is on political and economic choices rather than institutional mechanics, important though the latter may be. The book also looks at the broad picture, trying to fit together the different pieces of a complicated jigsaw puzzle. In times of narrow specialization, itself partly attributable to the enormous complexity of the world we live in, many contemporary social scientists prefer to distance themselves from the big issues, which it would surely be risky to tackle, and deal instead with the minutiae. Many years ago, a student of European integration likened the attempts of a few bold colleagues to make sense of the whole process to the attempts of blind men to figure out the shape of an elephant by touching different parts of the body. Since then, the elephant has grown much bigger and many observers have resigned themselves to studying its toenails, generally with a great deal of precision and the correct methodology.

In my opinion, we need the broad picture in order better to understand what the main issues at stake are and the big political choices associated with them. The approach is deliberately eclectic: it concentrates on some big themes that provide the lenses through which we can analyse specific policy areas and political dilemmas; otherwise, an encyclopedia would have been required— which takes time, and is also dull. Still, trying to make sense of trade and the single market, agricultural and competition policies, welfare issues and solidarity, financial markets and monetary union, not to mention the birth pangs of the common foreign and security policy, is extremely demanding for a single observer. There is a risk of too much generalization and oversimplification, but it is arguably a risk worth taking: the reader will judge.

Political choices have been repeatedly mentioned in the early pages of this book. One of the main arguments is that the European Union needs a strong dose of political oxygen to breathe properly. In trying to identify the key economic and political parameters of the wide range of issues discussed below, I make a conscious effort to highlight the different interests at stake and the choices available in the realm of the politically and economically feasible and not just the theoretically imaginable, and what they may imply. This book is addressed to the generally informed reader, and not just the specialist. It therefore tries to avoid the apocryphal language of modern social science, which helps to keep the uninitiated away from the ivory tower. The book is intended as a modest contribution to an informed public debate on European issues, a debate which is long overdue.

It is also what the French would call '*engagé*'; that is, it takes a political stand and does not shy away from normative statements, although these are based on a careful study of theory and empirical data, while alternative points of view are given as fair a treatment as humanly possible. This 'engagement' is manifested in two ways: through support for European integration in general, judged as having contributed substantially to peace, democracy, and welfare in Europe, without identifying with every manifestation of it; and with visible marks of the long social democratic tradition, thus attaching particular value to the public interest and the common good, as well as solidarity and internationalism. The book is not, however, intended to be partisan in the narrow definition of the term. The reader has been warned.

While covering a very wide range of issues, the book gives more weight to the economic and social aspects of European integration than to some of the relatively new areas of policy cooperation, most notably foreign policy and defence. This is deliberate and is based on the assumption that progress in those areas is likely to remain slow for some time to come, with important implications for the kind of Europe that develops and also who leads it. To put it simply, a common security policy, implying a clear commitment to sacrifice national soldiers for the common good, presupposes a truly common foreign policy, which is in turn difficult to envisage without a much stronger common European identity than is evident now and probably in the foreseeable future. The North Atlantic alliance used to have an identifiable enemy (no longer) as well as an undisputed political leader (it still does in a way, although some among the allies are clearly showing their unhappiness with the kind of leadership currently provided), and both helped greatly to mobilize the other members under a common policy. It is very different with the EU. This is the rational explanation for the relative bias in the book towards economic and social issues. There is also perhaps a hidden bias towards Europe as a 'soft power', which the uncharitable reader may attribute simply to an insufficient familiarity with the big issues of war and peace.

In the first part, the book takes stock of what has been achieved so far in European integration and the outstanding issues inherited from the past. Chapter 2 draws attention to the widening gap between economic and political integration; in other words, to the underdeveloped nature of the European political system, which does not at all match the economic functions this system performs. This has important implications: European societies may no longer be willing to follow what has always been an essentially elite-driven process. Chapter 3 adopts an unorthodox approach to the effects of integration, focusing on winners and losers. The conditions for a positive-sum game, the usually unrealized dream of the politician as well as the theoretical economist, are not there any more: they have gradually disappeared with the worsening of the economic environment, the deepening of integration, and the increasing inability of the nation-state to redistribute internally. What may be politically more relevant is that differences within countries tend to become more important than differences between countries. Chapter 4 looks at relations with the rest of the world: the EU as a mostly regional economic power, with some privileged and usually also weak partners, and a manifest inability so far to define a collective new relationship with the only remaining superpower across the Atlantic.

The second part follows logically: it goes into greater depth on specific issues and policies, concentrating on the main challenges facing the enlarged EU and the choices available. European integration has until now been mostly about the joint management of increasingly interdependent national economies, or, to put it differently, about the joint management of different models of capitalism that are compelled to interact with each other. The issues often appear too technical or too much driven by competition between national and European institutions. Yet there are important political trade-offs and also very concrete interests which do not always respect national dividing lines. Chapter 5 deals with some representative issues, ranging from economic liberalization and agricultural reform to social policy and tax harmonization. Chapter 6 is about economic and monetary union (EMU) as the single most important unifying factor for the foreseeable future. The single currency will further integrate economies, but it also risks dividing the members of the Union. EMU has come to life with a deliberately incomplete constitution that leaves key political decisions to be made later. Muddling through with inadequate institutions will have real costs. Last but not least, there is the question of appropriate policies and institutions for a powerful European bloc, an emerging political entity but still far short of a superpower, which has to deal with successive enlargements, a difficult periphery, increasingly global and unstable markets, and a powerful ally with a growing inclination towards unilateralism and fewer inhibitions in resorting to divide-and-rule tactics. The prospects and likely implications of a common foreign policy are discussed in Chapter 7; some aspects of it appear more feasible than others, but they all carry a political price tag.

The economics of European integration is intimately linked with the politics of it. Europeanization is not a neutral process: it involves choices, and it usually creates winners and losers. Chapter 8, as the concluding chapter, returns to the broad picture and the wider issues associated with the future of the EU. The European project is a fascinating one; it is, indeed, a revolutionary project aiming at a radical transformation of the economic and political map of the old continent, and also a way of strengthening peace, democracy, and welfare throughout Europe. Nowadays, it is usually taken for granted or perceived by the ordinary citizen as something obscure and distant—and, for some, also as threatening. There is not only one way of cooperating or integrating, and the political choices need to be made as stark as possible. Equally, the costs and benefits of non-cooperation need to be clearly understood. Professional Europeans and the grey suits of the Brussels bureaucracy have not been trained for this job. This is the role of political parties, old and new, as well as of other organized forms of civil society. They do, however, require both information and incentives. Economists and social scientists may help with the former, constitutions generally provide the latter. But there is little doubt that the European Union needs to become more political if it is to have a future.

PART I

☆☆☆☆☆☆☆☆☆☆☆

Taking Stock

2

☆☆☆☆☆

The Gap Between Politics and Economics—Or, Perception and Reality

European integration in the post-war period has been characterized by continuous expansion in terms of both geography and policy functions. It was born only a few years after a devastating world war with a highly ambitious attempt to integrate the coal and steel industries—then considered strategic sectors of the economy—in six countries of Western Europe. It reached adolescence with a still incomplete common market, and matured into middle age at the turn of the new century as a European Union of fifteen members performing (or sharing) most of the traditional functions of the nation-state. And arguably as a sign of the maturity that usually accompanies middle age, this European Union has decided to appropriate for itself one of the key attributes of sovereignty, namely, a currency of its own, thus casting the old currencies of European states into the dustbin of history.

After the end of the cold war that had divided Europe into two heavily armed camps, with only a few countries trying to preserve some kind of neutrality, a new prospect has opened up of integration (or unification, for some) extending to the whole of the European continent. Ten more countries are now ready to join, and others are already in the waiting room. This new round of enlargement is a slow process, as it has been in the past. And as before, most member countries are seeking ways to combine this widening of membership with the further deepening of the process of integration—this being at least the proclaimed objective of most members, with a minority apparently thinking otherwise. Widening and deepening has been a recurrent phenomenon of European integration; but this time it is a greater challenge than ever before.

This process of continuously widening and deepening integration has radically transformed the political economy of Europe and its constituent parts. It has fundamentally changed the ways in which states, markets, and societies interact. Here we examine how this has happened over the last fifty years or so, concentrating on four main themes: the gradual evolution of the policy agenda at the European level; the geographical expansion of membership; the changing nature of common institutions and 'governance' (a relatively new but highly fashionable term indicating something much fuzzier but also wider than governments) in Europe; and, last but not least, the changing attitudes of the citizens of the Union and its member states. This will lead to some general conclusions about the state of European integration, stressing in particular the growing gap between politics and economics or, put differently, between politics and policy, or between perception and reality. This is a crucial issue for Europe and its citizens.

☆ All the Way to Monetary Union—And More

It all started more than fifty years ago, with coal and steel. Of course, nobody would choose those two sectors now; they have both been declining rapidly in importance for quite some time. The plan submitted in 1950 by the French Foreign Minister, Robert Schuman, led to the creation of the European Coal and Steel Community (ECSC) consisting of France, West Germany, Italy, and the Benelux countries (Belgium, the Netherlands, and Luxembourg). The main features of the Schuman plan had a long-lasting effect on European integration. It was a French attempt to deal with the German problem after the end of the Second World War; it was an economic means to a political end; and it was elite-driven, since the large majority of citizens, and even much of the political class of European countries, were clearly not yet ready to throw bridges across national borders after such a long and bloody war. One is tempted to mention another aspect of the plan with long-lasting influence, namely, the tendency of the British to underestimate the seriousness of their continental partners' commitment to regional integration.

It was all part of managed capitalism and the mixed economies that were emerging in post-war Western Europe, especially in the case of coal and steel

14

with their long history of government intervention and cartelization. The next, more ambitious step had to be more liberal in its economic approach. The Treaty of Rome, signed in 1957, led to the establishment of two more communities, the European Economic Community (EEC) and the European Atomic Energy Community (Euratom). The latter proved to be stillborn, while the former was essentially about the establishment of a common market, albeit highly incomplete, with the emphasis on the elimination of cross-border controls on the movement of goods.

For many years, the EEC—by far the most important organization of the six signatories to the Treaty of Rome—was about the liberalization of trade in goods among its members, concentrating on the elimination of national tariffs and quotas, while trying to reconcile free trade with the reality of mixed economies and extensive government intervention within national boundaries. It was heavily qualified free trade; yet it contributed to the growth of intra-EEC trade, which grew much faster than production and also trade with the rest of the world.

In the process, the foundations of common European governance were laid through the operation of common institutions and joint rule-setting. The incomplete common market in goods was complemented with the first attempts at a common competition policy, mostly of an anti-trust character inspired by American experience, and a common commercial policy which bound the Six together in the General Agreement on Tariffs and Trade (GATT). This incomplete common market also included a highly interventionist agricultural policy as a key element of the overall package deal supporting the EEC, and as the only possible way of incorporating a sector which represented a very significant part of national output and of the labour force of continental economies. Indeed, the overall package deal of European integration at the time appeared to make little sense in terms of neo-classical economics; but did national economic reality make any more sense seen through the eyes of virgin economists?

The Golden Age of high growth and monetary stability lasted for almost thirty years after the end of the war—the *trente glorieuses* frequently referred to by the French. A subsequent period of stagflation brought with it new protectionist pressures and tensions inside the European Community (EC)—a term increasingly used to refer to all three Communities. This period of stagflation coincided with the first round of enlargement, with the accession of three new members in 1973. It also prepared the ground for a change in prevailing economic ideas and the inauguration of a new phase of European integration.

This centred on the programme for an internal (or single) market, which was introduced in 1985 and led to a major Treaty revision the following year. The internal market programme was first of all an acknowledgement of the highly incomplete nature of the common market, by far the most important economic achievement so far of European integration. It recognized the uneasy symbiosis between free trade and mixed economies, in which state interventions in the domestic economy unavoidably create distortions in cross-border transactions, whether in the form of state aids or different kinds of regulation: all those things that used to be bundled together in economics textbooks as 'non-tariff barriers' to be eliminated sometime before the second coming.

The decision to deal with the large variety of non-tariff barriers (in other words, with the multiple manifestations of the European mixed economy) ushered the EC into a new phase of deregulation and re-regulation at the European level. Since then, much joint European decision-making and legislation has been about new regulatory frameworks concerning technical standards for industrial products, telecommunications, transport, or financial services. This has expanded economic integration beyond trade in goods to include services and capital, which had been, to all intents and purposes, previously left out. Services had a long history of public regulation; and the uncoordinated (and often explicitly protectionist) character of national regulation had meant that most services had been virtually excluded from cross-border transactions. As for free capital movements, they were supposed to be one of the so-called four fundamental freedoms that lawyers are so fond of (the other three being freedom of trade in goods and services, and freedom of establishment, meaning the freedom to take up and pursue activities as self-employed without any discrimination on grounds of nationality). Yet any capital liberalization that had taken place inside the EC before the internal market programme was adopted had been introduced unilaterally by individual member countries. A key element of the internal market programme was precisely the complete liberalization of intra-EC and extra-EC capital movements.

The result has been a fresh boost to the growth of all kinds of economic transactions across national borders, including now services and capital, bringing a quantitative and qualitative change in intra-European economic interdependence. Today, exports of goods and services represent more than 30 per cent of GDP for the average EU member, and between 27 and 35 per cent for the big countries. The opening of European economies was, indeed, spectacular during the second half of the twentieth century. Figure 2.1 shows that exports of goods and services, expressed as a percentage of GDP for the fifteen

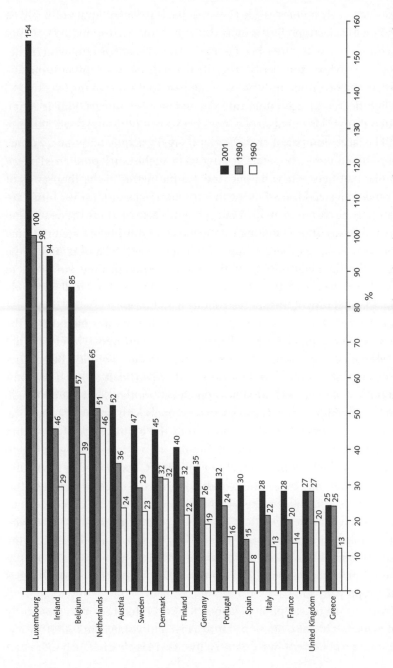

Figure 2.1. Trade openness 1960, 1980, and 2001 (exports of goods and services of EU-15 as a percentage of GDP)

Source: European Commission.

members of the EU, registered a very large increase—more than doubling in most cases—between 1960 and 2001. Ireland and the Benelux countries are by far the most open economies, while Greece is the least open. Approximately 60 per cent of total trade in goods (it is more difficult to find corresponding statistics for services) is done with other EU members. Thus, we are dealing with highly open economies whose prosperity crucially depends on developments outside their borders and predominantly on what happens in the rest of the Union.

This high degree of economic interdependence (or integration) is manifested not only in trade but also increasingly in terms of capital flows and production. The large number of cross-border mergers, acquisitions, and various other forms of economic cooperation, ranging from the much publicized megamergers like that between Vodafone and Mannesmann to the thousands of small- or medium-sized trans-European firm marriages or joint ventures, are daily changing the corporate map of Europe, while also marking the death (and subsequent reincarnation?) of long-established and much-venerated national champions. Cross-border mergers and acquisitions reached a peak before the bursting of the financial bubble of the 1990s. Although they are likely to remain at lower levels in this new period of sobriety, they will probably constitute a key feature of further restructuring in Europe.

One of the very few markets that remain predominantly national is the labour market, not so much because legislators at the European level have not tried to eliminate remaining barriers to cross-border mobility, but rather because of linguistic and cultural barriers that are difficult to legislate away. The operation of national welfare states constitutes another significant impediment to labour mobility across frontiers. Professionals with exportable qualifications and students have benefited most from the elimination of legal and other such barriers. An integrated labour market is, indeed, beginning to emerge in places like London, Brussels, or Frankfurt, but only for a small and successful transnational elite. The paradox is that the large majority of foreigners in European labour markets come from countries that do not benefit from the freedom of movement that EU membership brings with it. Those who have the established right to move rarely do so, while many others on the immediate or more distant peripheries of the Union are only too keen to jump the barriers, legally or otherwise. The labour market, at least at its lower end, is very much supply-driven.

Thus, with the major exception of labour, the EC/EU has become a more truly common market. It has also developed into a regulatory state. But is that an adequate description of current European reality? There is clearly much more to it than that. A crucial and arguably revolutionary element of the Single European Act, the Treaty revision of 1986, was the inclusion of redistribution as part of the overall European package deal. In Community jargon, this is called 'economic and social cohesion'. Thus, liberalization has become directly linked to redistribution, and in practical terms it has meant significant transfers of funds to less developed countries and regions of the Union through the Structural Funds and, later, the Cohesion Fund. This important link has been repeatedly confirmed in subsequent rounds of budgetary negotiations, and it extends at least until 2006. The next crucial decisions will have to be taken in the context of an enlarged EU.

With the European Monetary System (EMS), and now much more with Economic and Monetary Union (EMU), the EU has also acquired a large part of what economists call the 'stabilization function'. Monetary and exchange rate policy have been transferred to a new central institution and most national currencies have been replaced by the euro in a major and highly successful changeover operation. This has important implications for national fiscal policies. To the extent that there is still room and desire for active macroeconomic management, the terms of reference are already partially set at the European level, thus imposing further constraints on national economic sovereignty.

European integration started with economic instruments, and the EU remains largely an economic organization. In Europe, the interaction between the state and the market is very much—and increasingly—determined by European institutions. This is true of the allocation (and regulation) function. The European dimension, however, varies significantly from one policy area to another: from competition policy and agricultural policy, characterized by a high degree of centralization, to several other policy areas, notably environmental and social policy, where the role of the EU is usually limited to setting general principles and/or minimum standards, thus leaving significant room for national policy discretion and hence also for competition among regulatory systems. With EMU, the stabilization function and macroeconomic policy in general have been given a strong European dimension. In monetary policy, the EU has opted for centralization, while in the case of fiscal policy the division of powers between the Union and national institutions is not yet settled, although the emphasis clearly lies on national discretion. As for redistribution, the main responsibility still lies with the nation-state, and most aspects of welfare and social policies remain a national prerogative, despite sizeable inter-country transfers within the Union.

Economics is, of course, politics par excellence. Economic growth and regional development, inflation and job creation, environmental protection and welfare provision comprise much of the stuff that politics is made of in developed European democracies. This is now crucially affected by EU membership, although some aspects of economic life are affected more than others. Europeanization does not stop there: other functions of public governance have not remained untouched. Almost every national minister is now directly involved in and affected by membership of the Union, although again to different degrees. This has been true of education and culture for some time, but it is also increasingly true of justice and home affairs, which entered the European scene in the 1990s through the Maastricht and Amsterdam Treaty revisions in 1992 and 1997 respectively. Visas and immigration as well police cooperation are now part and parcel of regular transnational cooperation in Europe. In fact, with the war against terrorism a policy priority, justice and home affairs may provide the new (and largely unexpected) driving force of integration. Defence ministers have joined the feast last. It remains to be seen how fast they will try to catch up with the others. A common foreign and security policy is still much more of a goal than a reality. The European agenda has indeed expanded in an impressive way; yet economic issues still constitute the core of it.

☆ How Many Members Can We Take?

There were only Six in the beginning, embarking upon a daring project. And they remained Six for more than two decades, thus being able not only to lay the foundations but also to build the first floors of this ever-growing European construction. Those who came afterwards were thus forced to adjust their preferences for their own accommodation to the overall design agreed upon by the founding members.

By 1960, there were clear lines of division on Europe's political map. There was, first of all, the thick line separating the two opposing camps of the cold war, with their own common institutions, and led by the two superpowers of the West and the East. As far as Western Europe was concerned (Western being not a geographical term, since countries like Greece and Turkey had to be transported politically to the other side of Europe), three sub-groups of countries could be distinguished. The Six had opted for closer economic integration and considerable transfer of powers to common institutions; the more ambitious among them used the term 'supranationality', which, however, appeared only once in the treaties. Seven other countries, led by the United Kingdom, had instead opted for a much looser form of cooperation, the European Free Trade Area (EFTA), with a joint secretariat and a limited free trade area as their main goal. And there were the others, later referred to by Jacques Delors, President of the European Commission between 1985 and 1994, as the 'orphans' of Europe. They were the countries left out of sub-regional cooperation efforts because of their lower economic development or weak democratic credentials, and in some cases both. Much of southern Europe belonged to this group.

Thirty years later, most of the dividing lines had been erased. What used to be Western institutions, such as the Council of Europe, gradually developed into pan-European ones; and this seems to be rapidly happening also with the North Atlantic Treaty Organization (NATO), which is taking in more and more new members from central and eastern Europe: is this, indeed, a sign of grow- ing strength or growing irrelevance? On the other hand, the EU as the reincar- nation of the three old Communities (ECSC, EEC, and Euratom) in a much more developed form and with wider membership has clearly emerged as the most important regional organization, an organization which almost all European countries aspire to join. There are still several orphans waiting to be adopted. Yet the boundaries of Europe remain to this date (deliberately?) undefined.

All this did not happen in one single stroke. The EC/EU has gone through suc- cessive rounds of enlargement as different political barriers have come down. The first, and arguably the most difficult one so far, happened in 1973, when Denmark, Ireland, and the UK joined the Six. They had to wait for many years because of the veto of General de Gaulle, President of France, on British accession. Thus, the first enlargement brought in a country, namely, the UK, which was clearly unhappy with the overall package deal, being forced to accept en bloc the whole of Community legislation. As for the Danes, they showed precious little enthusiasm for the wider political goals of European integration, concentrating on the more concrete economic benefits associated with membership.

The first enlargement substantially increased political and economic diversity inside the Community, while coinciding with a major adverse change in the international economic environment. Oil shocks and the collapse of the post-war international monetary order (agreed at Bretton Woods in 1944) changed the fundamentals for European economies, while the internal polit- ical consensus also came under severe strain. The result was lower growth, higher inflation and unemployment, widening economic divergence, and political divisions. Long and bitter budgetary disputes about relatively small sums of money dominated most of the 1970s and early 1980s. There was, how- ever, one bright spot on this bleak picture, namely, the setting up of the EMS as

21

a means of restoring monetary and exchange rate stability in Europe while also laying the foundations of a regional currency bloc.

The second round of enlargement, moving south, was very different. The applications from Greece, Portugal, and Spain arrived at a time of crisis for the Nine. Although these young democracies displayed a flattering confidence in the EC, they did not offer much that could raise the spirits of existing members in the midst of stagflation and much bickering in European councils. Weak economically and fragile politically, the southern European candidates presented the EC with a new and difficult task. Being unable collectively and categorically to say 'no', the Nine bided their time while also opting for two instalments of this new round of enlargement. Greece joined in 1981; Spain and Portugal followed in 1986.

Some useful lessons can be drawn from this southern enlargement. The first and perhaps simplest lesson is that it is virtually impossible to refuse membership to any applicant that is both European and democratic; but you can certainly keep the applicants waiting for a long time. This lesson has, of course, much relevance for the large number of countries from central, eastern, and southern Europe waiting to join. The second lesson is that the EC/EU has acquired an extremely important role, which is to act as catalyst for the economic and political modernization of its new members. This has been true of the two Iberian countries, which have undergone a radical transformation since the fall of their long-lasting dictatorships and their subsequent opening to the world. It has been true, in a different way, of Ireland, and also of Greece, although with more difficulty and pain, especially in the early stages. The third lesson is that the widening of membership, even when it involves relatively weak new entrants, does not necessarily lead to the weakening of integration. Southern enlargement provided the extra push for the adoption of the internal market programme, while also being highly instrumental in establishing the subsequent link between liberalization and redistribution. For all these reasons, the southern enlargement can be considered the most successful so far. The three new entrants had no doubts or existential questions about the desirability of being part of the European construction; and this also seems to have made a great deal of difference.

Twelve was considered a good number and there was agreement to freeze membership at least until the completion of the internal market programme in 1993. Consolidation did seem to make sense, but the unexpected and rapid disintegration of the Soviet empire and the collapse of communist regimes on the eastern side of the notorious Iron Curtain changed everything. German unification in 1990 produced a new mini-enlargement, with the absorption of the five eastern *Länder* with their 17 million people into the Federal Republic of Germany, and hence also the EC. This set in motion a succession of events which radically changed the shape of the European construction.

The unification of Germany led to an important shift in the European balance of power, which became directly linked to the unification of Europe. EMU was adopted as the main economic means to this political end. Interestingly enough, talk about political union produced less precise and far-reaching commitments in terms of institutions, the development of a common foreign and security policy, as well as cooperation in justice and home affairs. That was Maastricht, the most ambitious revision of the European treaties ever, signed sixteen months after German unification. Thus, a small enlargement, which did not even change the number of national representatives sitting around the table in European councils, became linked to the most important deepening of integration.

In a paradoxical way, German unification also led to the biggest crisis of the EMS, while also exposing further the asymmetrical nature of the system. What was good (and necessary in view of growing budgetary deficits) for Germany in terms of monetary policy at the time was clearly not good for the other members. There was nothing in the EMS that could resolve this difference, and the markets quickly perceived the problem. In the midst of the major exchange crisis of 1992–3, few people would have dared to prophesy what was to happen only a few years later, namely, the setting up of the European Central Bank, coupled with the irrevocable fixity of bilateral exchange rates and leading to the adoption of a single European currency. True, the Maastricht Treaty said so, but with speculators in exchange markets running wild and central banks capitulating to market pressure, many Europeans would have been forgiven for thinking, like General de Gaulle, that treaties are like young girls and roses, and consequently last as long as they last. They were to be proved wrong in this particular case.

On the road to EMU, the Twelve were joined by three new members in 1995. This time it was the turn of the neutrals, who, of course, realized that neutrality had lost much of its meaning in the post-cold war period. Proud of their high level of economic development and their advanced welfare systems, and with confidence in their long-established corporatist traditions, Austria, Sweden, and, to some extent, Finland had seen little reason until then to pay the price in terms of a loss of national sovereignty (whether formal or real is another, big question) associated with membership of the EU. Their self-confidence was shaken when unemployment levels started rising in the 1990s, while the EU kept raising the stakes with Maastricht and the rest. In the end, they closed their eyes and took the big jump. Membership of the EU was not a question of love for the new members. It was more a question of fear of being left in the wilderness; and for the Finns EU membership offered a way of compensating for their peripheral position, which was too close for comfort to their unpredictable Russian neighbour. This latest round of enlargement has not so far caused any major upheavals, nor has it acted as a catalyst for any new major policies or developments, except perhaps for more enlargement. After all, the three new members are small, rich, and relatively well-behaved, Austria's Jörg Haider and friends excepted.

At the turn of the century, the EU of Fifteen was very different indeed from the three Communities of the Six formed back in the 1950s. The policy agenda had grown at a rapid pace and so had the size of the tables in European councils, to accommodate the arrival of new members. Thirteen candidates have been squeezed for some time in the waiting room, and ten among them are now scheduled to join as full members on 1 May 2004. The Union has been in a continuous process of change. Have common institutions adjusted to this remarkable expansion of the Union's membership and its policy agenda?

☆ A Political System Without a State . . .

There was a big discrepancy between the heavy institutional set-up provided for by the Treaty of Paris and the kind of decisions the ECSC was expected to tackle, even when one allows for the strategic importance of the coal and steel sectors as perceived at the time. This discrepancy was, however, intentional, since the institutional provisions for the first Community of the Six can be understood only in connection with the long-term political objectives of the authors of the Treaty.

What has come to be called the 'Community method', or the general process of decision-making in the EC/EU, traces its origins to the ECSC: a supranational executive in the form of the High Authority, the precursor of what is now the European Commission, in continuous dialogue and interaction with an inter-governmental law-making body (the Council of Ministers), an independent court, and a consultative parliamentary assembly. The discrepancy between institutions and policy outputs was significantly reduced in the Treaty of Rome. This time, the supranational ambitions of the authors, expressed mainly through the powers given to the Commission, were scaled down, while the policy scope of the new Communities, and most particularly the EEC, became much wider.

This Community method has always distinguished the EC/EU in its different incarnations from traditional international organizations, although very different expectations and analyses were to develop in connection with the integration process. The academic community gave them formal shape and intellectual respectability. There were those who believed that economic and welfare issues should be the priority on the policy agenda of pluralistic Western European societies; in other words, that the safest way to the heart of the voter would be through his or her pocket. The loyalties of citizens were expected to be gradually transferred to common European institutions as these proved to be more efficient in delivering the goods. The supranational Commission would and should act as the motor of integration. The final outcome and objective was clear: individual nation-states would be subsumed sometime in the future in a European federal state. These commentators formed the so-called neo-functionalist school of thought; they agreed with federalists on the final objective, although not necessarily on the emphasis on economics as the main instrument of integration.

Of course, not everybody was convinced by this logic of an automatic spillover effect of the integration process. The intergovernmentalist school saw the three Communities as forms of regional cooperation limited essentially to economics, which was part of what they rather disdainfully described as 'low politics'. As they saw it, security and defence, common values, and symbols—the essence of sovereignty—would continue to remain the exclusive responsibility of the nation-state, which was simply not going to fade away. This was very different indeed from the neo-functionalist analysis and the kind of development of regional institutions it predicted. Yet in both cases predictions, scientific or otherwise, were difficult to distinguish from usually undisguised preferences.

Contemporary European reality is, of course, much more complex than the black and white picture depicted in theoretical models. The institutional set-up of the three initial Communities, later the EC and now the EU, has undergone a major transformation through periodic revisions of the treaties, incorporating new policy areas and/or new members, as well as through everyday practice and accumulated experience. There is now, undoubtedly, a European political system in the sense that there is a stable and clearly defined set of institutions and common rules which have gained wide acceptance. It is coupled with an extensive network of organized economic and political interests, collective decisions that affect much of the everyday life of citizens, and a continuous interaction between the demand for and the supply of new decisions and laws.

It is clearly a very different political system from any other encountered in a European or non-European nation-state; but it is also fundamentally different from international or even regional organizations, be they the International Monetary Fund (IMF), the World Bank, or the North American Free Trade Agreement (NAFTA).

The EU is a highly decentralized system in which the representatives of member governments remain the key power brokers. The Council is the main decision-making and legislative body of the Union. Although there is only one Council in law, it brings together national ministers with different portfolios who meet their counterparts and decide common actions or policies in their respective areas. Foreign ministers meet more than once a month in the General Affairs Council, which was meant to be—and indeed once was—the senior Council with a coordinating role. This coordinating role, however, has been seriously weakened as policy areas have expanded, as has the number of specialized councils. Foreign ministers cannot even pretend to give marching orders to their economics and finance colleagues. Not surprisingly, this is one of the issues currently on the reform agenda.

The Council also has an important executive function, and the lines of demarcation between the Council and the Commission are not always very clear. The executive function of the Council is clearly more important in the new policy areas. The Council is supported by a wide range of committees, more or less specialized, in which many of the decisions are taken. Government by committee? True, to some extent, although in this respect the European political system would not be substantially different from modern national democracies. Perhaps it is just a matter of degree.

National governments and national administrations are actively engaged in every step of the EU political process, from the early exchange of ideas and the preparation of draft legislation to policy implementation. In fact, the decentralized nature of the implementation of common decisions and laws has become a growing problem in itself as the process of integration deepens. National administrative cultures and relative efficiencies in terms of law enforcement differ widely inside the Union, and this sometimes leads to the unequal treatment of its citizens. Scandinavians have a somewhat different understanding of the rule of law from some of their southern partners, for example; and they are usually much quicker in applying it. Thus, Scandinavian countries usually occupy the top ranks in the league tables for implementation of the internal market legislation regularly published by the Commission as a way of naming and shaming the laggards.

26

National governments are actively involved in the European political system up to the very top. The fifteen heads of government (including the head of state in the case of France, and also Finland for some purposes) plus the President of the Commission sit on the European Council, following the institutionalization of summits. This is different from the Council of Ministers, thus adding further to the layman's confusion. In recent years, the heads of government and state have met at least four times a year in 'formal' or 'informal' Councils. They do not legislate and they rarely vote; instead, they set by consensus the main medium- and long-term goals of the Union and, when necessary, strike the difficult political bargains which their ministers cannot deliver. The European Council is where the buck stops in the Union; and in the process it has become the key motor of integration, also attracting the spotlight of media and public attention. Decisions are reached by consensus (and, frequently, exhaustion), thus involving long negotiations, often through the night; and they also include complicated package deals, which ministers in their own councils subsequently have to translate into legislation.

Responsibility for the big decisions as well as setting the broad guidelines for the development of the EU now lies with the European Council. Typical examples are the seven-year budgetary deals, decisions on EMU and enlargement, treaty revisions, and key foreign policy pronouncements, not to mention the nomination so far of the President of the Commission and other key appointments in Union institutions. An intergovernmental body par excellence, with inadequate administrative backing and relying largely on the varying efficiency of its six-month rotating presidency, the European Council has shown strong signs of suffering from policy overload. This is an inefficient and cumbersome way of trying to run the Union, as became more than patently clear at the Nice meeting in December 2000, when the fifteen heads of government, together with their foreign ministers and the President of the Commission, were involved in the longest ever (and, arguably, among the most undignified) haggling match, lasting more than three days and nights, in trying to reach a compromise on yet another revision of the treaties. An example of the mountain giving birth to a mouse, many would argue; and an ugly mouse indeed. Dissatisfaction with the latest revision has led to strong pressures for reform, including the appointment of a President of the Council with longer tenure as a way of ensuring greater continuity.

The proper legislative task remains with the national ministers in the other Council of lesser mortals. In most policy areas, the Council (of ministers) can decide by qualified majority voting (QMV), which represents approximately

70 per cent of the votes. National votes are weighted; but relative weights take only partial account of the different population sizes of individual member countries, which means that small countries are over-represented. The latest treaty revision agreed at the Nice Council of December 2000 was meant to redress the balance in favour of the bigger countries, especially in view of the expected entry of mostly small and medium-sized countries in the new enlargement of the Union. It has done so, if only partially, while adding two further conditions to QMV, namely, that decisions should be backed by the majority of member states representing also the majority of the population of the EU. This triple majority will make decisions even more difficult to reach; hence the widely perceived need for a new revision.

The application of QMV has been steadily extended over the years through periodic revisions of the treaties, and it now covers most of the internal market legislation, with a few notable exceptions like tax harmonization and social security rights. New policy areas, which form part of so-called 'high politics', most particularly foreign and security policy, come under the unanimity rule, while justice and home affairs are already partly amenable to QMV. The unanimity rule also applies to all treaty revisions, including the accession of new members. But even when QMV is applicable, the Council usually operates by consensus, votes being the exception rather than the rule. Although the search for consensus does lead to long-drawn-out negotiations and to slow decision-making, it is true that the legal possibility of recourse to QMV helps generally to concentrate the minds of ministers and ultimately generates consensus, even with abstentions. Unanimity usually produces deadlock.

Thus, the use of the national veto as the ultimate weapon in the defence of the national interest has been seriously curtailed over the years; and it will probably be even more curtailed after the next treaty revision. It is, of course, only democratically elected governments that have the right to define the national interest. Yet in an increasing number of cases it has become really difficult to talk meaningfully of the national interest. There are, first of all, so many issues of a technical nature comprising much of the agenda of advanced capitalist democracies and hence also the EU, requiring expert knowledge rather than political sensitivity to decide. Furthermore, since membership of the EU means participation in a process of continuous negotiation over a very wide range of policy areas, complicated package deals, peer pressure, the long-term gains associated with credibility, and the osmosis of new ideas and benchmarking are all part of the decision-making process and the policy outputs of the European political system. National representatives need to keep

their electorates back home satisfied, but they are also influenced in their attitudes by the European institutional context in which they operate. And with
growing interdependence, the 'national interest' often defended by national
governments consists of little more than the entrenched positions of
well-organized minorities and interests.

The European Commission has experienced several ups and downs in the
history of the EC/EU. The ups are usually associated with Walter Hallstein, the
first President of the EEC Commission, and Jacques Delors, who served as
President between 1985 and 1994. After Delors, it has been only downhill.
What has hardly changed throughout this long period are the attempts made
by national governments to influence the internal decision-making processes
of the Commission. Supranationality sounds noble, but it is a long word and
sometimes hard to swallow.

The Commission remains the main executive body of the Union, although in
practice it shares many executive functions with the Council. Its main responsibilities include the drafting of legislation, making rules and regulations in
specific policy areas, ensuring the implementation of Union legislation by
national administrations, managing the budget, and representing the EU in
bilateral and multilateral trade negotiations. It consists of the European civil
service and a political body at the top: the college of Commissioners, headed by
the President, who have so far been appointed by the Council (each
Commissioner by his or her government in practice) for fixed five-year periods.
Decisions are taken by simple majority and Commissioners are bound by collective responsibility.

In good times—and with good presidents—the Commission has helped to
shape the overall policy agenda. It happened with the internal market in 1985
and it also happened to a smaller extent with *Agenda 2000*, a general policy
document that aimed at establishing a link between the new enlargement and
the further deepening of integration. The specific powers of the Commission
vary significantly depending on the policy area. Broadly speaking, it has a key
role in all aspects of Union legislation that had been provided for in the Treaty
of Rome; in other words, everything related to the functioning of the internal
market as subsequently redefined, with more far-reaching implications, by the
Single European Act of 1986. It is impossible even to imagine the operation of
the internal market on an intergovernmental basis, something that many
British Conservatives, for example, completely fail to understand. Limited free
trade areas can be administered by international secretariats, but not the kind of
internal market that the EU has developed in the context of mixed economies.

In specific areas, the powers of the Commission are particularly important. This is especially so with competition policy, but also with agricultural policy as well as external commercial policy, accession negotiations with candidates, and financial aid to third countries. The Commission has played a key role in the development of Structural Funds and in setting the criteria for the distribution of structural aid. It has been even more instrumental in the regionalization process in some of the recipient countries of the Union. It is bad enough losing powers to Brussels, but losing them also downwards to regional authorities inside your own country is to add insult to injury, some would surely say.

On the other hand, the political weakening of the European Commission witnessed since the mid-1990s may be more than a simple question of personalities. In all the major new areas of policy added in Maastricht and later in Amsterdam, the role envisaged for the Commission is small at best. This is largely true of EMU and even more so of foreign and security policy as well as justice and home affairs. If we add the growing pressures for at least a partial re-nationalization of agricultural, competition, and structural policy, then we may be observing a serious long-term decline of the Commission as one of the major institutions shaping the integration process. If so, this is bound to have wider consequences. The relative balance between the Commission and the Council constitutes a key element in the ongoing debate concerning the reform of European institutions.

The European political system has become more democratic in the process through repeated extensions of the powers of the European Parliament (EP). Starting with only a consultative role, the EP has increasingly acquired many of the functions of a real parliament, including legislation, expenditure powers, and control of the executive. The 626 members of the EP (a maximum of 732 members has been set in the Nice treaty for the future enlarged Union) are directly elected by citizens of the EU on the basis of proportional representation and for a fixed five-year term. They enjoy considerable, although still legally constrained, powers over the Union budget. They also share legislative powers with the Council in what is now, at least partially, a bicameral system, with more powers still reserved to the representatives of states in the Council than to the representatives of the citizens of the Union sitting in the European Parliament. As is typical with the EU, the legislative powers of the EP vary significantly among different policy areas, usually a function of history and political sensitivities, thus making the European political process a paradise for lawyers and consequently an impenetrable world for ordinary people.

The EP now ratifies international agreements and the accession treaties of new members. It also approves the appointment of the new college of Commissioners—and in future it may be asked to elect the President of the Commission. It makes active use of its powers of parliamentary scrutiny of both the Commission and the Council, and, after repeated threats over the years to make use of its old power to censure the Commission en bloc, it finally did sack the Santer Commission in 1999 for financial mismanagement. Yet it does not possess the same power vis-à-vis the other part of the executive, that is, the Council, and this reduces democratic accountability.

In order to make effective use of its powers, the EP requires large majorities, which means in turn that it usually operates on the basis of large coalitions. Political formations in the EP are formed mostly along left-right lines, with two major party groups dominating the scene. They are the European People's Party and European Democrats (EPP-ED) on the centre-right, consisting mostly of Christian Democratic parties plus British Conservatives and a few others, and the Party of European Socialists (PES) on the centre-left. In search of large majorities, cross-party alliances often include the European Liberal, Democrat and Reform Party (ELDR), a much smaller group representing a wide spectrum of political opinion since 'liberalism' and 'reform' usually mean different things in different countries; the ELDR has often proved to be a pivotal player. Some of the other small party groups in the EP have a stronger national, as opposed to ideological, character.

Thus, for the large majority of Members of the European Parliament (MEPs), political/ideological divisions are usually more important than territorial divisions in determining where they sit and how they vote, which may be taken as yet another indication of the relative maturity of the European political system. Much of the bargaining takes place within the large party groups, and the internal cohesion they exhibit in voting is actually quite high, usually comparing favourably with internal party cohesion in the US Congress. Yet, as also witnessed with the Council, the EP needs to operate on the basis of large majorities, and hence broad party coalitions in its case. The conflict is often inter-institutional (Parliament versus Council, Parliament versus Commission), and this requires large majorities, not only by law. On the other hand, given the nature of the EU decision-making system and the EP in particular, there is much scope for organized lobbying. In this respect, at least, the EP resembles the US Congress more than any other parliamentary system in Europe.

The European construction is a legal construction par excellence. Given the diversity of its constituent parts and the shortage of mutual trust, at least in the early stages of integration, it requires explicit and detailed rules governing interaction between its members, and it also requires arbitration and authoritative interpretation of the law. This is provided by the European Court of Justice (ECJ). Since the EU still lacks a proper constitution, the ECJ has been quick to establish some of the key legal principles generally found in federal constitutions. One of them is the supremacy of EU law over any other law in the Union; another is the direct effect of EU law on individual citizens. This is federalism that dares not speak its name; and it has been accepted in practice by national governments and courts, not always without resistance. 'Creeping constitutionalism' may be another way of describing what has been happening, with the ECJ as the main instrument and key integrator. Does judicial 'activism' imply an ideological or other bias, apart from being pro-integration? This is a highly sensitive issue relating to many decisions of the ECJ, which have acted as catalysts for economic integration, including most notably the liberalization of state-controlled sectors and the wide application of the principle of mutual recognition. Clearly, judges do not operate in a political vacuum, but who is to judge them?

The jurisdiction of the ECJ includes cases brought against member states, judicial review of EU legislative and executive acts, preliminary rulings on references by national courts (thus establishing a close link and continuous dialogue between the ECJ, as the emerging supreme court, and lower courts of the Union), and actions against EU institutions. The number of cases dealt with by the Court has increased rapidly over the years, and so has the number of cases dealt with by the Court of First Instance created in 1989 to lighten the load of the ECJ. The EU legal order relies on respect for the rule of law in member countries, since it has no direct powers of enforcement. Since Maastricht, the ECJ can also impose fines on member governments for not applying the law, thus adding an important sanction in a Union where, with ever-growing numbers and areas of activity coming under its jurisdiction, implementation and enforcement of the law is becoming more of an issue every day. The importance of the ECJ is duly recognized by both advocates and opponents of integration; hence the ferocious resistance of the latter to any attempt to involve the ECJ in new and sensitive policy areas, such as foreign and defence policy or the 'area of freedom, security and justice'. The ECJ is an absolutely crucial part of the 'Community method' of governance and all that it implies for integration and national sovereignty.

The wider institutional setting of the EU includes several other organizations or agencies with a variety of tasks. Some are of a consultative nature, such as the Economic and Social Committee (ESC) (a rather failed attempt at institutionalized corporatism at the European level whose history goes back to the founding treaties) and more recently the Committee of Regions; others are entrusted with specific tasks, such as the European Police Office (Europol) and the European Central Bank (ECB), in charge of monetary policy in EMU. If ever there was a supranational institution, it is the ECB—with precious little democratic account-ability. In a world of high capital mobility, central bankers are the high priests of international finance, and politicians are not even allowed to enter the temple.

This is a brief summary of how the European political system operates: a political system without a state and thus with no external sovereignty legally enshrined, even though the EU is already entitled to sign international treaties; and a political system with no direct powers of coercion. It is also a political system so far without a constitution, yet operating as if a constitution of sorts did exist: a 'constitutional charter', according to the ECJ, perhaps too fine a distinction for non-lawyers.

This European political system has some structural characteristics which influence both the way it functions and its policy outputs. It is a highly complex system that relies heavily on rules rather than discretion. In recent years, and especially after the Lisbon meeting of the European Council of March 2000, a deliberate attempt has been made to promote the so-called open method of coordination as an alternative to the old rule-based approach to integration, relying more on peer pressure, benchmarking, and also, inevitably, opt-outs instead of specific rules applying to everybody. Although opt-outs and differ-entiation have become more common (and necessary) with the further deepening and widening of regional integration, rules and formal negotiations still constitute the distinguishing features of EU decision-making, especially in the more traditional areas of responsibility. In a political system consisting of (semi-) sovereign states, which retain in most cases the monopoly of imple-mentation of joint decisions, discretion and brainstorming are usually a poor substitute for rules, although they may have wider application in some new policy areas where national governments want to preserve a wide margin of manoeuvre. The management of EMU will also provide a testing ground for the shift from rules to discretionary policy, although this will largely depend on how strong and effective the central institutions are.

It is a political system based on broad consensus and large majorities for its policy outputs. Some observers see it as an example of 'consociational' democ-racy, a term invented to describe the Dutch political system operating on the basis of consensus and wide representation of different elites as a response to the several important, cross-cutting cleavages in Dutch society, at least before the Dutch political system was hit by the meteorite named Pim Fortuyn.

Naturally, consensus and large majorities are much more difficult to build at the European level. The consequence is therefore a slow and conservative system (conservative in the sense of being resistant to change), leading mostly to reactive and disjointed policies. Political leadership and strategic vision do not easily come out of such a system.

New decisions need to go through many possible veto gates on the way; they also need to mobilize many national and transnational interests. Once bargains are struck and become translated into EU law, they are very difficult to undo. Thus, the system carries a heavy historical load, which discriminates against newcomers and new political majorities. It also reduces the ability to adjust to changes in the external environment. But how can we then explain the actual experience of continuous deepening and widening of integration? Is the demand for integration almost insatiable, or are there specific factors that may explain the rapid developments of the last one and a half decades in particular?

Some people contend that in the European political system liberalization measures are easier to adopt than common policies which try to shape economic outcomes through active regulation or redistribution rather than simply correcting market failures. In other words, positive integration is politically more difficult than negative integration; and this is further strengthened by the liberalization bias of the founding treaties. It remains a controversial argument, but, if valid, has very important implications.

Last but not least, in its attempt to minimize conflict the European political system has shown a strong tendency towards depoliticization and rule by experts— and judges, one might add. It is a system that favours bureaucratic compromises rather than political initiatives and strong leadership, and that emphasizes national divisions at the expense of all other kinds. Democratic accountability is limited, not only because of the still circumscribed powers of the European Parliament, but also because of the dual nature of the European executive. Much of the legislative process is completely non-transparent, while its complexity, combined with the geographical distance of decision-making centres from the very large majority of European citizens, makes it inaccessible to the wider public. Hopes for a more efficient and democratic way of taking decisions at the European level have shifted to the European Convention and the new treaty that will follow.

☆ . . . and With Less Permissive Citizens

Regional integration in Europe started as an elite-driven process, with little popular participation or excitement. At the turn of the century, the fundamentals are still the same. The Schuman Plan and the negotiations which led to the Treaty of Paris in 1951 concerned a very small number of people from the six participating countries, who had tried to keep it as far as possible from the political limelight in order to secure the ratification of the treaty. The negotiation of the Maastricht Treaty forty years later bore a considerable resemblance to the secretive diplomacy of the first years of European integration: interminable discussions behind closed doors and precious little public debate. The transition from diplomacy to democracy seems to be a long and arduous process. Ten years after Maastricht, the European Convention marked a conscious effort to accelerate this process, a belated acceptance of the limitations of the old approach.

For many years, national elites did not have to reckon with integration-sceptic publics, as they had feared, justifiably, would be the case after the end of the war. Observers of the European scene soon began to talk of a 'permissive consensus', at least in the six founding member states, meaning that the large majority of citizens had a generally favourable attitude towards European integration but did not know much about it or consider it a matter of high priority. They were thus ready to leave it to their governments to decide.

Wide popular support for European integration was subsequently and repeatedly confirmed through public opinion surveys, most notably those undertaken regularly by the *Eurobarometer*. These surveys showed high levels of support for integration, usually ranging from 65 to 80 per cent of the population in member countries, although the figures were persistently lower when people were asked whether membership of their own country was a good thing. This seems to suggest that in the minds of most European citizens integration commanded support, although membership of the EC/EU was not always perceived as producing concrete benefits. Opposition to integration was confined to a small number. Public opinion surveys as well as the data drawn from the small number of referendums that have taken place so far suggest that the rich, the educated, and the young are more likely to support European integration throughout the EU. Managers, white-collar workers, and the self-employed show significantly higher levels of support than unskilled workers and the unemployed. It also appears that the more informed are more likely to be supporters than the less informed.

Popular support for European integration has never relied on a strong sense of European identity; but how could it, given Europe's troubled history and its long-established nation-states? Thus, few people identify themselves first as European citizens, rather than declaring themselves to be German, Irish, or

Portuguese. The same used to be true of former Yugoslavia, where, with few exceptions, people identified themselves first as Serbs, Croats, or Slovenes, and not as Yugoslavs. We all know what happened to Yugoslavia in the end; but surely this is not a valid comparison to make with the EU—or so we hope!

For a long time European integration enjoyed wide public support in at least the large majority of member countries, with sizeable and vocal minorities in the former members of EFTA. This public support, however, did not act as a mobilizing factor in politics. Citizens were happy with this wide-ranging project, the fine details of which mostly escaped them, as long as it was seen to deliver the goods in the form of prosperity, peace, and also democracy on the European continent. And they also appeared ready to allow their political leaders considerable leeway in collectively managing the European project. There were few opportunities to test this popular support or the particular preferences of citizens in terms of European integration.

Broad consensus was particularly pronounced at the political level in most member countries: mainstream national parties did not differ much on European issues. With few exceptions, such as the UK and Denmark, elite consensus meant that there were no proper public debates in parliament or outside, even on concrete issues that did not necessarily command wide popular support. The old Treaty of Paris syndrome had thus left many traces: national elites know best and they genuinely lead their societies in terms of European integration. On the major issue of EMU there was little public debate in most countries, either before or after the signing of the Maastricht Treaty, even though public opinion was not so enthusiastic about the project. This observation certainly applies to Germany and the Netherlands, where public opinion on EMU was largely negative, at least in the beginning. Would the Maastricht Treaty have been ratified if more countries had tested public opinion through referendums? Significant doses of Euroscepticism may have at least one concrete advantage: they generate public debate, which is generally good for democracy.

Democracy in the EU and the legitimacy of its institutions are still mostly of an indirect kind: it is the national constituent parts that are democratic and thus also give legitimacy to common European institutions. This has become increasingly problematic with the continuous deepening of integration, majority voting in the Council (albeit limited), and the growing difficulties national governments have in compensating domestic losers. Direct elections to the European Parliament and the steady extension of its powers were meant to deal with the democratic deficit of the Union. They have been only partially successful. Direct elections to the EP have not generated any Europe-wide debates on issues dealt by EU institutions; and such debates that have taken place have been confined to small sections of the political elite, experts, and intellectuals. European construction remains an affair for the *cognoscenti*; the people are expected to follow.

Direct elections to the EP have been fought as second-order national elections, on national issues and by national parties. Although the EP is mostly divided along left-right rather than national lines, European party groups have behaved as loose confederations during European elections, with very general common platforms and little influence on electoral campaigns in individual countries. Thus, electorates have been asked to vote on national party lists with many candidates qualifying as the unknown famous who are supposed to represent European citizens in what is generally seen as a faraway parliament with obscure powers. It is therefore not surprising that the participation rate in European elections has been declining, from 63 per cent in the first direct elections of 1979 to 55 per cent in 1999—though this is still respectable by US standards. But participation rates in many national elections in Europe have also been declining, which may suggest a more general problem of popular participation and public confidence in democratic institutions.

In the meantime, attempts have been made to go beyond the narrow definition of economic freedoms in the old treaties, thus giving substance to European citizenship as something more than the sum of its national parts. The concept of EU citizenship, accompanied with enforceable yet limited rights, was first introduced at Maastricht. It has provided the launching pad for subsequent bolder initiatives. Citizens of the Union are nationals of member states. They have the right to reside freely anywhere in the EU; to vote or stand for office in local and EP elections wherever they reside; and to enjoy consular protection in third countries by the embassy of any EU member state. Revisions of the founding treaties have also made democracy and respect for human rights and fundamental freedoms an integral part of EU membership. Although this was understood from the very beginning, the treaty now provides for the suspension of the rights of membership in case of breach, thus adding an element of sanction. The Charter of Fundamental Rights (a European bill of rights) was finally adopted at Nice in 2000, although it is still not legally enforceable because of strong opposition from a small number of member states. This will probably change in the new treaty. On the other hand, citizens' rights are already directly affected by the recent extension of policy cooperation/integration into the area of 'freedom, security and justice'.

These developments have not, however, delivered the goods in terms of tackling the democratic deficit of the Union. Democratic accountability remains weak; EU-wide issues usually suffer from low public visibility, and are rarely debated as such. National political debates therefore contain a strong dose of unreality, since they assume that the nation-state has many more powers than is actually the case. During the 1990s, popular support for European integration suffered a major and unprecedented decline throughout the Union. *Eurobarometer* surveys show that it fell to less than 50 per cent of the population; and although it made a small recovery, reaching 55 per cent in the autumn of 2002, it is still very much lower than the 69 per cent registered at the beginning of the 1990s. The decline was particularly pronounced in France and Germany, the two countries which had traditionally been the main pillars of regional integration, but also in countries such as Italy and the Netherlands (Figure 2.2).

Admittedly, a large majority of European citizens still believed that membership of the EU was a good thing. The 'no' answers were mostly given in the former EFTA countries (if nothing else, there has been remarkable consistency in the anti-integration feeling of a sizeable section of the population of those countries), while the Benelux countries, the south, and Ireland continued to serve as the main depositories of Euro-enthusiasm. And there was also EMU: as the E(uro)-day approached, *Eurobarometer* surveys pointed to at least a partial recovery of popular support for European integration.

Signs of serious cracks in the permissive consensus, a characteristic of public attitudes to regional integration for many years, have multiplied. The weakening of popular support has been manifested in several referendums linked to successive treaty revisions. Danish voters did it twice: first when they rejected the Maastricht Treaty in 1992 and again in 2000 when they said 'no' to their country's participation in EMU. There had been another Scandinavian 'no' in the meantime, when the Norwegian population voted against accession to the Union in 1994. They had done the same in 1972, again with a small majority. Those negative votes could no longer be dismissed as Scandinavian eccentricities: 'they have never believed in European integration, have they?'. The French electorate produced only a 51 per cent majority for Maastricht, while the Irish, always considered fervent supporters of European integration, said 'no' in 2001 to the new treaty revision agreed at Nice, although only a small minority bothered to vote. This pointed to yet another problem: pro-European majorities are difficult to mobilize. The second attempt in Ireland at the Nice Treaty was more successful: in October 2002, more people turned out to vote, under heavy prodding from the main political

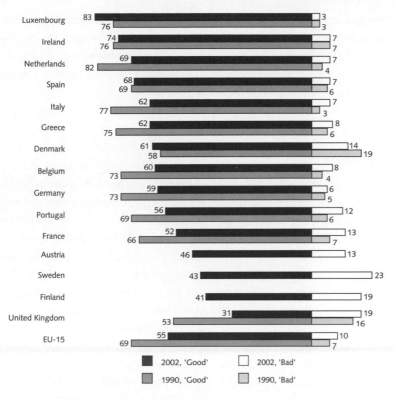

Figure 2.2. Popular support for EU membership, 1990 and 2002 ('Is membership a good thing?' (%))

Source: Eurobarometer (Autumn 2002, December 1990).

parties, and this time they produced a clear majority in favour of the new treaty and further enlargement.

In all cases, the negative vote appeared to be largely an 'anti-establishment' vote; and there have been further signs of this trend in several national elections held recently. While the old elite consensus on Europe seems to have survived, some of the new forces emerging on the political scene, usually on the extreme or populist right, are challenging this consensus, thus giving expression to new undercurrents in European societies. The immigration issue has served as a catalyst. European societies may have become less permissive in the sense of being less willing to give their national politicians carte blanche to proceed further with integration and to continue taking decisions on their behalf with little transparency and accountability. They may have also become less permissive in the sense of no longer perceiving European integration as a 'win-win' game (even better than a Pareto-optimum in economic terms), with potential losers clinging more and more to old, familiar national institutions as a shield in a more adverse and rapidly changing environment.

☆ Does It Matter?

During the second half of the twentieth century, European economies became much more interdependent. Autonomous market forces combined with rapid technological change and conscious political decisions to bring this about. We can in fact go one step further. European integration has led to the development of a regional economic system that is, both quantitatively and qualitatively, more than a set of highly interdependent national economies, and on whose survival the continued prosperity of European citizens largely depends. Most of the barriers have been eliminated, while responsibility for public policy has been at least partially transferred to the European level. In the process, market forces have been strengthened at the expense of government, whether national or European. This is, of course, entirely compatible with economic orthodoxy, although not equally backed by popular consensus. It is also highly compatible with the parallel process of globalization, the main difference being that with globalization there is market but virtually no government.

Thus, economic reality has become increasingly European and also global. The EU has developed a system of government at multiple levels in order to manage it. Delors may have been right in saying that approximately 80 per cent of legislation affecting socio-economic issues is already taken at the European level, although this does not preclude a high degree of decentralization and differentiation. The crucial question is what kind of government—and what kind of economic management—the European political system is capable of producing, and who the likely winners and losers are. But there is something else too. If European governance has at least partially adjusted to this new economic reality, societies have hardly done so. Public attitudes and expectations are still very much geared towards the nation-state as well as to the regional and local levels. Europe provides the focus of political attention for only a few.

True, welfare and social solidarity are still essentially the prerogatives of the nation-state, and they also remain the most salient issues for European citizens. National governments have preserved the symbols, but they also have kept tight control over the public purse, leaving only a few crumbs for expenditure at the Union level. Nevertheless, many important decisions affecting the everyday life of citizens are already taken outside the boundaries of the nation-state, and the number has been steadily increasing over the years. Individual and collective prosperity largely depend on decisions taken in Brussels and other such faraway(!) places by the travelling circus of European decision-makers and legislators. But the democratic process of popular participation and accountability has not caught up with this development.

The result has been a growing gap between politics and economics in Europe. Despite the continuous expansion of its policy agenda, the EU remains largely an economic system, with an increasingly complex institutional set-up but no proper political base. European governments have been talking for years about establishing a political union as a counterpart to economic and monetary union; and what they have delivered in the process is cooperation in a wide range of new policy areas, including foreign policy and internal security, as well as limited institutional reforms. Though important, all this has little to do with political union. Can or should this political union—and of what kind?—be constructed from above, as has happened all along with European integration? And how does one make the European system more democratic and hence also more legitimate? These are difficult questions, and there are no model answers to be found in history or current experience in other parts of the world. Yet they are the questions with which all those taking part in the debate on the future of Europe have to grapple. The gap between politics and economics has important consequences for our societies as well as our national and European institutions. It directly affects the functioning of democracy and the legitimacy of our institutions; it may also have distributional consequences.

Usually cloaked in their technical garb, European issues remain out of bounds for the ordinary citizen. Political parties, still very much national in their outlook and internal organization, have failed so far to act as two-way transmission belts. After all, why should we expect them to rise to this challenge, when there has been no office with real power to fight for at the European level? The European Parliament as it stands offers only a poor substitute. There can be no European political parties as long as there is no European political marketplace. And, certainly, it is not the harmonization of technical standards or even of tax which will send people waving banners into the streets of Brussels, Manchester, or Cagliari—although pig farmers have done so in the past and EMU may act as a mobilizing force in the future. Would 'social Europe' provide the recipe, as some on the left of the political spectrum have been arguing for years, so far with little success?

The gap between politics and economics can also be presented as a gap between politics and policy, or perhaps more appropriately as a gap between perception and reality. It can only cause disappointment and frustration, leading to populist reactions and protest movements with mixed and often confused messages. The growing protests against globalization may therefore assume a more specifically European expression, while 'anti-establishment' votes may become a more recurrent theme. Permissive consensus for European integration is no longer to be taken for granted.

3

☆☆☆☆☆

Winners and Losers . . .

For many years, talking about winners and losers in European integration was not considered the done thing. It was surely not politically correct. After all, integration was meant to be about fundamentals, such as peace and democracy and, though to a lesser extent, welfare; and they could all be more safely secured through close cooperation (many preferred the word integration) across national borders. National elites, at least in the six founding members, quickly espoused this kind of logic, learning some hard lessons from the bitter experience of the first half of the twentieth century. Social Democrats joined Christian Democracy in supporting the European cause; dissenting voices became few and far between, and were often treated as eccentrics and more often branded narrow-minded nationalists, which they usually were. Thus, talking about possible losers would risk undermining the consensus. After all, post-war states had developed many ways of compensating losers within their borders.

Economists discovered in economic integration a rapidly growing field for their theories and their empirical studies, but they were hardly trained to deal with distributional issues. Their attention was concentrated on economic efficiency and Pareto-optimal situations. For most, redistribution, when necessary, was supposed to be delivered by an imaginary benevolent dictator. Thus, the question of winners and losers hardly appeared in earlier economic studies on the effects of regional integration. But over time a growing minority of economists began to rise to the challenge.

The conspiracy of silence was first broken by the British in the 1970s. Unhappy with the deal they had been forced to accept as the price for joining, they soon discovered that they had more possibilities of changing it once inside. They began asking awkward questions about who gains and who loses from the Community budget, finally forcing the Commission to start doing the sums it had always resisted doing, at least in public, because they were considered to be against the Community spirit. Thus, the British were the first to let the cat out of the bag, because they rightly did not like what they had got. In her inimitable way, Margaret Thatcher led the attack on the budget, raising the question of who wins and who loses from it. Of course, budgetary gains and losses are only a small part of the broader balance sheet of membership of the Union. But Thatcher was ideologically incapable of asking the broader and more interesting question about winners and losers. After all, she did not believe in the political dimension of integration, nor did she think (or care) about the losers from market integration.

Many things have happened since then. Although the fundamentals of European integration have not changed much during the last fifty years or so, the internal balance of power in Europe has changed, with significant effects on the perception of national interests and the matrix of potential alliances between countries. This is surely important, and it has not yet been fully reflected in the overall European package deal. Another important change will come with further enlargement, the scale and effects of which have so far been generally underestimated. The tidal waves of the breakdown of the post-war political and economic order in Europe continue to reach our shores; and the biggest ones may be yet to come.

This is not all. Most people are used to thinking in terms of balancing different national interests in the European context. The predominantly intergovernmental character of the European decision-making system has, after all, always highlighted divisions between countries rather than divisions within countries. Things are changing here too as a result of three main developments: the continuous deepening of European integration, which is now having wide-ranging effects on society as a whole; the deterioration of the economic environment, characterized by low growth and high unemployment in times of rapid change; and the increasing difficulties of national welfare states in providing an effective safety net for the losers and a warm embrace for those who fear the different and the unknown. Thus, internal divisions within countries begin to acquire a new political importance. Who benefits and who loses? Who has a stake in Europe? More importantly, what kind of Europe do we want? The answer to these questions can no longer be given exclusively at the national level and in the name of the 'national interest'.

☆ Virtuous Circles and Economic Integration

The founding treaties were extremely complex in their attempt to include something for everyone ('everyone' being understood as the signatory states). The EEC treaty, for example, contained provisions for the liberalization of industrial trade, a common agricultural policy (CAP), a common transport policy, and the setting up of the European Investment Bank (EIB) and the European Social Fund (ESF). Different provisions catered for different interests. Furthermore, the six founding members constituted a fairly homogeneous economic area with similar levels of development; the only big exception was the Italian south (the *Mezzogiorno*), for which the ESF and the EIB were meant to provide financial support.

The post-war Golden Age for the Western European economies lasted until the early 1970s, and produced rapidly rising levels of prosperity. The growth rates and unemployment levels achieved during that period have never been matched since (Figure 3.1). It was truly exceptional, with average annual growth rates of real GDP reaching 5 per cent, while unemployment was close to 2 per cent. How things have changed since then! The only macroeconomic variable that has improved in recent years, as compared with the Golden Age, is inflation; and this improvement has been far from dramatic, since annual rates of inflation remained around 3–4 per cent in most Western European countries until the late 1960s.

International trade grew faster than output during that period, and intra-EEC trade grew faster than international trade. Economists were very quick to try to establish links between these variables. To the extent there can ever be

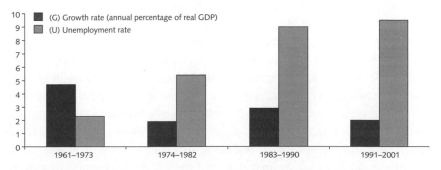

Figure 3.1. Growth and unemployment in EU-15, 1961–2001

Source: European Commission.

unanimity among economists, they achieved it on the relationship between trade liberalization as a result of regional integration efforts, and the growth of regional trade. Moreover, economists agreed that most of this trade was the result of trade creation (a good thing) as opposed to trade diversion (a bad thing), the latter being associated mainly with the CAP. There was, however, less agreement about the link between the growth of trade and GDP. Early studies on integration suggested that the welfare effects of trade growth were very small. If true, this would imply that, after all, integration had little to do with economics, since trade cannot be an economic good in itself. Later, economists began to study the so-called dynamic effects of trade and, in so doing, they were able to establish a much closer link between intra-European trade on the one hand and growth and welfare on the other. They probably still underestimate those effects.

The causal link between trade and growth is not only one-way, as is usually assumed. The rapid elimination of intra-EEC trade barriers between 1958 and 1968 was made possible largely by the favourable macroeconomic environment, characterized by high rates of growth and low unemployment. Increased exposure to international trade brings with it adjustment costs for both labour and capital. These costs are much more easily absorbed in times of rapid growth, thus minimizing resistance from potential losers. This suggests a virtuous circle: the favourable macroeconomic environment of the 1950s and 1960s, attributable to various factors such as catching up with the more advanced US technology and high investment ratios coupled with wage moderation, created the conditions that permitted the signing of the Treaty of Rome and the successful implementation of its trade provisions. Liberalization then led to more trade and this, in turn, contributed to the remarkable growth rates of the period.

So far so good. But another piece of the puzzle challenged conventional thinking. Trade liberalization, much faster at the regional level but also quite significant at the international level with GATT as its main vehicle, coincided with the emergence of mixed economies and welfare states, especially in Western Europe. During that time, the role of the state became increasingly pronounced at both micro and macro levels. 'Keynes at home and Smith abroad', as someone very ingeniously put it. While Western European countries were eliminating their border controls, mostly affecting trade in goods, they were busily developing domestic instruments for macroeconomic stabilization, redistribution, insurance against risk, and the provision of public goods. In some countries, notably France and Italy, the state also directly controlled whole sectors of the economy, ranging from public utilities to the banks.

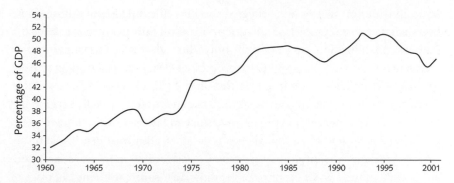

Figure 3.2. Total expenditure of general government in EU-15,[a]
1960–2001 (as a percentage of GDP)

[a] 1960–9: EC-6; 1970–94: EU-15 excluding Luxembourg.

Source: European Commission.

General government expenditure as a percentage of GDP is a simple yet quite reliable indicator of the size of government. For the average EU country, that measure rose by almost twenty points between 1960 and the early 1990s, reaching more than 50 per cent of GDP (Figure 3.2); since then, it has fallen a little, although remaining above 45 per cent—still not bad for capitalist economies! The political contract of the post-war period was the apotheosis of social democratic values, usually coupled with the growing power of trade unions and heavy regulation of labour markets.

At the time, the Keynesian state facilitated trade liberalization and European integration, not the opposite, as economic purists might have thought. The mixed economy and the welfare state helped to smooth domestic adjustment resulting from the opening of borders and greater international competition; it also helped to buy social acceptance by alleviating the effects of adjustment on potential losers inside each country. It was therefore part and parcel of the virtuous circle: the domestic political contract was inextricably linked with the international economic environment and regional integration.

It was only in the agricultural sector that the main responsibility for inter-vention and adjustment was, from early on, transferred to the European level. In the 1950s, the agricultural sector in all the founding members was very large in terms of the numbers of persons employed, although less so in terms of out-put. When the founding treaties were signed, farmers represented 23 per cent of the total labour force in the Six, reaching 35 per cent in Italy. Now, they are down to 4 per cent in EU-15. It would therefore not have been at all easy to leave

47

agriculture out of the overall package deal. Given the long history of intervention in and external protection of agriculture in all European countries, intra-regional liberalization was possible only through the establishment of a common policy, which was bound to reproduce at least some of the elements of the national policies it replaced. It thus had little to do with laissez-faire. The price was to be paid by consumers and taxpayers alike, as well as by foreign producers. High intervention prices for European farmers were coupled with a very effective system of variable levies on imports. But the overall cost of the CAP skyrocketed as productivity growth accelerated and European self-sufficiency in food products also rose rapidly. In a sense, this was the price of success; but for how long would it be worth paying, as overall CAP expenditure kept rising?

With the rapid deterioration of the economic environment in the 1970s (in other words, with the end of the Golden Age), serious tensions developed inside the Community of Nine. They manifested themselves in long budgetary squabbles coupled with covert protectionism in the form of non-tariff barriers. In the process, distributional issues among the members also came to the fore. The setting up of a new European Regional Development Fund (ERDF) was initially seen as a means of partially compensating the British for their large net budgetary contribution.

The new economic reality, characterized by low economic growth and high unemployment (Figure 3.1), in most cases accompanied by high inflation, gradually brought about a shift in economic ideas in Western Europe. The new emphasis on macroeconomic stabilization, including fiscal consolidation after several years of large budgetary deficits, coupled with supply-side measures and deregulation of markets, lay behind the internal market programme put forward by Delors in 1985. The accumulation of budget deficits pointed to the limits of expansionary fiscal policies as a remedy for the recession, while the first years of the EMS confirmed German monetary policy as the anchor of monetary stability for all members. Meanwhile, big business in Europe came to perceive the fragmentation of the European market, caused by persisting government intervention and various forms of non-tariff barriers, as the main reason for the lack of competitiveness in international markets. Thus, economies of scale and cross-border restructuring became the key objectives, and the elimination of intra-European barriers the main instrument to achieve them. Supply-side measures and deregulation were ideas mostly imported from the United States of President Reagan, with Margaret Thatcher acting as the main and highly energetic European agent. Academic economists had laid the

48

groundwork earlier. Those ideas were gradually adopted by other European leaders, although with a mixture of anticipation and embarrassment characteristic of young virgins. European institutions served to facilitate the new economic orthodoxy.

This was the background to the adoption of the internal market programme, which marked a major turning point in regional economic integration. It was, first of all, an admission that the common market was largely incomplete almost thirty years after the signing of the Treaty of Rome. It was also a recognition of the limits of liberalizing trade by eliminating border controls in the context of mixed economies. But this meant that the national mixed economy was no longer untouchable: a new formula would have to be found for John Maynard Keynes to be able to coexist with Adam Smith. Intruding into the mixed economies of individual member states implied that national economic sovereignty would become an even more relative concept, unless the internal market programme became tantamount to deregulation. This is precisely what people like Thatcher had in mind: wrongly, of course, as was to be proved later. Last but not least, the internal market programme brought services and capital into the European picture, since they were most affected by domestic government intervention, which in turn created distortions in intra-European transactions.

This helped to create a new virtuous circle, involving both governments and the marketplace. The internal market and the Single European Act (SEA) signed in 1986 coincided with a steady improvement in the economic environment. The modest export-led recovery gradually turned into a self-sustaining process, with a steady increase in investment. The shift towards a more dynamic macroeconomic environment made governments more ready to accept the adjustment costs associated with further liberalization. This political readiness to go ahead with what was basically perceived as a supply-side programme contributed in turn to a further improvement in the economic climate. It had, of course, much to do with credibility and market perceptions, which were regularly massaged by national governments and the Commission. The necessary ingredients of a virtuous circle were all there; and there was close similarity to what had happened back in the 1950s and 1960s. But, like all good things, the economic boom was soon to end. Virtuous circles are not for ever; and this particular one was short-lived.

The 1992 programme, as it came to be known because of the termination date (31 December 1992) for the adoption of all the measures included in it, was backed by many economic studies pointing to the benefits of a larger European market and an effective marketing campaign (the two not always being clearly distinguishable). The biggest and most comprehensive study of the likely effects of the internal market—the 'Costs of Non-Europe', otherwise known as the Cecchini report, published by the Commission—covered a large area and ventured into quantitative estimates of the effects of the internal market programme. These proved to be wildly optimistic as judged by the results of *ex post* studies on the effects of the internal market—or is it simply that our measurement tools are still highly inadequate? Interestingly enough, the Cecchini report had virtually nothing concrete to say about the likely distribution of costs and benefits, apart from acknowledging the problem and expressing the hope that redistributive policies, supported by an active macroeconomic policy, would provide adequate compensation to losers or, even better, help weaker economies and regions to face the strong winds of competition unleashed by the elimination of barriers.

This was, indeed, a politically sensitive issue, and most economists did not want to touch it. The same story was repeated some years later with EMU. Being agnostic about the likely distributive effects but also fearful of a worst-case scenario, the Commission led by Jacques Delors insisted on an explicit link between the internal market and redistribution. And it succeeded, through the inclusion of the economic and social cohesion chapter in the SEA and even more importantly through the Structural Funds. In the first big negotiation in 1988 on the operation of those Funds and the amounts of money to be spent through them, the role of Germany was absolutely crucial. Germany had always been the biggest net contributor to the Community budget; it continued in this role while also setting the level for more explicitly redistributive policies. The same happened again some years later, although German generosity seemed to weaken with time, especially as the costs of Germany's unification grew while its war guilt faded away.

Are the Structural Funds, together with the Cohesion Fund which was born at Maastricht, a straightforward side payment (or bribe, in plain English) to poorer countries to buy their support for the internal market programme and later also for EMU? Alternatively, are they a kind of development policy of the Union? Many people have debated this issue at great length; but does it really matter? As with many other subjects, there is the official truth and the other. For the Commission, armed with the relevant treaty articles, it is all about a European development policy addressed to problem regions (not countries) of the Union chosen on the basis of universal criteria. This development policy is frequently justified with reference to the new growth theories. Unlike their neo-classical predecessors, these theories postulate increasing returns and agglomeration effects. They incorporate technological progress and advances in human knowledge in their growth models. Last but not least, they recognize a coordinating or supporting role for governments.

Yet it would be naive to dissociate the large amounts spent through Union structural policies, now accounting for approximately 35 per cent of the total budget, from intergovernmental bargaining in the Council. There is clearly an element of side payment in structural policies as part of complex package deals; and the criteria adopted for the use of funds are not only the product of technocratic brainstorming. This should come as no surprise. After all, this is the way European integration has so far moved along. Structural policies have also had an effect on devolution inside member countries by offering regions a new margin of manoeuvre in relation to the national centre. In this respect, the EU effect varies significantly from country to country, depending on the size of EU transfers compared with regional transfers inside national borders and also on the degree of political decentralization each country started with. Thus, the effect on regions in Greece, Portugal, or even the UK has been greater than in federal Germany, where, if anything, the main concern of the *Länder* has been about losing power because of European integration: not the way it is seen in Epirus, Alentejo, or the Highlands. The power of the regions in an integrating Europe has become indeed an important political issue. However, the effect of the EU on the regions has often been grossly exaggerated. We are still far from a Europe of the regions, even though in some countries, such as Belgium, Germany, and Spain, the process has gone much further than elsewhere.

When the debate on EMU started back in 1969–70, the creation of a monetary union was closely linked with a bigger Community budget and the so-called automatic stabilizers and inter-regional transfers to be found in all national or federal budgets of Western capitalist democracies. This was a time of plenty, rich also in Keynesian ideas. Revisiting the subject twenty years later, the official report which prepared the ground for the Maastricht treaty paid much attention to the link between monetary and fiscal policy; but it had precious little to say about fiscal federalism and redistribution. There was a political drive for EMU, but hardly any agreement to move to anything resembling a federal budget. Side payments were not deemed necessary this time: the new monetary orthodoxy did not recognize any long-term costs associated with stabilization, while most of the poorer countries were not expected to join EMU for some time. Economic preconditions for joining, which were indeed new in regional integration, seemed to make side payments quite unnecessary.

51

The main concession offered to the economically weaker was a new agreement on the Structural Funds, coupled with the creation of the Cohesion Fund, which brought about a further increase in the amounts to be spent over the next seven years. This was repeated in 1999, although with no net increase in the total amounts to be spent until 2006. Redistributive policies were thus confirmed as an integral part of the European package deal, but there was no major quantitative or qualitative change.

The transition from EMS to EMU in 1999 constitutes the next important—undoubtedly, the most important—turning point in European integration. From relatively fixed intra-EU exchange rates, we have moved to a single monetary policy and a single currency managed by a supranational central bank. In practice, the central bank is more independent and politically less accountable than any other central bank, including its role model, the Bundesbank, for the very simple reason that there is no equivalent political interlocutor: in other words, no European government. The centralized monetary policy will operate in the context of a decentralized fiscal system, since the Union budget remains very small (slightly more than 1 per cent of total output in the Union), while provisions for the coordination of national fiscal policies are mostly of the soft kind, with the exception of limits set for national budget deficits as a percentage of GDP.

Thus, the Union has finally acquired a major, albeit partial, stabilization function through EMU. As it stands, EMU changes the traditional balance between monetary and fiscal policy, this being the result partly of political expediency (or feasibility) and partly of the new economic orthodoxy prevailing at the time of its conception. Keynes was finally(?) out, and Milton Friedman was in. Back in the Golden Age, European integration developed in a way compatible with the mixed economy and the welfare state. Things have changed since then. The internal market, and especially EMU, influence and constrain the ability of states to shape economic events. The domestic political contract in European countries has been changing, and regional integration has often acted as a catalyst. Sometimes it has also served as a scapegoat for national politicians forced to take unpopular measures at home. The process that began in Lisbon in 2000, aiming at structural reforms through soft intergovernmental coordination and benchmarking, is meant to provide both the catalyst and the scapegoat.

Although the Union has acquired new and important functions in terms of market regulation, redistribution, and macroeconomic stabilization, it has only partially compensated for policy instruments which have been weakened or simply made redundant at the national level. This is surely consistent with the new global economic reality (usually referred to as globalization) and with new ideas about the relationship between the state and the market: economic events and economic ideas generally moving in the same direction and reinforcing each other. It remains, however, to be seen whether this is a stable state of affairs and, if so, for how long.

In earlier years, liberalization measures at the European level helped to create a favourable economic environment, which not only contributed to growth and welfare but also helped to shape positive popular perceptions of integration. Thus, virtuous economic circles kept the European project spinning. It has not been like this for more than a decade. During the 1990s, the road to the single currency was paved with restrictive macroeconomic policies in an attempt to meet the convergence criteria and also to undo the accumulated mistakes (and debts) of the past. This was not, however, the case in countries with a poor record of monetary stability, such as Italy or Greece, where the commitment to EMU—and tying themselves to the Deutschmark/euro mast— helped to reduce the cost of deflationary adjustment.

The euro arrived at a time of low growth and further rapid restructuring, which naturally brings with it adjustment costs and political resistance from potential losers. In the same way that European integration became identified with prosperity in the first decades, it now risks being associated with economic adversity, painful changes, and uncertainty for an increasing number of citizens. A return to healthy rates of economic growth would probably make the crucial difference, but is it likely? And it surely does not help when national politicians resort to easy blaming of Brussels for unpopular measures at home.

☆ Who Loves Europe?

In my early years as an academic, when the EC was preparing itself to receive three much poorer countries from southern Europe, theories of centre and periphery were popular, especially in left-wing circles. They drew their inspiration from the wider family of economic divergence theories, which predict a worsening of inequalities as a result of free trade, and hence a growing economic gap, following the southern enlargement, between the centre of Europe, comprising most of the EC of Nine, and its new southern periphery. Rich countries (or regions) tend to get richer and poor ones poorer with the free interplay of market forces, or so such theories contend. Markets do not behave in the way described in neo-classical textbooks. Economies of scale and different kinds of externalities can have cumulative effects leading to wider inter-country or inter-regional disparities.

The end result has been very different, and this largely explains why the European periphery loves Europe. If anything, the EU seems so far to have acted as a convergence machine, leading to a substantial reduction of inter-country income disparities. This is particularly true of the so-called Cohesion Four, comprising Greece, Ireland, Portugal, and Spain, which have been identified as the main targets and beneficiaries of the Structural and Cohesion Funds. The case of the Republic of Ireland is by far the most spectacular: starting with 68 per cent of the EU-15 average in 1988, the year when the first major reform of the Structural Funds took place, Ireland reached 122 per cent in 2001. These figures represent per capita income calculated on the basis of purchasing power standards (PPS), thus adjusting for different price levels. During the same period, Spain climbed up the ladder from 74 per cent to 84 per cent, Portugal from 59 to 74, and Greece from 60 to 68 (Figure 3.3). True, the Irish performance would appear less spectacular if measured by gross national product (GNP) and not GDP figures, since net profit repatriation from foreign-owned companies in the Republic usually accounts for more than 10 per cent of GNP; and the figures for Greece would be less encouraging if we took into account the downward trend during the early years of accession (1981–8). Yet the overall picture does not significantly alter. During this period, the poorest countries of the Union have succeeded in narrowing the income gap separating them from their partners; and Ireland has actually overtaken most of them.

Is economic convergence a validation of liberal economic theories? This is impossible to prove, although EU and national economic policies during this period can hardly qualify as models of economic liberalism. Membership of the EU has meant the opening of national markets, in some cases after a long history of protection. It has also meant large inflows of funds, both private and public. Private inflows, mostly in the form of foreign direct investment, fit nicely with traditional theories: free trade and lower wage costs bring foreign investment, thus leading to higher growth. This is at least a partial description of the Irish economic miracle of the last ten years or so. To complete the picture, however, one should add the advantage of the English language, large investment in education and training, a favourable tax regime (is there a free-rider problem?), and political consensus, including a wide-ranging agreement between the government and the social partners.

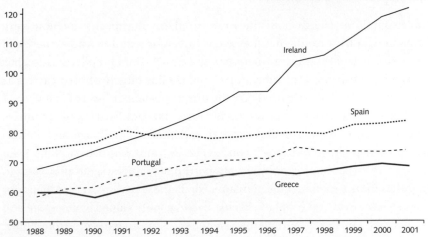

Figure 3.3. Economic convergence, 1988–2001 (GDP per head of population of cohesion countries as a percentage of EU average)
Source: European Commission.

There have also been large transfers of public funds: in the case of Greece and Portugal, transfers from the Structural and Cohesion Funds reached 3.5 per cent of GDP every year during this period, going mostly into infrastructural projects and investment in human capital (education and training). There is little agreement among economists about the real contribution of these transfers to economic growth in the recipient countries; and there has also been considerable wastage due to inefficiency or corruption (usually both). Admittedly, it is extremely difficult to distinguish *ex post* the effects of EU structural policies from all the other factors that may have influenced growth in the European periphery; but can they be ignored? We also need to add transfers through the CAP in countries where agriculture is still an economic sector of considerable importance. With the exception of Portugal, cohesion countries have benefited from the CAP, although at a price for their consumers. Transfers from the EU budget have also gone hand in hand with the growth of government expenditure and the welfare state in the three southern European members, although not in Ireland.

On the other hand, there has been more to EU membership for the peripheral countries than growth and transfers. Membership has meant opening up to the rest of Europe and the world in more than an economic sense; in other words, greater exposure to modernity. It has also meant the consolidation of democracy in countries which had been cut off for shorter or longer periods from Europe's post-war democratic core; and it has meant different benchmarking and the import of higher standards of public and corporate governance.

55

The Republic of Ireland and the three southern Europeans are now very different countries from what they were fifteen or twenty years earlier; and they owe much of this transformation to the EU. Of course, modernization has not just been imported; membership of the EU has mostly offered carrots as well as sticks which helped to change the internal balance of forces in favour of the modernizing elements of the society. Last but not least, these countries have acquired a new role on the European and international stage, and this has been a tremendous boost to self-confidence in countries that had long been objects rather than subjects of international diplomacy. The same also seems to apply to a more recent member, Finland. For all these reasons, it is perhaps not an exaggeration to argue that the EU has become more valued by the small and peripheral countries of Europe than by the old Carolingian core from which regional integration has sprung and where the gains of the previous generation now tend to be taken for granted.

This has been reflected in popular attitudes towards European integration. The four countries, namely, Greece, Ireland, Portugal, and Spain, have consistently ranked among those with the highest levels of support for integration, with Portugal still, slowly and somewhat hesitantly, rediscovering Europe (Figure 1.2). On the other hand, the attitude of the Cohesion Four towards EMU is both interesting and typical. Hardly any of them was considered a serious candidate for early membership, at least by Germany, which was insisting on strict admission criteria. After all, their record on inflation and budget deficits had not been very impressive. Yet their subsequent adjustment effort during the 1990s in order to meet the convergence criteria and thus secure admission tickets to EMU was impressive indeed. While unemployment rates remained high in most of the countries, deflationary policies were justified by governments as the necessary price to pay in order to avoid exclusion from EMU and hence marginalization within the Union. Precisely the same thing happened in Italy. The EU has often served as the justification, the external catalyst, or even the scapegoat for unpopular measures at home. But this can work only as long as EU membership remains popular and continues to be perceived by the large majority of the population as crucially important for the country. The negative Irish vote in the first referendum on the Nice Treaty in 2001 indicates that popular support cannot be taken for granted anywhere, although the result of that referendum should be treated with caution because of the very low turn-out. Supporters of European integration are not easily mobilized, especially when faced with such unattractive political propositions as the Nice Treaty. Admittedly, the second try in Ireland proved more successful.

The EU as a convergence machine? This is a hypothesis that needs to be tested further in the context of EMU and further enlargement, while international competition continues to grow fast. On the other hand, this convergence machine has not worked for everyone. Inter-country income disparities have indeed shown a tendency to narrow, especially in times of high growth. It had also happened during the Golden Age. Convergence does not, however, apply to inter-regional disparities, which, after all, are supposed to be the main concern and target of EU structural policies according to the book (that is, the treaties). There are very few generalizations we can make about how disparities among the 211 regions of EU-15 have changed over the years, whatever the indicator used (income, employment, or productivity). Two hundred and eleven is the precise number of regions (or basic administrative units) classified by the European statistical service with the rather unfortunate name of NUTS2 (no insult intended: the initials simply stand for 'nomenclature of territorial units for statistics'). These are also the most relevant units for the purpose of EU structural policies and hence for EU funding. The number is large. Furthermore, many of those regions are hardly comparable entities. How can we compare, for example, the cities of Hamburg and Bremen (two NUTS2 regions and also two of the sixteen German *Länder*) with Andalucia or Sicily, which are also NUTS2 regions? Statistical information usually needs to adjust to administrative practices and political realities, but it may end up having little comparative value.

Subject to all those limitations, there is no clear trend of inter-regional disparities being reduced, even among the Cohesion Four countries, where inter-country convergence with the rest of the Union has clearly taken place. In simple terms, what has been true for Lisbon or Athens has not necessarily been true for the rest of Portugal or Greece. Only for Spain has there been some evidence of a reduction in inter-regional disparities; as for the Republic of Ireland, there are no comparable statistics, since the whole country was treated as a single region until 2000, when it became convenient to divide it into four regions in order to continue to qualify for EU structural aid. No noticeable trend of convergence has been discerned either in the case of other less developed regions of the Union, such as the Italian south or Northern Ireland. It has, however, happened in eastern Germany after unification, but this surely has most to do with inter-German transfers. In the 1990s, subsidies from the rest of the country usually accounted for more than half the total income in the new *Länder*. So much for relying on market forces for income convergence, although admittedly German unification has been in many respects a special case.

Reducing inequalities has been one of the key priorities of the Union. It is proclaimed in the treaties and it is regularly repeated in public statements. Since the treaty revision of 1986, the Union has acquired some policy instruments to help bring it about. The money spent through the Structural and Cohesion Funds goes entirely for investment rather than consumption, in contrast with the CAP, in which the bulk of expenditure takes the form of price or income subsidies. In practice, however, the difference is less stark than it may appear, since money is fungible and the so-called principle of additionality in the case of structural policies (which means that EU funding should be additional to what the recipient normally spends on investment) is not always easy to apply.

The emphasis on reducing inequalities and the inclusion of redistribution as an integral part of the European economic package deal reproduce, on a much smaller scale, what has been happening within individual Western European countries since the end of the Second World War. European societies continue to attach much importance to equality and social solidarity, as political practice and opinion polls have repeatedly shown. But how much solidarity can there be across national borders, even in the context of the EU? The answer to this question will be one of the key determining factors for the future of European integration. Market integration has become closely linked to redistribution in the EU, which is indeed a remarkable development for an emerging polity consisting of nation-states. Strong political pressure from the poorer countries, which successfully linked redistribution with the further deepening of integration through the internal market programme and later EMU, was backed by the Commission and accepted by Germany, by far the biggest provider of funds. This package deal will go through a difficult test with the accession of a large number of poorer countries, as the rich members, especially Germany, try to cut back on their own net contributions to the common budget.

As a key part of the bargain in the 1990s, redistribution coincided with a substantial reduction of inter-country disparities within the Union. The precise link between the two is impossible to establish, although it is perhaps safe to argue that it has been more important for the slower members of the convoy than for the faster ones. Flows of foreign direct investment into Ireland, for example, have been a multiple of Union transfers. On the other hand, there is little doubt about the political effects of redistribution, which has acted as a catalyst for opening up and modernizing the periphery, while also facilitating the implementation of the internal market programme and later the transition to EMU.

The main responsibility for redistribution and reducing inequalities among regions or social groups still lies with national governments. The EU provides the extra bit; in some cases it is the bit that makes the difference, while in others it is more symbolic than real. Since the 1980s, earnings inequalities have grown within countries, and in some cases they have been translated into an increase in after-tax income inequalities. This trend has been more pronounced in the UK, a country that has gone further than others in terms of economic liberalization, including the liberalization of its labour market and tax cuts concentrated mostly on the top end of the income ladder. The experience of the United States has been similar; indeed, inequalities there have become even greater. At a time of slow growth, high unemployment, unfavourable demographics, and widening inequalities in terms of earnings, the welfare states of Western Europe are being faced with an almost impossible task. Something will have to change.

Measures of inequalities are notorious for their diversity; yet most studies point in the same upward direction for the recent period. It is difficult to agree on the magnitude of the problem and even more difficult to agree on the causes. Has regional integration contributed to the widening of intra-country disparities in recent years? There is very little evidence of that, though it is almost impossible to separate the effects of regional integration from the effects of globalization and technological change (which are among the main determining factors) on income distribution inside the member countries of the EU. On the other hand, it is clear that tax and welfare policies do make a difference: some countries have been much more successful than others in containing the upward trend of income inequality.

We know that economic integration puts a premium on cross-border mobility and arbitrage. It therefore favours professionals, the younger, and the better educated, who can more easily take advantage of the opportunities provided by the dismantling of national barriers than those whose assets and skills are tied to domestic markets. It favours the big and the better organized, who can more easily take advantage of size in a large market and of the lobbying opportunities provided by the European political system. This is already reflected in political attitudes. European integration—and European identity as well—remain essentially a matter for cosmopolitan (Europeanized?) elites. They have been growing in numbers, but elites they remain, all the same.

Integration also undoubtedly favours capital more than labour and, in general, the more mobile factors of production, to use the sterilized language of economics rather than the value-laden language of politics. This has important distributional consequences, both before and after tax. And to the extent that political power in Western European democracies tends to counterbalance the inequalities produced by the market, the underdeveloped nature of the European political system will also have distributional consequences. These simple truths were well understood by, among others, Jacques Delors, who therefore insisted on a close link between economic liberalization on the one hand and redistribution, together with the strengthening of the European social dimension, on the other. He was only partially successful.

European farmers deserve a separate mention, since the CAP has long been the most developed sectoral policy of the EU. Farmers have been heavily subsidized at the expense of consumers and taxpayers, not to mention producers outside Union borders. Remote villages have thus become very conscious of European integration, as they regularly receive their cheques with the compliments of the European taxpayer. Because they are among the least mobile internationally, European farmers are therefore the main exception to the rule that integration mostly benefits the mobile. Since the average income of those engaged in agriculture remains even today significantly below the EU average, agricultural transfers would appear to have a positive redistributive effect, thus making the CAP, if not a model of economic efficiency, at least some kind of social and adjustment policy in a declining sector. But this is only part of the story. The CAP has in fact increased inequalities within the farming sector: the bigger the farm, the greater the subsidies, although this has been changing slowly with successive reforms. On the other hand, the political importance of the CAP has diminished as the size of the farming population has been rapidly falling.

With few exceptions, and most notably the farmers, the distributional effects of European integration among different economic and social groups were not very noticeable in the past, for two simple reasons: the pie was growing fast, while the nation-state was more able to influence developments inside its borders and also to compensate the losers from economic adjustment. We may add a third reason: the effects were limited as long as integration was mostly about the elimination of border controls on trade in goods. Inter-country and inter-regional redistribution through EU structural policies acted subsequently as a lubricant for further integration in times of slower growth. The political and economic environment has been changing at an accelerating pace in recent years.

Increasing Europeanization and globalization of the economy necessitate rapid adjustment, while at the same time reducing the capacity of states to influence economic developments. Slow growth, low levels of employment, and ageing populations have certainly made matters worse. Evidence from European elections and opinion polls suggests that losers, potential losers, and risk-averse people in a world of rapid change tend more and more to rally behind national flags, the state emerging once again as the only potential, although objectively much weaker, source of protection. The division between winners and losers thus tends to become a more important issue within countries than between countries. Further enlargement is expected to bring into the Union an eastern periphery which is much poorer than the one in the south. Will it happen in the same dismal economic environment, or will Europe succeed finally in creating the conditions for more growth and higher employment? All these factors will influence the way in which European countries, individually and collectively, attempt in the next few years to tackle the trade-off between efficiency and equality, and also how the new division of labour among European, national, and sub-national institutions shapes up in this context.

☆ The Broader Equation

European integration reaches parts of the body politic that mere economic policies cannot reach. The big historic agreements that have shaped European integration—the signing of the Treaty of Rome, the adoption of the internal market programme, EMU—undoubtedly have a strong economic content, but also much broader effects. On issues of strategic interest—and high politics, the international relations expert might add—national interest seems easier to define. And on such issues European decisions have been essentially the product of intergovernmental bargaining, usually based on broad consensus among the main political parties in each country.

It is, however, impossible to understand how national policies led to those agreements by reference simply to real or perceived narrowly defined national economic interests. EMU is a good example. Of course, we need to consider the importance of fixed exchange rates for open economies; the desire to safeguard the competitiveness of domestic producers; the need for monetary stability and the usefulness of the external anchor as a means of achieving it; and several other economic variables in the equation considered by economics and finance ministers. Yet heads of government, with the final say in those negotiations, had a much broader equation in mind. It included the deepening of integration and the strengthening of common institutions as a means of

61

achieving wider political goals as well as restoring symmetry among participants, to mention only a few but extremely important factors in the negotiations leading to EMU.

Thus, the German Chancellor, Helmut Kohl, accepted the link between German unification and a stronger Community/Union, and the price attached to it, namely, a common European currency (and monetary policy) to replace the Deutschmark, which until then had been the key currency of the EMS. On the other hand, the French President, François Mitterrand, saw in EMU a way of tying the now united Germany more securely to a stronger European system, while also achieving a greater balance between France and Germany in the monetary field. As for the Italians and the other southern Europeans, EMU fitted well with their policy of active engagement and participation in regional integration as well as the search for an external discipline and catalyst for domestic economic restructuring and stabilization. The British did not share these political objectives, and they also believed they had different economic interests. So they decided to stay out, at least for the time being.

EMU is representative of how regional integration has developed over the years. Even in the earlier stages, when integration was almost entirely about economic issues, the big decisions reflected wider political considerations, the political and the intangible being intimately linked to the material and the specific. European integration has been generally perceived as a positive-sum game, involving the joint management of economic interdependence for increasingly open economies; the intermeshing and interlocking of sovereign political entities as a means of consolidating peace and security on a continent with a long history of national rivalries and bloody conflict; and, last but not least, the strengthening of democratic institutions. There has clearly been an element of spillover, integration in one policy area bringing about pressures for integration elsewhere. With time, member countries have also developed a strong coordination reflex in response to external challenges, whether globalization and international competition or the collapse of the economic and political order on their eastern frontier. Otherwise, the internal market programme, EMU, and the two new 'pillars' of the Maastricht Treaty, representing the new common foreign and security policy (CFSP) as well as justice and home affairs, would be extremely difficult to explain.

European integration also means, fortunately, different things to different countries. It has helped Germany to regain credibility as a responsible member of the European system and a status quo country, enabling it in the process to secure full sovereignty and reunification. For many years, the French had a decisive influence on the European agenda and the way European institutions were run. It was therefore not a complete illusion for French presidents to think '*l'Europe, c'est moi*'. A sophisticated French political elite, supported by a highly organized civil service, produced ideas and initiatives that helped to match the rising economic power of Germany; and as a result the Franco-German couple served for many years as the locomotive for the train of European integration. For Italy, Europe provided its much-needed Leviathan: a solid framework and an anchor for an unstable (and often unruly) nation-state. This observation also seems to apply to the other southern Europeans, although perhaps more to Greece than to Spain.

Small and medium-sized countries have been over-represented in all common institutions. Through the EU, they have also acquired a role and an influence in European and international affairs they would never have enjoyed otherwise. This explains why, with only few exceptions such as Denmark, they have tried to resist moves towards more intergovernmentalism, which they perceive as a device for restoring the predominance of the big powers. For the periphery and the less developed, European integration has provided the catalyst for modernization and development, while for regions aspiring to greater autonomy or independence, Europe has offered a favourable environment and a framework within which they would try to reconcile international interdependence with regional autonomy or even sovereignty.

Thus there have been important common interests, but also more specific ones catering for the needs of different national actors. The combination has proved truly powerful, and it helps to explain the remarkable extension and deepening of regional integration over the years. Democracy, welfare, peace, and security remain, of course, key objectives, although the political and economic environment in which they operate has changed considerably over the years, especially since the end of the cold war—and so have perceptions among participants, including the perception of the relative contribution of the EU to the achievement of these objectives. For example, unified Germany has become a more 'normal' country, with greater clout than the others. How much will this influence German perceptions and policies in the context of the EU? On the other hand, French leaders have often experienced difficulties in adjusting to a Union in which they cannot always define the agenda. And there is more: Berlusconi's Italy may not, after all, prove to be only a short-term aberration in a long history of undiluted Euro-enthusiasm, while Spain may find it hard to reconcile the interests of a cohesion country with its ambition to be treated as a fully paid-up member of the group of big ones—the kind of experience that Poland also is likely to go through in the future. Meanwhile, all cohesion countries of EU-15 will be forced to redefine their interests in a further enlarged Union, in which they will cease to be the poorest members and also the beneficiaries of significant intra-Union transfers.

In the list of broader national interests outlined above, there are some notable absentees, among them the UK. Membership of the EU has been marred by periodic crises, various opt-outs from common policies, divergence from mainstream opinion on several important issues, and generally low levels of popular support for unification. Memories of the lost empire, the more international and offshore character of the British economy, and the 'special relationship' with the United States have all played a role. They have combined with a strong tradition of parliamentary democracy, a historical mistrust of continental Europeans, and the fact that, by choosing to stay out, the British had no influence in the early but crucial phases of integration, when the overall package deal took its first concrete shape. They have been trying hard to secure a leading role in European affairs, but for that to happen they will need a different kind of European Union in the future, which is closer to a more traditional concert of powers than a proper Union. What is true of the UK in general is not, however, necessarily true of Scotland. For the Scots, as for the Catalans, Brussels provides a safe anchor for regional autonomy (and ultimately independence?) as well as an alternative reference point to the old national centre. Scottish independence has no credibility outside the EU.

The Scandinavians constitute the other difficult part of the Union puzzle. Although small in population and open in trade, these countries have behaved very differently from others who share the same characteristics. A long tradition of neutrality and social democracy, coupled with high standards of living and governance, has produced a certain superiority complex and an unwillingness to share sovereignty with the other countries of the European continent. This seems an apt description of Sweden in Europe, although less so of the other countries. A rich periphery with a strong sense of regional identity, backed by close cooperation, and a consciously kept distance from the rest of continental Europe is a more general description that seems to apply to all Nordic countries, including Norway and Iceland, which have so far rejected the option of EU membership but not that of NATO. If anything, Scandinavian countries are likely to feel more comfortable in a European Union with more democracy and higher social and environmental standards.

There are, indeed, powerful forces for change in European integration—and they do not all work in the same direction. For some decades, the Franco-German couple led the Community, and then the Union, through successive rounds of widening and deepening. Regional integration was generally perceived as a win-win game, both between countries and within countries; the most notable of the few exceptions was the UK, where European policy was more often determined on the basis of the costs of exclusion than the benefits of inclusion. The Franco-German couple have been through a difficult period in recent years: it happens to most couples. Will they continue to be able to lead in an enlarged EU? And, if not, will they be gradually replaced by a concert of the big powers, including the British and perhaps others, imposing a more intergovernmental model of integration? If so, what will happen to the smaller partners who have tended to identify more—and rightly so—with the European project and the Community method? And how will the new members fit in? Leadership is, of course, closely linked to what the Union does. So, in a Union with a stronger role in foreign policy and defence, the British would secure a more prominent place.

High politics has not disappeared from the European scene, nor is it likely to for a long time. In this context, nation-states will continue to play an important role. On the other hand, many aspects of European integration have long ceased to be just an affair concerning sovereign countries with a clear definition of the national interest, especially as integration begins to reach the 'nooks and crannies' of our societies. This is bound to have an effect on the way European politics is being conducted. Ideological divisions, together with class or group interests, should be expected to express themselves more strongly at the European level, thus cutting across the more traditional inter-country divisions that have long dominated—and naturally so—the process of European integration.

4

☆☆☆☆☆

. . . and the Rest of the World:
Americans and Others

European integration does not take place in an international vacuum. Size and history combine to ensure that what happens within the region does not go unnoticed outside. The EC started as a trade bloc; its nature as a customs union, incomplete though it had remained for many years, long determined its external dimension. This was enshrined in the treaties, and the Commission was given the power to represent the Community in international trade negotiations. As regional integration deepened, covering an ever-increasing number of policy areas, relations with the rest of the world were bound to be affected, raising some fundamental questions about external representation and the definition of the common interest in relation to others.

Between trade and high politics, relations with the United States have been the single most important determining factor of a common European policy. This has been true of GATT negotiations, in which the Americans were very critical of what they described as European protectionism and the repeated violations of multilateralism and the most-favoured-nation clause of GATT; and it is even more true of recent attempts by EU members to develop a common foreign and security policy (CFSP). This is only natural, since the United States remained the undisputed leader of the Western alliance during the long period of the cold war (all the original members of the EU being also members of NATO, plus the majority of those who joined subsequently); and this has been followed, after the disintegration of the Soviet empire, by the primacy of American power in what appears to be, in many respects, an increasingly unipolar world.

Of course, this crucial relationship with the American superpower goes further back. The foundations of regional economic cooperation in Western Europe were laid during the reconstruction period immediately after the end of the Second World War. The initiative and the money came from the United States in the form of the Marshall Plan. American aid to the dollar-hungry economies of Western Europe provided the finance for large payments deficits. At the same time, US aid was conditional on effective cooperation among European governments and the progressive liberalization of intra-European trade and payments. The first regional organizations, such as the Organization for European Economic Cooperation (OEEC), later transformed into the OECD, were the result of American pressure on the European recipients of Marshall aid; and the United States was apparently ready to make a big exception to its pursuit of multilateralism in order to promote the economic and political integration of the old continent. Yet the rich and powerful godfather did not succeed in having a decisive influence over the upbringing and development of the child—or so it appears. Although US pressure was at least partially responsible for the French initiative leading to the ECSC, this organization hardly conformed to American wishes.

As an international economic actor with a constantly expanding range of policy responsibilities, if not necessarily political influence, the EU has tried to reconcile the principle of multilateralism, meaning non-discrimination in trade matters, with its instinct for regionalism and privileged partners. It has also struggled to make the transition from economic power to political power, thus stepping with much trepidation into the area of traditional foreign policy and security. In so doing, it constantly needs to define and redefine what, if anything, distinguishes it from the rest of the world, and the means through which this should be defended. Do Europeans believe that they have common interests which they agree to pursue collectively through common instruments and policies? And does this agreement extend all the way from trade to defence? The development of a common European foreign policy necessarily proceeds by way of defining a common policy vis-à-vis the most important ally and partner, the United States. Europeans have usually tried to fudge this issue, only to be reminded of its key importance in times of transatlantic tension.

☆ Trade Policy as a Model?

The EU is big and influential in trade matters—and there is still a considerable difference between trade and most other aspects of relations with the rest of the world. The reason is simple: in trade the EU has a common policy that operates along federal lines, with a single representation ensuring that its nego-tiating power is commensurate with its collective weight. This does not apply to other areas of policy.

The Union now accounts for approximately 20 per cent of world exports, excluding intra-EU trade. Its share will increase further with the new enlarge-ment. In terms of world trade, it is already more significant than the United States. The EU, the United States, and Japan—the so-called Triad—together represent approximately one-half of world trade. This clearly illustrates the dominant position of the three big players. Their dependence on external trade in goods as a percentage of GDP has converged over the years around the 10 per cent figure, with the United States gradually catching up with the other two (Figure 4.1). However, averages of exports and imports often hide large trade imbalances, as has traditionally been true of Japan and increasingly so of the United States in recent years. Given their economic size, it is not surprising that the members of the Triad still have a high degree of self-sufficiency. However, somewhat surprisingly, over a period of thirty years the external trade of EU-15 has registered only a slow upward trend as a percentage of GDP. Intra-EU trade, even when adjusted for successive enlargements, has been growing at a much faster rate; in other words, the regional has been growing faster than the global.

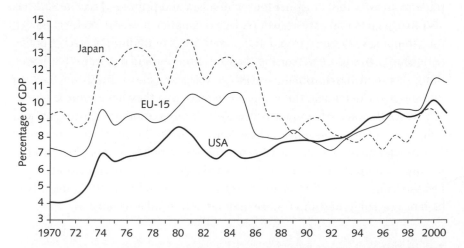

Figure 4.1. External trade in goods in EU-15,[a] Japan, and USA, 1970–2001 (average of exports and imports as a percentage of GDP)

[a] excluding intra-EU-15 trade.

Source: European Commission, IMF.

European regional integration was from the very beginning meant to be an exception to the principle of multilateralism, which had been one of the main planks of US policy in the post-war economic order. Article XXIV of GATT, allowing for free trade areas and customs unions, served as an instrument of legitimization. In fact, the Europeans have gone much further, interpreting this article very liberally in the conduct of the common commercial policy. Their American partners were greatly annoyed by this until they decided to follow the European example.

The EEC started as an exception in the world of GATT, and it very quickly emerged as a leading partner in international trade negotiations because of the collective trade weight of the six founding members. During the Kennedy Round (1963–7), the Six, represented by the Commission, matched the negotiating power of the United States, thus marking the end of a period of unchallenged American leadership in the post-war international trading system. The British got the message quickly, and drew the necessary conclusion: 'if you can't beat them, join them.' The collective negotiating power of the Europeans was further confirmed in subsequent trade rounds.

The European Commission negotiates on behalf of the Union and on the basis of mandates agreed by the Council, which also retains the power to approve the results. To be sure, the EU is not an easy partner to deal with, because it is big, has a cumbersome decision-making system, and is highly decentralized; but are the Americans easier to deal with? The powers enjoyed by Congress in matters of international trade certainly make US policy rather inflexible and often prone to be taken hostage by organized lobbies. However, those powers also ensure greater transparency and accountability, which is certainly not true of the EU. The European Parliament has no powers with respect to the common commercial policy, while national parliaments usually find it extremely difficult to penetrate the complicated and closed system of EU decision-making. True, the system has generally delivered the goods and, if anything, delivery has improved with time and accumulated experience. It has also improved because the old ideological battle between free traders and protectionists has become much less pronounced. Yet it remains a system that is not open to democratic control and scrutiny.

The Kennedy Round led to a major liberalization of international trade. The common stance of the Six was not based on the lowest common denominator, while their collective weight forced bigger trade concessions from other GATT members, including most notably the Americans. This seems to have been generally true of subsequent international trade negotiations. The further deepening of European integration, combined with the addition of new members, has often acted as a catalyst: third countries trying to anticipate and minimize the trade diversion effects of EC decisions, and then the Community's involvement in the negotiations helping to bring about a shift, albeit partial, in the attitudes of the less liberal-minded members. This leads to the conclusion that European integration has had an overall liberalizing effect on international trade, contrary to the fears expressed by many economists bound to the altar of multilateralism and the repeated complaints made by Americans and others. There is, of course, an important exception to this general observation, and it is called CAP. In agriculture, 'Fortress Europe' has survived several rounds of international trade negotiations, even with some more recent significant changes in its external protection; but this is the exception and not the rule.

Trade effects are easier to measure, even though with variable degrees of accuracy, than the effects of international negotiations. There is broad consensus among economists, drawing on numerous econometric studies, that trade creation resulting from European integration has been much greater than trade diversion, thus having a positive welfare effect for those inside the regional bloc as well as for those outside it. This is true of earlier studies in the 1960s and also of subsequent studies on the trade effects of the internal market. Agricultural goods remain the main exception: the CAP operates partly at the expense of outsiders, with trade diversion far outweighing trade creation. But in this respect the EU is not very different from many other developed countries.

The common external tariff, a by-product of the customs union, has served as the main instrument of the European common commercial policy; it has been progressively reduced as a result of successive rounds of GATT negotiations, thus losing much of its effect as an instrument of external protection. The average EU tariff for industrial products is now around 4 per cent. Yet averages are often misleading, and this also applies to EU tariff protection. Higher tariff rates have survived in some sensitive sectors. Furthermore, effective rates of protection calculated on the basis of value added are almost invariably higher than nominal rates. As tariff protection gradually lost its bite, non-tariff barriers (NTBs) in their many different manifestations and incarnations began to occupy centre stage. With the implementation of the internal market programme, a good deal of market regulation came under the direct control or scrutiny of the EU, although there is still a grey area in terms of the division of powers between nation-states and the Union.

The extension of the European integration agenda has often gone hand in hand with the GATT agenda, although the results remain substantially different. The latest example was provided by the Uruguay Round, which started officially in 1986 and ended with an agreement signed in Marrakesh in 1994. There was close similarity between the European internal market programme and much of the agenda of the Uruguay Round, dealing with the multitude of NTBs, usually falling into the category of economic regulation, and the extension of jurisdiction to new areas, most notably services. Although the Uruguay Round has produced important concrete results, leading also to the creation of the World Trade Organization (WTO), it is hardly surprising that these results are far short of what has been achieved in the context of the Union. There is a big difference between what is feasible at the regional (more precisely, the European) level and the global level; and this difference has to do with the similarity of economic and social values, the long history of cooperation, the existence of an elaborate institutional machinery, and a well-established legal order, among other things. There is much greater scope for joint governance of the economic interdependence achieved within the EU than is the case at the global level; and this should have long-term consequences for market integration within Europe and globally.

Largely because of its collective experience, the Union has defended, though with exceptions, multilateral rules in international trade. It pushed for the establishment of the WTO and the strengthening of the dispute-settlement procedures of this new trade organization, which are also its most important distinguishing feature. There is apparently an unofficial contest going on between the Europeans and the Americans regarding the cases brought before the WTO panels; and the Europeans pride themselves in being far ahead in the number of cases they have won so far. It is a laudable competition, as long as compliance follows. Wisely enough, perhaps, the WTO rules provide for retaliation but not necessarily for compliance.

It is certainly not all bright and clear. The Union has sometimes (increasingly?) succumbed to the attractions of unilateral or arbitrary action, thus taking advantage of its own relative weight and the big gaps in international legislation. One prominent example is the use of anti-dumping, an important instrument of so-called commercial defence in the hands of the Commission. GATT rules still allow relatively wide scope for the use of anti-dumping against 'unfair trade practices' by third country exporters. Since neither economic theory nor international regulation offers clear guidance on this issue, the resulting gap is unavoidably filled with a mixture of unilateralism and arbitrary action. The Union has frequently been accused of using anti-dumping as a protectionist instrument; indeed, countervailing duties or different kinds of

71

undertakings with exporters are usually a much more effective form of protection than tariffs, while the threat of anti-dumping action can serve as a powerful instrument of deterrence against rapid import penetration of the internal market. Who can give an impartial definition of discriminatory pricing in a world of imperfect markets or provide a correct answer to what constitutes 'injury' to domestic producers? The Commission has been given the responsibility of providing the answers to those questions in the context of the EU, although many people would prefer an independent authority deliberating with greater transparency.

A similar problem arises with respect to the extraterritorial dimension of competition policy, another common policy of the EU though not part of its trade policy. The increasing globalization of production and economic exchange, coupled with the inadequacy of international rules, inevitably leads to unilateral actions and the attempt to give an extraterritorial dimension to competition policy. The Commission, for example, could argue in the past that price fixing among paper producers in Scandinavian countries, even before their accession to the EU, had an effect on the internal market, thus justifying the imposition of heavy fines on them. Similarly, the Commission can also argue that the proposed merger between Time Warner and AOL, or between General Electric and Honeywell, all of them large multinational companies with their headquarters in the United States, will have an important effect in terms of competition in the European internal market. And this justifies imposing strict conditions on those mergers and ultimately reserving the right to prohibit them if the conditions are not met, as in the case of General Electric and Honeywell.

A European body pronouncing on the proposed marriage between two American champions, and on the basis of what kind of criteria? What has the world come to, many Americans and others may wonder. And there is no answer to the question, since international rules are highly inadequate for dealing with this problem of overlapping authorities. US legislators and courts have in fact acted as pioneers in the game of extraterritoriality, especially with regard to anti-trust laws and taxation—and they continue to do so. Unilateralism and extraterritoriality are, indeed, the privilege of the strong; and the Europeans, like the Americans who started earlier, have developed a taste for such luxuries, at least in trade matters. Increasingly recognizing the dangers for the international economy, the two sides have been trying to cooperate with respect to the extraterritorial dimension of their respective competition policies. There is arguably more scope today for bilateral cooperation between the two biggest players in this area than for trying to reach an agreement at the WTO.

Trade in services has been growing faster than trade in goods in recent years, and this has bitten harder into Europe's mixed economies because of a long record of extensive state intervention and/or state ownership. Financial markets in particular have acted as a driving force of economic globalization. Internal EU measures have followed suit through the internal market programme and subsequent legislation. In this area, the Union seems to have adjusted to external events rather than trying to shape them. Regional integration has therefore become part and parcel of, and in some cases virtually indistinguishable from, global developments. Is there really so little scope for regional differentiation in the context of increasingly global financial markets, or is this due more to the inability so far of Europeans to adopt a common policy?

There is, in fact, a more general problem arising from the continuous extension of the international trade agenda, which has not been matched by a corresponding transfer of powers to EU institutions with regard to external policy. The Commission has legal powers to negotiate on behalf of the Union only with respect to trade in goods. New areas of policy, such as services, intellectual property, investment, labour standards, cultural issues, and the environment, are either the subject of so-called mixed competences, where the Commission does not have exclusive responsibility for representing the Union and decisions in the Council have to be taken by unanimity, or they remain in the hands of member states. One example is the bilateral 'open skies agreements' concluded by individual member countries and the US, later found contrary to EU law by the European Court. As a result, the Europeans' negotiating power has been almost invariably greatly weakened. Illusions of national sovereignty die hard.

For many years, the EC was a trade actor in the international system, a powerful actor but little else. Within GATT, now the WTO, it has had to deal with a much wider range of issues, while regional integration has been moving even faster. This change on both fronts has not as yet been fully reflected in the external policies of the Union. The new major challenge comes from EMU. As the launch of the euro approached, American incredulity concerning the prospects of EMU was being steadily replaced by apprehension about the possible effects on dollar supremacy in the world of international finance, only to be tempered by the early weakness of the euro. Does it make sense for individual member countries to continue to define and represent separately their national interests in international financial forums, having already transferred full responsibility for the conduct of monetary policy to the ECB and also aspiring to a more closely coordinated macroeconomic stance? There is also, of

73

course, high politics widely defined. How quickly will the logic of internal integration translate itself into common external policies, and to what extent will this be accompanied by the strengthening of internal democratic accountability? The common commercial policy could provide a good reference point, but there is surely much more at stake in other areas of policy.

☆ Privileged Partners

Trade preferences are contrary to the principle of multilateralism and the most-favoured-nation clause of GATT, according to which any trade concession offered to one country should automatically be extended to all other members. Yet the Europeans have acquired a rich collection of different kinds of preferential agreements with other countries, including association agreements with stronger political connotations. They have usually tried to justify them through a very liberal interpretation of Article XXIV of GATT. At the time of writing, 118 countries had bilateral agreements of different kinds with the EU. And this is not the end of the story, since other countries or regions have adopted similar practices in more recent years, including the United States, which has also lately come to appreciate the benefits of bilateralism and regionalism in trade. Article XXIV has therefore become a fig leaf which barely covers the nakedness of participants engaged in a game played allegedly in the name of multilateralism. But does it really matter?

The EU has traditionally had three groups of privileged partners with whom it has signed different kinds of preferential agreements. The first consists of European non-member countries, starting with EFTA, and later, after the fall of communism, covering virtually the whole of the European continent on its eastern frontier. It notably includes countries that have applied for membership and are expected to spend the requisite number of years in the waiting room, plus others that may follow later. In other words, the first—and in practice the most privileged—group consists of candidates or potential members of the Union. The second group includes countries of the Mediterranean region, whose number has been diminishing as those on the northern shores of the Mediterranean made the transition to full membership, starting with the southern enlargement of the 1980s and continuing with the imminent accession of Cyprus and Malta, and perhaps also eventually Turkey. This leaves a core group consisting of Arab countries plus Israel. The third group is much more numerous and diverse. At the latest count, it amounted to 77 countries, usually referred to as ACP (African, Caribbean, and Pacific countries), comprising former colonies and dependent territories of European members. This group includes most of the poorest countries of the world.

Through this pyramid of privilege constructed on the basis of trade preferences, close institutional relations, and financial aid, the EU has established a policy of discrimination vis-à-vis the rest of the world; and this, of course, applies to industrialized as well as developing countries. On the assumption that preferences do make a difference, the great paradox is that the least privileged among the Union's partners appear to be those simply enjoying most-favoured-nation treatment (a diplomatic misnomer) under GATT rules. This category includes all the non-European members of the OECD, and most notably the United States, as well as China and large parts of the Third World. Russia, like other countries, does not enjoy most-favoured nation treatment since it is not yet a member of the WTO.

EFTA started as a rival organization to the EEC in Western Europe and as an alternative for countries opting for the intergovernmental model of cooperation. For its few remaining members, its main present function is to manage their relations with the ever-enlarging EU. On the eve of the first enlargement in 1973, the rest of EFTA signed bilateral free trade agreements with the Community covering most industrial products, while the agricultural sector was virtually excluded as it was also excluded within EFTA. Later on, the internal market programme acted as a catalyst for a new set of agreements meant to ensure for EFTA exporters unrestricted access to the wider European market without internal frontiers, thus signalling the birth of the European Economic Area (EEA). Agriculture was still left out, and EFTA countries continued with their national policies, even more costly than the CAP. The price they were forced to pay for free access to the internal market was the acceptance en bloc of Community rules and regulations; in other words, a kind of second-class membership without participation in joint rule-making. Three of the remaining Eftans finally drew the logical conclusion, and this led to the accession of Austria, Finland, and Sweden to the EU in 1995. Norway, Iceland, and Liechtenstein are now members of the EEA, having incorporated most EU legislation related to the internal market. As for Switzerland, the second biggest trading partner of the EU after the United States, economic relations are governed by bilateral agreements with the Union.

With the fall of communism, preferential agreements were signed with a new group of European countries, which made clear, early on, their desire to join the Union, starting with simple trade and cooperation agreements and moving to the so-called Europe agreements and finally to accession partnerships as the final step before full membership. Eight countries in central and eastern Europe, together with two Mediterranean islands, are now ready to join, having already adopted a large part of EU legislation. And this will not be the end of the story: others are already waiting in the queue, and the queue will become longer with time while the Union tries to devise new formulae and different kinds of agreements for aspiring members. In the midst of dramatic changes in the political and economic map of the old continent, the Union has developed, albeit slowly and not always consistently, a European policy vis-à-vis candidates or potential members, with different gradations in terms of institutional cooperation and preferences. Agreements signed with European nonmember countries have had a liberalizing effect in terms of trade and economic transactions more generally, while the carrot of EU membership has acted as an important catalyst for domestic reforms (and not only economic ones) in those countries aspiring to join. Measuring the various agreements with other European countries with the yardstick of Article XXIV of GATT would thus be inappropriate, if not irrelevant.

There is another side to this story: trade with the rest of Europe accounts on average today for approximately three-quarters of the total external trade of member countries (Figure 4.2). This includes intra-EU trade as well as trade with the candidate countries, the remaining members of the EEA, and also Switzerland. Strictly speaking, intra-EU trade can no longer be considered as external trade. However, from the point of view of individual countries, the above figure is a clear illustration of the large regional concentration of trade transactions on the European continent, an important factor explaining the strong regionalist instincts of European policy-makers. The United States, as the biggest trading partner outside the EU, accounts for less than one-tenth, and the corresponding figures of trade with countries such as Japan, Russia, and China are much smaller.

The picture is no longer very different in terms of financial transactions, and most particularly in terms of foreign direct investment (FDI). Both inward and outward flows of FDI increased substantially during the 1990s, especially during the second half of that decade when the Union as a whole also became a big net investor in the United States (Figure 4.3). At the same time, portfolio investment grew very rapidly. These were the days of great confidence in the dynamism of the (new) US economy, and everyone was trying to take advantage of it. History teaches us that prolonged booms have the tendency to produce bubbles; but who has the time to read history when money appears so

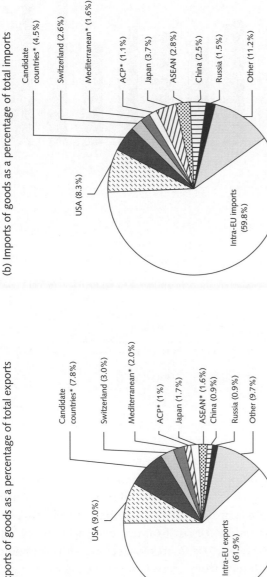

(a) Exports of goods as a percentage of total exports

Candidate
countries* (7.8%)

Switzerland (3.0%)

Mediterranean* (2.0%)

ACP* (1%)

Japan (1.7%)

ASEAN* (1.6%)

China (0.9%)

Russia (0.9%)

Other (9.7%)

USA (9.0%)

Intra-EU exports
(61.9%)

(b) Imports of goods as a percentage of total imports

Candidate
countries* (4.5%)

Switzerland (2.6%)

Mediterranean* (1.6%)

ACP* (1.1%)

Japan (3.7%)

ASEAN (2.8%)

China (2.5%)

Russia (1.5%)

Other (11.2%)

USA (8.3%)

Intra-EU imports
(59.8%)

Figure 4.2. Main trading partners (average EU-15, 1998–2000)

*Candidate countries**: Poland, Hungary, Czech Republic, Slovakia, Estonia, Latvia, Lithuania, Slovenia, Bulgaria, Romania, Cyprus, Malta, Turkey.
Mediterranean: Morocco, Algeria, Tunisia, Egypt, Jordan, Lebanon, Syria, Israel.
ASEAN: Thailand, Vietnam, Indonesia, Malaysia, Brunei, Singapore, Philippines.
ACP: Angola, Antigua and Barbuda, Bahamas, Barbados, Belize, Benin, Botswana, Burkina Faso, Burundi, Cameroon, Cape Verde, Central African Republic, Chad, Comoros, Congo, Congo (Democratic Republic), Cook Islands, Côte d'Ivoire, Djibouti, Dominica, Dominican Republic, Equatorial Guinea, Eritrea, Ethiopia, Fiji, Gabon, Gambia, Ghana, Grenada, Guinea, Guinea-Bissau, Guyana, Haiti, Jamaica, Kenya, Kiribati, Lesotho, Liberia, Madagascar, Malawi, Mali, Marshall Islands, Mauritania, Mauritius, Micronesia, Mozambique, Namibia, Nauru, Niger, Nigeria, Niue, Palau, Papua New Guinea, Rwanda, St Kitts and Nevis, St Lucia, St Vincent and the Grenadines, Samoa, São Tome and Principe, Senegal, Seychelles, Sierra Leone, Solomon Islands, Somalia, South Africa, Sudan, Suriname, Swaziland, Tanzania, Togo, Tonga, Trinidad and Tobago, Tuvalu, Uganda, Vanuazu, Zambia, Zimbabwe.

Source: Eurostat.

(a) Intra EU-15 FDI inflows and outflows*

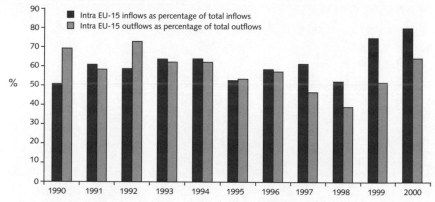

(b) EU-15 and USA FDI flows*

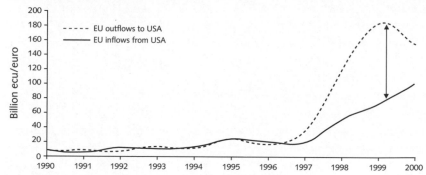

Figure 4.3. Foreign direct investment (FDI), 1990–2000

*Excluding reinvested earnings.

Source: European Commission.

easy to make? Lessons are learned later, usually the hard way. The gap in FDI flows between the EU and the USA was absolutely huge before the turn of the century, and this also largely explains the weakness of the new European currency in its early years. More recent data show a substantial reduction in transatlantic FDI flows as the bubble began to burst, accompanied by an increase in the share of intra-EU flows. The figures for regional concentration in FDI are no longer very different from corresponding figures for trade (Figure 4.3). If we include the candidate countries of central and eastern Europe, where companies from EU-15 have become the biggest investors since the fall of communist regimes, the figures are even higher.

It has been different with the second group of privileged partners in the Mediterranean. The first preferential agreements were signed by the Six soon after the establishment of the EEC in 1958, starting with Greece and Turkey. Most of them were renewed and extended in the context of the so-called global Mediterranean policy during the 1970s. The term 'global' was essentially a euphemism, and 'policy' proved to be too ambitious a word to describe the mosaic of bilateral agreements with limited concrete effects. There was also a desire to make preferential relations with the Mediterranean countries more palatable to the Americans, in form if not necessarily in substance. Following its southern enlargement of the 1980s, and with the prospect of a new and bigger enlargement to the east and the south, the EU has subsequently tried to preserve some balance with respect to the non-European countries of the Mediterranean. The result of this effort is the so-called Barcelona process initiated in 1995.

The aim is to create a large free trade area comprising all European and Mediterranean countries by 2010—a conveniently distant target at the time of the signing ceremony, the cynical observer might add. In the new bilateral agreements signed between the EU and individual Mediterranean countries (candidates for EU membership receiving different treatment), there is more reciprocity in trade liberalization and also greater emphasis on cooperation in the regulatory sphere, including environmental protection. In practice this means that Mediterranean countries are being asked to adopt the regulatory norms of their European partners as the necessary price to pay for securing access to the internal market. The new Mediterranean policy includes substantial financial assistance, no longer tied to individual projects, thus following the example of internal structural policies; and financial assistance is also linked to internal reforms in the Mediterranean countries. Drawing from their own experience, the Europeans have for many years been encouraging regional cooperation within other parts of the world; and they have tried to do the same with the Mediterranean countries in the context of the Barcelona process. Respect for human rights, the strengthening of civil society, and the development of links at the non-governmental level are also important features of the new approach adopted by the EU. Last but not least, for a group comprising Arab countries and Israel there is strong emphasis on the establishment of peace and security in the region.

The Mediterranean is strategically important for the EU—more for France, Italy, Spain, and Greece than for Sweden and Finland—and it is about much more than narrow trade or economic interests. After all, exports of goods to the

Mediterranean, excluding candidate countries, account for only 2 per cent of the total exports of member countries (Figure 4.2); and FDI has also been relatively small. There is, of course, oil. The Mediterranean is important as a route for oil supplies to Europe, and what happens in the Middle East has a considerable effect on Europe's access to oil supplies as well as the price of oil. It is less important as a direct supplier, since Algeria and Libya are neither among the biggest producers nor among the most dependable. Having gradually adjusted to the oil shocks of the 1970s, Europe's attention has shifted to other Mediterranean issues. The large majority of countries in the region have developed an explosive mix of rapidly growing populations, economic underdevelopment, and political instability. Europeans and others have learned from bitter experience that instability is easily exportable and that the Mediterranean Sea is not wide enough to act as an effective barrier. The same applies to potential immigrants looking for an escape from economic misery, and often also political oppression at home. The Mediterranean has become a key transit route for immigrants into Europe, thus constantly adding to the large numbers of those already residing in EU countries.

It looks quite different from the other side. All Mediterranean countries, including Israel, which is by far the most developed country in the region, are heavily dependent on the EU in terms of their external trade. On average, more than 50 per cent of their trade is conducted with the EU, which is hardly surprising given geography and the size of the European partner. For several Mediterranean countries, tourist revenues and migrant remittances from the EU also represent a very substantial part of their foreign exchange receipts. Thus, in economic terms at least, the relationship between the two sides is highly asymmetric.

The limitations of the varieties of Mediterranean policies adopted by the Community, and now the Union, have become all too clear over time. Trade has developed at a slow pace, and so has European investment in the developing countries of the region, whose general economic performance has been anything but spectacular. The economic distance between the north and the south of the Mediterranean has been steadily growing. As well, little progress has been achieved in terms of democratization and political stability; authoritarian regimes, usually highly corrupt and inefficient, continue to prevail in most countries. As for peace and security, the picture remains dismal: the prospects for a peaceful and viable solution to the Middle East problem are still not good, while human suffering has been growing by the day. Surely, the EU cannot be blamed for all those failings. Yet the gap between the grand objectives in the colourful rhetoric adopted at high-level meetings and the meagre results achieved so far is painfully wide.

There is only so much that the EU can deliver in terms of economic development, democracy, peace, and security in the region. The instruments employed are of limited effect: trade preferences have lost much of their meaning because of the steady reduction of the common external tariff; concessions in agricultural trade continue to be constrained because of the CAP—and this is after all a sector of the economy where Mediterranean countries retain a comparative advantage; and, last but not least, preferential access to European markets becomes important when there is something to export from the other side. Unfortunately, the domestic conditions for economic development are still absent from the large majority of countries in the region. Structural reforms are long overdue, and the combination of carrots and sticks used by the Europeans has not delivered the goods from the other side. Economic and political conditionality has been an important feature of the new wave of agreements signed with the Mediterranean partners, but it has proved difficult to apply in practice. This is true of trade concessions and even more so of financial aid, which has been marked by low absorption rates. Dealing with the non-European countries in the Mediterranean, as with the rest of the world outside Europe, the EU cannot employ its most effective instrument, namely, the prospect of membership.

Because of geographical contiguity and historical ties, and also because of their high dependence on imported oil from the Middle East and the Gulf, European countries have a strong interest in peace and stability in the Mediterranean region. This is clearly impossible to achieve as long as the Arab–Israeli conflict continues. Surely, solutions cannot be simply imposed from outside; even the Americans have been trying to learn this lesson. However, it is equally important to recognize that the mediating role of the Union has been extremely modest until now, verging on the insignificant. The explanation is simple, even though painful for the Europeans: it has been difficult to reach a common stance, not to mention a common policy; and when this has happened, neither the Israelis nor the Americans have been ready to play ball, which has automatically put Europe's mediating effort in the deep freeze. Everyone in the region knows where the real power lies, and it is certainly not in Brussels. So the frustrated Europeans have been left with trade and little influence; and, adding insult to injury, they have often been asked to pick up the bill. The EU is a major donor in the region, and this includes aid to the Palestinian territories. Many of the buildings destroyed by Israeli tanks during the latest and most tragic phase yet of the *intifada* had been built with European taxpayers' money.

The third group of privileged partners is geographically more distant and strategically less important. Periodic negotiations between the EU and the ACP countries have been an interesting exercise in international diplomacy. In the latest round of these negotiations, which led to the agreement in Cotonou, Benin, signed in 2000, fifteen of the richest European democracies were co-signatories with a large number of very poor countries from sub-Saharan Africa plus a few island states in the Caribbean and the Pacific: 77 is the latest count of ACP associates. The huge inequality in negotiating power between the two sides is arguably the single most important factor explaining how such negotiations have actually led to agreements. In the pyramid of privilege which the EU has built over the years, the ACP countries formally occupy one of the highest positions, together with Mediterranean countries. Those agreements can be seen as an attempt at collective management of post-colonial economic ties. Numbers have been increasing with successive rounds of enlargement of the EU. Yet many former colonies are excluded from this group, notably South Asian and Latin American countries, at least partly because of higher levels of economic development and greater export possibilities which would have enabled them to take better advantage of EU preferences.

Earlier agreements contained trade liberalization on the European side with no reciprocity on the other, preferential rules of origin, complex arrangements for sugar exports, stabilization schemes for export earnings for several commodities and minerals, as well as financial and technical assistance. They were sometimes hailed as a model of economic relations between North and South. But this attitude was clearly not shared by those developing countries that were left out, not to mention the Americans, who constantly cried foul, accusing the Europeans of violating GATT rules and trying to establish spheres of influence. More recent agreements reflect a shift of emphasis towards more reciprocity in trade liberalization, closer South-South cooperation, and tighter conditionality, including domestic reforms and human rights.

The practical limitations of these agreements have here too been all too obvious. The ACP group includes too many economic and political disasters: oppressive regimes, widespread corruption, and declining living standards; in other words, many weak or failed states for which the agreements signed with the EU cannot on their own serve as the mechanism to extricate them from the vicious circle of economic and political underdevelopment. Despite preferences, the share of the ACP in total EU external trade has been steadily declining.

It now represents a mere 1 per cent of total trade for the average EU-15 country (Figure 4.2).

There is no doubt that the EU has been one of the worst, if not the worst, offender among developed countries against the principle of multilateralism in international trade, because of old habits and occasional absent-mindedness. True, preferences have often served as a poor substitute for a more encompassing policy, unattainable because of the internal limitations of the EU. Some of the agreements signed with third countries have been anodyne, at least in terms of their economic effects, although they did provide photo opportunities for politicians and another excuse for the Commission to waive the EU flag. It has, of course, been different with the more privileged partners. The Union has indeed gone further than any other developed country or region in meeting some of the demands made by the developing world; but in so doing it has added to its many divisions, distinguishing between privileged and less privileged partners. European attitudes and policies have evolved, becoming more compatible with the multilateral system as many EU protective barriers came down and preferences began to fade. European policies have also retained a distinctly European flavour relating to the protection of the environment, labour standards, and human rights, although with limited practical effect. On the other hand, European integration has served as a model for many developing countries, and the Europeans have consciously promoted its export. But again, results have so far been poor essentially because European conditions are not easily reproducible in other parts of the world.

Have the Europeans been in the business of trying to create spheres of influence following the disintegration of their colonial empires? If so, they have chosen badly and with little success. With few exceptions, the countries belonging to the two most privileged groups among developing countries have been on a downward slope in both economic and political terms. More correctly, perhaps, history and geography seem to have chosen for the Europeans their privileged partners. Successive Mediterranean and ACP agreements have produced limited results and growing internal differentiation. The share of trade of the Union's privileged partners among developing countries has been declining by comparison with the share of, say, south-east Asian countries, which have traditionally been the object of negative privileges from Europe. This may lead to the conclusion that some countries trade and others sign trade agreements. But, surely, preferential access to markets is not the only determining factor for export success or for economic development more generally.

With time, EU financial assistance has arguably become the single most important element of such preferential agreements. The EU and its member states account today for more than half of all official international development assistance. It is by far the biggest donor in many parts of the world. Here again, a qualification is necessary. The efficiency of EU development assistance leaves much to be desired, suffering from lack of coherent strategy as well as from heavy bureaucratic procedures and a serious shortage of Commission staff entrusted with the management of multilateral assistance. It has not been very efficient in terms of the use of economic resources and the outputs delivered. Furthermore, the considerable amounts of money spent have generally bought the Europeans little political influence in the recipient countries, for better or worse. Have the Europeans been willing to part with their money just in order to keep their collective conscience clear? Or is this poor result yet another by-product of their highly imperfect political system? Having finally realized the shortcomings of their external aid policies, the Europeans have recently begun to take some measures to make the system more efficient.

☆ New Pillars in a Postmodern Construction

European integration started with economic instruments because traditional foreign policy and defence, the main constituent elements of what is often referred to as high politics, were considered out of bounds. After all, the defeat of the French plan for the creation of a European Defence Community by the French National Assembly in the early 1950s signalled the limits of the integrationist ambitions in the more sensitive areas of national sovereignty. The French came back, only a few years after the signing of the Treaty of Rome, with a new and more modest initiative on foreign policy cooperation among the Six. It too failed, although some of its main characteristics proved to be less ephemeral: a French initiative, an intergovernmental model of cooperation—to be distinguished from the Community model—and a direct challenge to American leadership. Gaullist France was trying, unsuccessfully, to mobilize the rest of the Six in an attempt to change the balance of power within the Western alliance.

European political cooperation, meaning foreign policy cooperation but excluding defence, was launched in 1970 as a concession to France in the first big package deal to combine widening and deepening. It lasted for slightly more than twenty years. It was entirely intergovernmental, based on consensus, and

84

kept separate from Community institutions. It was managed by diplomats, mostly in the old secret style, and hence with little public exposure and even less democratic control. European political cooperation produced a complex network of committees and a rich collection of joint declaratory statements on a wide range of international issues. It also contributed to the socialization of national diplomats and foreign ministries to the idea of a common European foreign policy, by regularly exposing them to each other's prejudices and national interests, thus leading to some convergence of views. But it remained far short of a common policy. Joint statements were not always accompanied by joint actions, and they generally seemed to have little impact on the rest of the world. The Europeans talked a lot, but did they have a clear message and, more importantly, how many people were ready to listen?

The American variable in the equation remained crucial all along. European countries were more often than not divided on how far a common European position could differ from that of the Americans, and the latter did not help much either. The United States regularly repeated its unstinted (verbal) support for European unification—and the creation of a strong European pillar within NATO—always on the assumption that the Europeans would continue to provide unqualified support for US leadership within Europe and beyond. The two objectives are not necessarily compatible. Tensions were particularly pronounced when Henry Kissinger was in charge of US foreign policy. France reacted strongly to US attempts to dilute the autonomy of European political cooperation, while it remained formally outside the integrated military structure of NATO, thus leaving itself open to criticism as a free rider. Following the 1973 Middle East war and the subsequent Arab oil embargo, the Europeans launched the Euro-Arab dialogue independently of the Americans, who hardly appreciated it and reacted in strong terms. It has been the same whenever the Europeans have tried to steer an independent course of action in the Middle East, a part of the world where American and European perceptions and interests do not always coincide. This is clearly meant as an understatement.

Wiser with age and bigger in numbers, member countries decided to go further at Maastricht, committing themselves to a common foreign and security policy. German unification, the disintegration of the Soviet empire, and the Gulf War all acted as catalysts. Stripped of official rhetoric, however, the new CFSP 'pillar' of in the Maastricht construction did not contain much that was new. Defence was for the first time explicitly mentioned. The Western European Union (WEU), an organization also mature in age but very young in accomplishments, was taken off the shelf as the preferred instrument for European defence policy and the official link with NATO. Yet it remained unclear how all this would translate into practice. Persisting national differences were couched in diplomatic language and Euro-rhetoric, while there were only modest modifications to already existing institutional arrangements and an absolutely minuscule budget, not enough to pay even for EU special envoys in troubled parts of the world. The CFSP was meant to continue as an intergovernmental operation, with only a flimsy common structure and virtually no funds.

Its limitations were soon to become obvious. The handling of the Yugoslav tragedy, for example, left an enormous amount to be desired. The Europeans were often divided, slow to act, and painfully short of the ultimate instruments of persuasion in international diplomacy, including, of course, the use of force. They also made serious blunders, the premature recognition of Slovenia and Croatia under German pressure being one of them. This was 'the hour of Europe', in the ill-fated words of the Foreign Minister of Luxembourg and acting President of the Council during the first half of 1991, which never came. The war in Kosovo and the bombing of Yugoslavia later exposed the enormous gap between Americans and Europeans in terms of transport, communications, and intelligence capabilities; the relatively small European contribution to the war was also translated into a correspondingly small influence over its conduct and decision-making within the alliance more generally. It was more than abundantly clear who was in charge, leaving the other members in times of war with precious little choice. The European members of NATO were in more or less supporting roles, but there was nothing approaching a European policy or a common position with some weight. The experience in Kosovo, as well as in Bosnia-Herzegovina, did in the end mobilize a kind of collective EU action, while also making Europeans more aware of what could be done with or without the Americans. US military supremacy, making the support of European allies increasingly dispensable, was later confirmed in an even more blatant manner by the war in Afghanistan.

For many observers of the European scene, the CFSP thus exemplified the big gap between expectations and capabilities, or between rhetoric and action. There was later a new surge of optimism following the St Malo meeting in 1998 between the British and the French. The British showed greater interest in European defence cooperation, while France was seen as taking discreet steps towards a gradual rapprochement with the Atlantic alliance. The actual operational experience in former Yugoslavia seemed to have prepared the ground. This apparent convergence between the two key European players, with a more active foreign policy and far stronger military capability than the rest, could ultimately add real substance to the CFSP. After all, the Union already has a High Representative for the CFSP in the person of Javier Solana, very appropriately (and not only symbolically so) the former General Secretary of NATO, who should be better qualified than others to help define a European defence identity compatible with the Atlantic alliance. Some practical decisions have been taken in the meantime with the view of making the CFSP a more integral part of the Union and also more operational, although remaining very much intergovernmental in character.

The Helsinki Council of December 1999 added yet another abbreviation to the already long list for the Euro-initiated: the ESDP (European security and defence policy) was meant as an official declaration of the incorporation of defence into the Union's agenda. Defence ministers joined European councils in 1999. There is now the commitment to create a European rapid deployment force of 60,000 soldiers before the end of 2003, drawn from the member countries of the Union. Once put together, this European force will be on call to undertake peacekeeping and peacemaking operations, the so-called Petersberg tasks, which have been agreed upon as the concrete manifestations of a European defence policy; hence it is a 'soft' version of defence policy, the rest remaining the exclusive responsibility of NATO. Meanwhile, cross-border mergers and cooperation were changing the structure of the European defence industry.

However, irrespective of the acronyms and abbreviations used in traditional foreign policy and defence, a common policy remains even now more of an objective than a reality. National attitudes towards a common foreign policy, and particularly defence policy as something much more concrete, can be presented on a two-dimensional graph with one axis running from the Community model of integration to the intergovernmental, and the other from European autonomy/independence to Atlanticism (Figure 4.4). For a long time, member countries placed themselves on distant locations on this graph: among the Big Three, France was strongly intergovernmental and pro-European autonomy, Germany supranational and Atlanticist, Britain intergovernmental and Atlanticist—in fact, more Atlanticist than European, as the non-benign observer might remark. There were also major differences among the smaller members. Signs of convergence appeared in recent years, only to be exposed subsequently as both temporary and reversible. The war in Iraq brought France and Germany closer together, while Britain once again followed the American lead. All the arrows in Figure 4.4 did not point towards the centre.

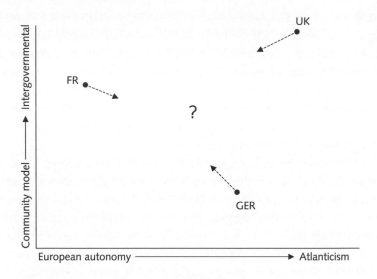

Figure 4.4. The 'Big Three' and the CFSP

For many years, there was an explicit division of labour between the Community in its different incarnations and NATO: even with far-reaching political ambitions and with mostly rhetorical exercises in traditional power politics, the Community continued to concentrate mostly on economic matters, while high politics and especially security remained *la chasse gardée* of the Atlantic alliance. This also explains why there are neutral countries inside the Union and European members of NATO outside it. The Americans provided the security guarantee for Western Europe, and many of the soldiers and the defence expenditure to back it up, while the Europeans seemed content with their role as junior (and protected) partners.

The Soviet threat is no longer there, although serious instability and sudden policy reversals in the new Russia cannot be completely excluded in the foreseeable future. New threats to security have appeared, including notably the threat from international terrorism. But perceptions and interests inside the alliance have begun to diverge more than ever. And all this time, the gap in terms of military capabilities between the United States and its European allies has been constantly growing. With few exceptions, defence budgets in Western Europe have not caught up with the spiralling costs of high-tech warfare; if anything, the pressures on defence expenditures are still downwards. National armies have large numbers of men and women in arms, but few of them can be mobilized at short notice. They are also poor in terms of logistics and communications, something that became glaringly obvious during the war in Yugoslavia.

It is inevitable that a proper European foreign policy and defence will require a redefinition of relations with the leader of the alliance, including a redistribution of responsibilities and the defence burden. The Europeans are still not there, or even close enough. And in the meantime NATO could be rapidly declining into irrelevance as a military alliance, with no clear mission in sight despite an expanding membership, which is in turn perceived as a formal admission ticket to the community of Western democratic nations. In this respect, NATO membership has become complementary to EU membership; arguably, a second-best for those countries that have to wait longer before being admitted to the Union.

Meanwhile, the issues under the third of the Maastricht pillars have been steadily growing in importance and so has the policy output of this new area of cooperation, which had been kept out of the public limelight until immigration and terrorism began to hit the headlines. This pillar is about justice and home affairs. More precisely, it was intended, first of all, to translate the objective of the free movement of people inside the Union into concrete reality with the elimination of internal frontiers. But this automatically leads to a common frontier vis-à-vis the rest of the world, and hence also a common policy towards foreigners treated as individuals and not countries. It is the equivalent of a customs union and a common external tariff on goods. In concrete terms, it includes immigration policy, visas, and asylum; it also includes policies against organized crime and terrorism. The determination to proceed with the elimination of internal frontiers for the movement of people inside the Union, the growing pressure of immigration from the east and the south, and the rapid growth of transnational criminal organizations, including terrorist groups, have acted as powerful driving forces for integration in a way that had not been anticipated by the signatories of the Maastricht Treaty.

Thirteen out of the fifteen members of the Union are now members of Schengen, named after a village in Luxembourg which is now very familiar to anybody travelling inside this large area without frontiers. On the road towards a 'union of freedom, security and justice', as official Euro-rhetoric goes, much of the business under the so-called third pillar of the Maastricht construction, including internal free movement of people as well as immigration, has become normal Community business. The UK has insisted on preserving its own system of border controls, thus staying out of the Schengen area, accompanied by Ireland because of the passport union between the two countries, although increasingly recognizing that the protection of the external borders of the Union is a matter of common concern. Like EMU, the Schengen agreement is therefore an important example of internal differentiation inside the Union; and this becomes even more complicated by the fact that Norway and Iceland are also de facto members through the Scandinavian connection.

At the same time, Schengen sets new tasks in terms of defining a common policy with respect to the rest of the world. Although 'Fortress Europe' has not materialized in trade terms, a growing number of European policy-makers as well as ordinary citizens would like it to happen with respect to the movement of people. The image of large numbers of immigrants pushing through the gates, continuous reports on the trafficking of drugs and people, and organized crime more generally have strengthened xenophobic tendencies in Europe and those political parties trying to capitalize on them.

In earlier years, several Europeans spoke with conviction and pride about what was then the Community as a 'civilian power', to be distinguished from more traditional players of the old game of power politics in which power is closely correlated with military might. It became increasingly clear with time that, to a large extent, they were making a virtue out of necessity. The Community remained an economic giant and a political dwarf, and often a highly frustrated one. European political cooperation, later metamorphosed as the CFSP, was meant to provide the transition to an international political role. But many Europeans were apparently still not ready to accept the consequences for national sovereignty, not to mention military budgets—and they were certainly not any closer to an agreement about how the CFSP would operate in the context of the Atlantic alliance. Progress therefore remained extremely slow, unless we count official declarations as a substitute for policy.

The deepening of integration, together with rapid changes in the external environment, especially in Europe's 'near abroad', may accelerate the pace. This is already happening in the domain of justice and home ministries—unexpectedly and also unglamorously. An aggressively unilateralist US Administration could also act as a catalyst, although it would take a lot of effort from the Americans. There are still many difficult decisions to be taken in the transition from low to high politics; and they include internal decisions about the democratic deficit of the Union, which is even more pronounced in the new areas of policy. The Union has been described as a postmodern political construction in the way it tackles sovereignty, because of its decision-making system and the policy instruments it employs. But the trouble is that a post-modern political construction may not always fit well in a world with many pre-modern characteristics. It remains to be seen how the Union will try to reconcile these two different realities.

PART II

☆☆☆☆☆☆☆☆☆☆☆☆

The Main Challenges Ahead

5

☆☆☆☆☆

Economic Governance
and Policy Choices

The EU has moved a long way in integrating national economies. In the process, it has acquired many of the policy functions—or at least a share in them—previously monopolized by national governments. Much of the debate in Europe has therefore concentrated on the appropriate division of powers and responsibilities between the European and the national levels, and also the regional and the local levels, especially for those countries practising decentralization at home.

It is only natural that the division of powers becomes a key issue in any federal or pre-federal system, and the Union could not escape this political tussle between competing levels of authority. Since Maastricht, subsidiarity has become a buzz-word (perhaps, more appropriately, a theological concept in view of its origins in the debate and practice of the Catholic Church) for those defending national sovereignty against what they perceive as excessive centralization at the Union level. Important though it may be, this debate about how much power should be given to European and national institutions often hides a whole set of other important issues and trade-offs.

This particularly applies to economic life. The division of powers in the European political system has direct effects on the way our national economies function and the institutions and rules that shape them. The fashionable term nowadays is 'economic governance', which is meant to cover both the public and the private spheres. Economic governance is about specific and often seemingly unexciting issues for the ordinary citizen, such as technical standards for products, capital-asset ratios for banks, as well as competition rules. Economists refer to market failures and the kind of intervention required to correct them. There is, of course, no single magic formula to deal with market failures; and in the past member countries responded in very different ways, a function of history and collective preferences among other things.

However, economic governance is also about much wider issues, which form the main stuff of everyday politics. Democracy and equality, for example, cannot be reduced to simple market logic. The legal obligation, or otherwise, on employers to consult workers in private firms is just one example; the distribution of income and wealth is another. Economic governance is about the appropriate mix between the state and the market, between public and private interests, as well as about trade-offs between economic efficiency, stability, and equity.

Choices about the distribution of political power and responsibilities between different levels of authority in the EU have implications for market integration (or fragmentation) in Europe and for the conditions under which economic agents compete for market shares. In many cases, they also imply certain choices about the nature of market regulation, the protection of consumers and the environment, the ability to tax, and hence also the ability to provide public goods or redistribute resources. On all those matters, there can (and should) be legitimate political differences. Such differences are, however, often buried beneath thick layers of greyish jargon (which characterizes most policy debates in the Union) and the essentially intergovernmental character of the negotiation.

The main argument in this chapter is that the distorted nature of the European debate simply hides or transforms many of the crucial trade-offs and policy choices relating to the kind of Europe, and the kind of society, we want to live in. The chapter will attempt to make at least some of them more explicit by examining specific policy areas in European integration. Decisions in the name of subsidiarity, or its opposite, often conceal implicit choices about economic governance and the kind of issues mentioned above. And those implications are, at best, only half understood by the wider public in whose name decisions are taken.

One thing is the transfer of powers to European institutions and the development of common policies; and this can be perceived as a zero-sum or a positive-sum game between the EU and its constituent national parts. There has also been convergence between national systems, itself the product of regional integration in the wider sense of the term; and this process has been analysed in the rapidly growing literature on Europeanization, another fashionable offspring of integration studies. This literature has tried to depict the narrowing of differences between economies, political systems, and societies in Europe. Economies have led the way; institutions and societies have followed slowly and reluctantly. How much convergence, and in which direction? How much diversity, and at what price? Answers to those questions are bound to differ, depending not only on the nationality of those questioned but also, and increasingly so with time, on political and ideological preferences, not to mention economic interests. Nationality may overlap with ideology or interests, but not necessarily. This should become clearer with the development of a proper European public space, meant as a forum for Europe-wide debates.

☆ Market Regulation and Level Playing Fields

In the good old days of the founding treaties, the overall approach to economic integration consisted mainly of the elimination of physical cross-border controls, which hindered the free circulation of goods, services, persons, and capital: the so-called four fundamental freedoms. Given the nature of national mixed economies, this meant in practice that, during the first three decades or more of European integration, the main, albeit limited, effect had been on the free circulation of goods. The elimination of national barriers, mostly at the border, was coupled with some harmonization when the mixed economy raised its ugly head (or pretty head: it is only a matter of taste) and as long as national governments could agree on common European rules as the necessary price to pay for the common market.

There were a few exceptions, however, for which the treaties had provided a federal type of structure for the development of common policies at the European level. Competition policy was one example, agricultural policy was another, and so was the common commercial policy. We could add transport to this list, although treaty provisions were never translated into actual policy; and also coal and steel, which had served as the foundation stones of regional integration, yet soon to be turned into tombstones for those rapidly declining sectors. In most cases, politics had played a much more decisive role than economics in shaping European policies.

The big turning point came with the internal market programme in the 1980s: the EC thus entered the world of mixed economies in a big way, and market regulation became a major issue on the European agenda. It was supposed to be based on a radically new approach to the elimination of all remaining barriers to the free circulation of goods, services, persons, and capital arising from a myriad of national rules and regulations, which, precisely because of their differences, created obstacles or distortions inside the common market. The new approach was both simple and radical, and it was meant to serve like the sword used by Alexander the Great to cut the famous Gordian knot. Instead of trying to harmonize everything, a process which had proved to be extremely long and arduous, it was agreed that the Community would rely as much as possible on the principle of mutual recognition, fully consistent with subsidiarity, coupled with common legislation limited only to essential objectives and requirements.

Mutual recognition had earlier been defined by the European Court: any good legally manufactured and marketed in one member country should be allowed to circulate freely in the rest of the Union. It was thus meant to provide the entry ticket for goods (and services) from other countries, and the burden of proof would henceforth fall on those wanting to block their entry. Meanwhile, European legislation would concentrate on the basics and leave it to national legislators to define the details and also decide on different ways to achieve the main objectives, be they for protecting the environment or for the safety of consumers. This new approach also contained another important element: the task of defining technical specifications would be left to private European standardization bodies.

A great deal has changed since the internal market entered the European agenda in 1985, largely as a result of it. Free circulation has indeed become much easier, and the European economy is now significantly more than the sum of highly interdependent national economies, which had already been the case for some time. Capital circulates freely, and so do European citizens, particularly in the Schengen area. Several of the previously protected national sectors have been opened to competition, such as telecommunications and transport, but also banking and financial services. There are many more cross-border company marriages (and alliances) in Europe than before and more effective instruments to control them. Even public procurement in member countries is now—if only a little—more open to other Europeans. Yet what we have clearly learned in the process is that the creation of a truly internal market in Europe will be much slower and more complicated than had been anticipated, while the effects in terms of competitiveness and welfare will be more spread out over time and often also difficult to identify or measure; clearly not the ideal combination for the impatient or the agnostic, searching for something big and tangible as the proper reward for their integration efforts. It surely does not help that the marketing campaign accompanying the internal market programme back in the mid- and late 1980s had promised quick and rather dramatic results.

By the end of 2001, the legal framework of the internal market consisted of approximately 1,800 legislative measures adopted at the EU level, mostly in the form of directives, which need to be transposed by national legislation, and fewer regulations which are directly applicable in all member countries. Too many? Given that the so-called new approach was meant to simplify the legislative task of EU institutions, thus leaving plenty of room for subsidiarity and mutual recognition, this large number may come as a surprise—or it may be seen as yet more proof of the centralizing zeal and the strongly interventionist bias of EU institutions. The latter would be indeed the most popular explanation among Eurosceptics and neo-liberals, who largely overlap. It is, however, difficult to believe that national governments would have so happily participated in a conspiracy leading to the creation of an interventionist European superstate. After all, relatively small minorities in the Council would have sufficed to block such a process.

A more plausible explanation lies in the complexity and diversity of Europe's mixed economies, which require some degree of European re-regulation as a precondition for the establishment of a true internal market. There were many hard-fought battles before the Union could reach a politically acceptable compromise between liberalization, regulation, and national differentiation. A similar observation can be made with respect to private standards. More than 80 per cent of standards are now the product of European or international standardization bodies, as compared with about 80 per cent produced at the national level only some fifteen years ago: another piece of evidence that some powers need to be transferred as a corollary to the establishment of a European, or indeed a global, market.

The internal market legislation has taken much longer than anticipated because of the nature of EU decision-making and the need to find a common denominator among different national systems. Sometimes, European directives have explicitly allowed for differentiation and also for different timetables in the application of common rules. In other cases, differentiation has not followed the road of legality. EU institutions sometimes legislate, but they never implement. Implementation is still exclusively the responsibility of national institutions, and the result is not always perfect. There have been, for example, many delays in the transposition of EU measures into national

99

legislation, and these need to be added to the usually long gestation period of the EU legislative process. Furthermore, laws are not always enforced, and some countries take law enforcement more seriously than others. It is largely a matter of administrative efficiency and civic culture, and ultimately an issue for national courts to handle. In many cases, associated countries, such as Norway and Iceland, which have joined the internal market without participating in the EU law-making process, have performed better than member countries in applying this law. Last but not least, the European Court of Justice takes a long time to deal with those infringements that come under its jurisdiction, because of overload; and when member countries are notified of its decisions, they sometimes take their time in complying.

Thus, decentralization carries a price, both in terms of market fragmentation (rules are not universally applied) and in terms of the ability of institutions to adjust regulation to changing economic conditions. Mutual recognition has helped to open up national markets, but it has certainly proved to be no panacea, especially when national institutions and regulatory regimes start from very different bases. It should not therefore come as a surprise that entrepreneurs have not always responded enthusiastically to integration efforts from Brussels, or that they still see many imperfections in Europe's internal market. Nobody has yet invented a magic wand for quick and painless integration. These problems are bound to multiply with further enlargement, not only because of sheer numbers but even more so because of the weaker administrative structures and the relatively soft approach to the rule of law in most of the prospective new members of the Union.

If the legal side is both slow and imperfect, so should be the economic effects of the internal market. Following the ambitious quantification exercise of the expected effects, which also served as an important marketing tool for the internal market programme, the Commission in 1996 came up with the first *ex post* estimates of the macroeconomic impact. They were not as impressive as it would have liked them to be: a 1.1–1.5 per cent gain in GDP, close to a 3 per cent impact on investment, and a 1–1.5 per cent reduction in prices; and, more encouragingly, a 20–30 per cent increase in trade in manufactures, and between 300,000 and 900,000 jobs directly attributed to the internal market. These estimates, being only a fraction of the effects anticipated before the introduction of the programme, were not terribly convincing. How can one isolate *ex post* the effects of the internal market when so many other changes have occurred in the meantime in the environment affecting European businesses? A way out for Europhiles would be to argue that the effects of the internal market will be long-lasting and inextricably linked with the ongoing process of economic restructuring at the European and global levels: a convenient argument, indeed, but perhaps also not far from the truth. In this long process of integration, the nationality of individuals and of companies will continue to play a role, albeit a diminishing one, in the economic life of the Union.

The EU has developed into a regulatory state, and it is therefore continuously confronted with the standard questions associated with market regulation: how much regulation, and of what kind; centralized or not, public or private? The main driving force for market integration has naturally come from those who have an interest in the opening of markets. Interest has been reinforced by ideology: the prevailing set of ideas in recent years lays the emphasis on economic liberalization and supply-side measures. Yet liberalization (and negative integration) has often gone hand in hand with some kind of re-regulation at the EU level. Calls for market integration are often inseparable from demands for the creation of level playing fields—a fancier term for what used to be referred to as fair competition. Fairness is, of course, in the eye of the beholder, and economic theory does not always give hard and fast rules as to what constitutes fair competition. There are many examples we can cite.

The rapid increase in cross-border mergers and acquisitions, facilitated by internal market legislation although not exclusively the product of it, has highlighted the different conditions applying to hostile takeovers in member countries; and this has led in turn to pressures for the introduction of Union legislation in order to deal with the resultant distortions. A disproportionately large number of firms in the UK have been the target of hostile bids, and this can be largely explained in terms of the legal and institutional conditions applying in different countries. The relative size and role of stock exchanges as providers of finance capital is surely important, and market capitalization in the UK is much bigger than in the rest of the Union. On the other hand, many restrictions, legal or otherwise, on changes of company ownership and control have survived in several European countries.

The trouble is that, although many of them can and should be treated as straightforward protectionist barriers waiting for the EU liberator to strike them down, some at least of those restrictions or regulations could be legitimately considered as integral parts of models of capitalism that differ from the Anglo-American model, which relies almost exclusively on capital markets as a means of correcting managerial failure. What is frequently referred to as the Rhine model—that is, the German model, variations of which can be found in several other European countries—puts the emphasis instead on long-term relations between investors, managers, and employees. Banks play a key role, and so does organized labour in a system designed to promote consensus through its institutions and rules. As well, the state retains a controlling share in some companies, although the number of such companies has significantly fallen following the wave of privatizations in the 1990s. There is not, at least as yet, compelling economic evidence or political consensus that the rest of Europe should adopt, lock, stock, and barrel, the Anglo-American model of capitalism. Many would argue that events are moving in this direction anyway, with globalization and the growing reliance of firms on equity finance; but it is surely a less convincing argument after the bursting of the financial bubble, the series of big corporate scandals in the United States, and the reappearance of the long-forgotten spectre of a prolonged economic recession or even depression.

Is European integration the catalyst for convergence towards the Anglo-American model of capitalism? This is not exactly what many Europeans thought they had bargained for when they endorsed the objective of establishing the internal market—perhaps wrongly, although the jury is still out. National capitalist models in Europe have become more market-oriented, but they remain national and hence different from each other. They also, arguably, provide the basis for different kinds of comparative institutional advantage: liberal market economies are more favourable to radical innovation, especially important for the fast-moving technology sectors, while other economies, in which non-market institutions play a strategic role, are better endowed for, say, the production of capital goods where incremental innovation and training systems constitute key elements of success. The process of convergence has proved to be, if anything, quite slow. The French state, although accepting some of the constraints resulting from globalization and European integration, has not been reduced as yet to the role of a benign regulator of markets: far from it. And the Germans show little willingness to abandon their 'social model' and corporatist traditions, while Lower Saxony continues to own a large chunk of Volkswagen, which itself remains an integral part of Lower Saxony. A similar argument applies to the various *Landesbanks*, another key element of the German capitalist model.

As for the EU directive aiming at level playing fields for hostile takeovers, it was still on the negotiating table at the time of writing. Thirteen years of frustrating negotiations now seem to be approaching a happy end, if only in a watered down form of common legislation. Convergence requires patience and strong nerves. After all, it took more than thirty years to agree on the

European company statute, mainly because of the need to include provisions for industrial democracy, much cherished by the Germans and despised by others. And the compromise reached in the end is unlikely to lead to a rush of companies wanting to take advantage of the new directive. Too much compromise sometimes defeats the whole purpose of the exercise.

The search for level playing fields is clearly behind the Commission's control of state aids. This is generally understood and accepted—an important factor behind the widespread support for the common competition policy—even though Chancellor Schröder, for one, has repeatedly objected to such controls on German state aids. Could the same argument about level playing fields apply to social standards or taxes? The French, for example, have long argued in favour of applying EU minimum standards to a wide range of social rules and regulations, thus calling for a 'social Europe' which would also help to eliminate 'unfair competition' arising from much cheaper social regulation in some countries. Similarly, the Germans and others insist on tax harmonization and the adoption of minimum rates, especially where there is high cross-border mobility, as with portfolio capital, and hence much room for arbitrage between national taxation systems. Does this constitute fair or unfair competition? We shall return to these questions below. Some answers are indeed given by economic theory; most will continue to be determined by the interaction of markets and politics.

Countries with high social or environmental standards, or with high taxes, have always feared that the absence of common legislation/regulation creating the conditions for competition among different systems would automatically lead to a 'race to the bottom', as capital, being far more mobile internationally than labour, looks for cheaper costs of production, while also taking advantage of the elimination of barriers to free trade in the context of the internal market. Should voters or the market decide on the optimum level of regulation or taxation? There is, of course, a third option: continued market fragmentation because of the diversity of national regulatory systems and hence the barriers resulting from this diversity; and this also needs to be made more explicit.

Integration comes with a price, which sometimes governments and/or voters may be unwilling to pay. At least we should be clear about the parameters of the choice that needs to be made. In many cases, the minimum standards adopted by the EU, as a protection against a race to the bottom, are much more than the lowest common denominator. This is particularly true of environmental regulation, and it has long been true of legislation against sex discrimination in the workplace. In other cases, integration has been so far more closely identified with deregulation, financial services being a good example. And there are also examples where the internal market is still very far from complete; this is particularly the case with the labour market.

The new approach to regulation, introduced with the internal market programme back in 1985, was taken one step further with the decisions reached at the Lisbon European Council in March 2000. The objective was to make the EU 'the most competitive and dynamic knowledge-based economy in the world by 2010', and this was to be achieved through a set of economic reforms aiming at further liberalization and the creation of a more business-friendly environment in the new e-economy. The Lisbon decisions were also meant to fill remaining gaps in Europe's internal market. And there were new ideas as to how this would be achieved: the emphasis would henceforth be on the 'open method of coordination', relying mostly on benchmarking and peer pressure, with the Commission acting essentially as a secretariat and sometimes as catalyst or cheer-leader.

Those who had criticized the Community method as too constraining on nation-states and heavy on rules hailed Lisbon as the new way forward for the ever-enlarging Union: essentially intergovernmental, allowing much latitude for national differentiation, relying more on discretion than rules, and emphasizing flexible markets and light social regulation. Interestingly enough, the decisions reached at the Lisbon Council also seemed to suggest that at least some European leaders were determined to employ the Union—and peer pressure—as an external catalyst and facilitator for domestic reforms.

Three years later, the limitations of this 'new, new approach' have become clearer. The Lisbon consensus on the general direction of economic reform appears extremely fragile in places. Indeed, among the more pessimistic observers, the target of turning Europe into the most competitive economy in the world by 2010 already looks like a bad joke. When the external catalyst collides with domestic political realities, victory is far from being guaranteed. As for the indicators used by the Commission to name and shame laggards, they clearly do not have the potency of, say, the convergence criteria which had forced macroeconomic adjustment as a precondition for entry into the final stage of EMU.

The 'open method of coordination' may have its uses in some policy areas, but it cannot serve as a general instrument of integration; perhaps it should be seen more as a precursor for 'harder' forms of coordination in the future. Benchmarking, for instance, has been imported from the world of business and public utilities. Applied within a company, benchmarking draws its strength from a decision-making system where there is hierarchy and enforcement, or at the very least an environment where people are used to comparing results. It is still quite different inside the Union. Proponents of 'soft' coordination thus often appear to assume (wrongly) that there is already strong convergence of systems and preferences in a particular direction: a precondition of its effectiveness. The more cynical interpretation would be that they do not expect or want much from such coordination. The same people may be all too keen on hard rules when it comes to their own favourite level playing fields. And this is how integration usually proceeds.

☆ Different Rules for Common Policies . . .

Presented in graph form, the division between national and EU responsibilities across different policy areas would produce many peaks and troughs; and the economist from Mars would find it hard to make any sense of it. Rationality, as defined by economists, including those from outer space, does not always help much in understanding the ways of European integration.

CAP: Ready for Reform?

The CAP is, undoubtedly, one of the best examples of the divorce between policy and economic rationality. Considered as an essential part of the original package deal behind European integration and by far the most important common policy, which still represents almost half of the total budgetary expenditure of the EU, the CAP has been under severe attack from many quarters and for many years. True, it has not remained unchanged; and the pace of change has clearly accelerated since the early 1990s. Yet what has been most remarkable is its capacity to survive and preserve many of its key characteristics for so long.

It was initially meant to integrate the large farming population of the Six in a common market, operating on the basis of common intervention prices, a common protective fence against outside competition, and common financing. The CAP, following the tradition of the preceding national agricultural policies, was meant to be part of the welfare system developed in Western Europe in the post-war period, farmers being on average at the lower end of the income scale in most countries. But the combination of productivity increases, the slow rise in consumption, and high support prices for unlimited quantities soon proved to be explosive. The budgetary cost of agricultural support went up and up, while large amounts of produce had to be dumped in foreign markets or even literally in mountains of waste.

The CAP thus came under severe attack from foreign countries, which resented the loss of markets to European subsidized goods, and from national treasuries in member countries, especially those with fewer farmers, who saw their net contributions to the common budget rising constantly. Consumers should also be included in the category of losers from the CAP, since they are forced to pay higher prices for food than they would pay otherwise. However, consumers have never constituted a strong political force in the direction of CAP reform. The reason is simple: lack of mobilization. The battle for reform has been mostly waged by economics and finance ministers trying to impose ceilings on budgetary expenditure, and in GATT (later the World Trade Organization, WTO) councils by Americans, Australians, and others.

The CAP was meant to be redistributive from the very beginning, in favour of farmers and at the expense of consumers and taxpayers. In practice it has also proved to be highly redistributive among farmers and in the wrong direction. The bigger or more productive the farmer, the greater is the subsidy received from EU coffers, since the subsidy is a function of production. Thus, the CAP has been a regressive policy, contrary to its initial—and always officially claimed—welfare and social dimension. It has survived as such because of inertia, because big farmers have tended to monopolize the representation of European farm lobby organizations, and because some countries have invested a great deal of political capital in the defence of the agricultural status quo.

The CAP has been largely identified with France: a big agricultural producer and exporter, albeit with a steadily declining share of the labour force engaged in agriculture, and still an instinctive opponent of any attempt at radical reform. Many French politicians still treat the CAP as some kind of national product and one of the main pillars of European integration. Meanwhile, Germany has usually shied away from direct confrontation with France on this highly sensitive subject—and it has its own Bavarian farm lobby to take care of—while other net beneficiaries, such as Denmark and Ireland, have been only too happy to lend their support to the status quo. Interestingly enough, the countries that benefit from the CAP continue to resist giving the European Parliament any direct powers of control over agricultural expenditure, presumably believing that decisions taken behind closed doors by ministers of agriculture provide a better guarantee for the preservation of the status quo.

The agricultural sector has been steadily losing its share of total output and the labour force. Correspondingly, it should also be losing out in terms of political power. This seems to be already happening, although with a consider-able time lag. Farmers nowadays represent less than 5 per cent of those employed in EU-15, and they receive almost half of total budgetary expend-iture, although this says as much about the very low levels of expenditure in other policy areas where national treasuries still call the shots as about the gen-erosity or profligacy of the CAP. Certainly, nobody would expect that the budg-etary figure should converge towards the 5 per cent employment share. History, political reality, and the nature of the farming sector will jointly pre-clude pure laissez-faire reforms in the foreseeable future. This is not the issue. Furthermore, most partners of the EU are not exactly innocent of interven-tionism and financial support for their own agricultural sectors, including the Americans who, under the Bush Administration, have shown themselves ready to beat the Europeans at their own game through a very large increase in agri-cultural subsidies. As for the liberal Swiss, they have always excelled in this game: annual subsidies per Swiss cow—apparently holier than those in India—exceed the per capita income of many members of the United Nations!

Yet further reform of the CAP seems to be both necessary and urgent: enlargement and the new WTO round of negotiations, together with food safety and environmental considerations, could in the end act as catalysts. The first important steps in the direction of serious reform were taken in 1992. They have already brought about a major shift from price support to income subsidies for farmers, thus making the CAP more compatible with WTO rules while also transferring the main burden of support from consumers to taxpay-ers. This also explains why reform has not been translated as yet into any substantial reduction in budgetary expenditure.

The shift to income subsidies will have to continue. In order to transform gradually the CAP into a more explicit social policy, such subsidies should also be increasingly de-coupled from production. The Commission's proposals for reform go in that direction, although cautiously. The crucial point is that the bigger farmers should stop receiving the bulk of the subsidies. It will be a difficult political battle: there is much at stake for a small number of well-organized and politically influential people, and they have shown themselves capable of resisting change for very long.

Further enlargement makes the CAP even more untenable than before. The Fifteen have imposed long transitional periods on the new members, which means a slow phasing-in of agricultural subsidies payable to the large number of much poorer farmers in those countries now ready to join. They have tried to save the common agricultural budget from exploding, at the expense of those who did not yet have the right to vote in EU councils; but for how long? And there is also the world outside. The CAP, in its present form, seriously undermines the credibility of EU efforts to promote economic development in the Third World. Thus, the shift away from price support to income subsidies needs to be followed by further liberalization measures on the external front.

In addition, a set of new challenges faces the CAP. More and more people recognize that the emphasis needs to shift from production growth to more quality (and organic) products, more effective health and safety controls (remember BSE?), rural development, and environmental protection. These should represent the new policy priorities. Thus, the CAP will need to address more effectively the various externalities constantly mentioned by economists, instead of simply throwing money at more and more unwanted products as it did so much in the past.

As the social, structural, health, safety, and environmental dimensions of the CAP are strengthened—which already appears to be the direction in which the CAP has been moving, albeit slowly, in recent years—another extremely sensitive political issue is bound to crop up sooner or later. The CAP has been one of the most centralized among common policies, at least in terms of policy formulation and financing. As it comes to rely more and more on income subsidies and structural measures, it will also have to allow more room for national differentiation, especially in the context of an ever-enlarging Union with a much greater diversity of farm structures and incomes. This may mean, among other things, an increase in the share of national co-financing and greater differentiation in terms of income subsidies, which should also release funds for other policies financed by the EU budget. This will be sacrilege for some, including new members, and good enough reason for bringing the tractors out to block the motorways. Yet, if unemployment and other social benefits continue to vary significantly among different members of the Union, reflecting differences in standards of living as well as different political preferences, on what basis can we insist on uniform income subsidies for farmers?

More subsidiarity, therefore, appears to be the way of the future for the CAP. The Union will continue to set the main parameters of its (new) agricultural policy; beyond that, national (and regional) institutions should be expected to play a more prominent role than before. The exact balance between different levels of authority, including shares of the financial burden, will, of course, be determined in political councils, and, one hopes, with more effective control by parliaments and most notably the European Parliament. It will be a hard battle, and not necessarily one where the dividing lines are exclusively national.

It would be a huge mistake to lump the interests of all European farmers together, although those among them who benefit most from the existing policy have good reasons in doing so in order to better protect the status quo; and they have been so far extremely successful in this respect. It is high time to expose this political trick.

Competition Policy: Rule by Experts

If the CAP had not existed, surely nobody would have invented it, at least in its current form. The same is not, however, true of the other major common policy of the Union: competition policy. This is an old policy with increasing relevance and widespread acceptance. Nowadays, competition policy is beyond doubt one of the most important Commission portfolios. It all goes back to the Treaty of Rome, which gave the supranational Commission powers to deal directly with the collusive behaviour of firms, the abuse of dominant position, as well as with state aids. These powers were the means to strengthen competitive forces inside Europe's nascent common market. An American-inspired policy has gradually put down deep roots in European soil, and in the process it has developed into the most federal of European policies. It is also largely depoliticized: a technocrat's dream of a European regulatory state?

It has steadily grown in importance as the Commission has flexed its muscles, starting with anti-competitive behaviour of private firms and only much later beginning to tackle seriously member governments in their use of state aids. All along, it has received valuable support from the European Court. The strengthening of European competition policy has been very much a response to rapid economic concentration, a trend particularly pronounced since the 1980s, which has spilled over national borders. The Commission, with ample room for discretion in this area, has had to tread a narrow path between the desire to create conditions for economies of scale on the one hand, and its concerns about the weakening of competition on the other. It has not been at all easy: national politicians have frequently accused the Commission of excessive zeal, directed against any attempt to develop European and national champions in increasingly oligopolistic world markets, while others have considered the Commission's conduct as being too lax. It is largely a matter of taste—and different capitalist traditions (and interests).

The stakes have been raised significantly since 1990, when the Commission was first given powers to authorize mergers above a certain threshold of turnover. Until then, its powers had been limited to *ex post* intervention. The granting of more powers to the Commission—a pretty unusual event in recent

109

years—needs to be explained in terms of three main developments: the rapid increase in cross-border mergers and acquisitions, and hence the interest of private firms in having a 'one-stop shop' for competition decisions; the convergence of national competition policies, itself partly a product of regional integration and osmosis between national administrations; and the jurisprudence of the European Court, which opened the way for an *ex ante* control of mergers, combined with the anticipated effects of the internal market. Thus, the change in the economic environment produced the demand for a common policy. But that common policy would not have been possible if the necessary preconditions had not been met: member countries had already come closer together, while the ground had been prepared by earlier policies and institutions. A telling story about how policy integration proceeds, yet also not very typical since this combination of factors is not always available.

Merger control legislation has enormously strengthened the Commission in its role as the competition policeman for the Union as whole. As the number of mergers and acquisitions coming under its authority has grown over the years, so apparently has its readiness to block those deemed dangerous for competition. And the list of those who have been given the red light by the Commission includes big names in the world of business, such as Bertelsmann, Kirch, and Premiere in mass media, Volvo and Scania in trucks, not to mention General Electric and Honeywell, the two American giants—a decision which caused fury in the United States, especially since the proposed merger had been earlier waved through by the US authorities. Combined with highly publicized dawn raids on firms suspected of fixing markets and the record fines imposed on those found guilty, such as close to 1 billion euros for price fixing in the vitamins market (a cartel led by Roche of Switzerland), have given much prominence to the Commission's competition policy. The inclusion of US and Swiss companies in the list of those who have suffered suggests that the Commission has not shied away from extending its powers beyond EU borders, although of course foreign-based companies come under Commission jurisdiction only to the extent that their actions impact on Europe's internal market.

It has not been exactly the same with state aids. Here, the Commission finds itself face to face with member governments and not private companies, however powerful the latter may be; and this does make a difference. Legal powers may be one thing; political realities are another. In fact, the relevant treaty article contains a long list of exceptions; and it is all a matter for interpretation, a gold-mine for lawyers. Control over state aids has become more effective with time. The total amounts spent by member governments have declined in recent years, although this is hardly a straightforward case of cause and effect: budgetary consolidation may have had a greater impact. The control of state aids appears to be a clear attempt to create level playing fields in the European internal market. Interestingly enough, the German Chancellor seems to think otherwise, while state aids in Germany already far exceed in per capita terms those spent in the poorer countries of the Union. True, all are not equal, but can some be so much more equal than others?

One proposal for a radical reform of EU competition policy calls for the setting up of an independent agency, along the lines of the German *Kartellamt*, thus closing the door to any kind of political interference in the decisions taken. This raises a more general question about the boundaries of responsibility between elected representatives and independent experts in different policy areas. How much should remain out of bounds for elected representatives? This is a particularly relevant question in the case of the EU because of its strong regulatory dimension. And is the Commission's directorate-general for competition, with a commissioner in charge, to be treated as a political body or a glorified bureaucracy? It seems highly unlikely that responsibility for competition policy will move in the foreseeable future to an independent body outside the Commission. What is, however, more likely, and indeed desirable, is that the Commission's decisions in the area of competition become more transparent, and hence also more predictable, allowing for greater accountability. This is, undoubtedly, a weak spot in the Commission's record; and it has become further exposed as the result of a series of Court decisions in the last months of 2002, reversing earlier Commission vetoes on proposed mergers. Those decisions were a major and unprecedented blow against the credibility of the Commission's policy on mergers, and especially against the kind of reasoning and economic analysis employed by the Commission staff.

In view of its constantly increasing load of work—in a world where we seem to be moving fast from heavy regulation to excessive economic concentration—and its very limited resources in terms of both money and manpower, the Commission is now considering a more decentralized approach, relying on a 'regulatory network' of EU and national competition authorities. Many of those who would otherwise have been the first to wave the subsidiarity flag seem to have cold feet in this case. Greater decentralization (or partial renationalization) of competition rulings on cartels or proposed mergers creates serious risks of contradictory decisions taken by national competition authorities and different treatment of economic agents depending on the relative efficiency or culture of those authorities. Level playing fields? It all sounds very familiar. As market integration proceeds further and faster than institutional integration, the limits of decentralization in terms of competition policy become more apparent. On the other hand, there is pressure from different interested parties for a more relaxed approach to competition, which will have to be resisted for the sake of consumers in markets that resemble less and less the economist's dream of perfect competition.

The extraterritorial dimension of competition policy has been growing over the years, usually causing political friction between sovereign political entities, including the EU, which has a federal kind of structure in this area. The problem is almost always between the European Union and the United States, and the reasons are very simple: most global companies are either North American or European, while there is hardly anybody else who could face the potential cost of retaliation caused by an extraterritorial application of competition policy. This is a political minefield, which can only become more dangerous with the growing globalization of markets and production while multilateral rules remain extremely weak. Further cooperation between the two sides would be highly desirable; and, given its own experience, the EU should also find it easier to accept multilateral rules. It has, in fact, already shown a readiness to proceed in this direction in the case of competition policy. This is a good example of where the Union could lead the way towards stronger international agreements and rules.

Financial Services: Globalization Rules OK?

Financial services are a relatively new policy area for the EU, and a rapidly expanding one. For a long time, the financial sector had remained on the margin of regional integration. Capital restrictions in many member countries and very different regulatory frameworks had kept national markets insulated. It was therefore only natural that liberalization of financial services should be given such prominence in the internal market programme; and large benefits were expected from it. Yet this is also the sector where the elimination of national barriers needs to be accompanied by re-regulation at the EU level. The financial sector is a textbook case of what economists call market failure (where free markets do not necessarily produce optimum economic outcomes).

It is all about confidence and asymmetric information between producers and consumers. Regulation is needed to protect the consumer, and hence public savings. As well, given the fragile and volatile nature of public confidence,

112

provisions are required for public intervention in order to protect the stability of the whole financial system: in other words, the lender of last resort function undertaken by central banks to deal with systemic crises. This in turn creates moral hazard: financial institutions are tempted to take excessive risks in the search for higher profits, knowing that if things turn out badly they are likely to be saved through public intervention; the bigger they are, the greater the chances of this happening. The privatization of profits and the socialization of risks would be the dream of every entrepreneur, including financiers, who have frequently proved more able than others to make it come true. Hence the need for prudential supervision.

The above is only part of the long story of extensive public intervention in the financial sector. After all, macroeconomic stability, as well as economic growth, is directly affected. Furthermore, political power has always been intimately linked with financial capital, in turn a determining factor in the different forms that national models of capitalism may take. This is hardly the stuff that democracies are inclined to leave to markets to handle; at least, never entirely.

The decade of the 1980s was marked by a process of deregulation of banking as well as the financial sector more generally, coupled with a further strengthening of the internationalization process, the two being mutually reinforcing. Liberalization measures in individual countries paved the way for legislation subsequently adopted at the European level. The lifting of all restrictions on capital movements, a decision taken in 1988 and extended to all third countries, was one of the most important in the context of the internal market programme. It was soon followed by a set of banking directives, based on the well-tried formula of common basic requirements and mutual recognition and leading to a single banking licence for the EU as a whole. Thus, the EU went further than an old federal country such as the United States had gone until then in creating the legal conditions for an integrated banking sector inside its borders. More directives for other financial services followed.

The first directives began to be applied in the mid-1990s. The whole process of new EU legislation has been slow and arduous; not surprising, given the need to reconcile very different institutions and interests in a sector where the stakes are high. Economic concentration has continued at an accelerated pace: mergers, acquisitions, and strategic alliances have been the key characteristics. But most of this has happened within national borders, especially when it comes to retail banking. Thus, in a context of rapid globalization and increasing concentration, coupled with the development of a common EU regulatory framework, we have witnessed the strengthening of national champions, often aided by the active (and hardly invisible) hand of national central banks and/or national politicians. There have, however, been some exceptions, including most notably foreign acquisitions of domestic banks in candidate countries; the latter seem to play in a different league in this game. Furthermore, cross-border integration has been manifest in several areas outside retail banking: most investment banks and securities houses in the City of London have already been bought by foreigners, while European bourses have been busy establishing close links and strategic alliances.

It is in fact difficult to distinguish European from global developments: deregulation has gone hand in hand with technological change in information technology and communications, leading in turn to rapid consolidation and the emergence of very large and complex financial institutions. So far, little evidence has emerged of economies of scale or managerial efficiency, or of any obvious gains especially for the small consumer. At the same time, systemic risk and the chances of global contagion in times of crisis have dramatically increased. For the majority of European countries, the shift from banks to financial markets has also meant a serious change in the functioning of their mixed economies, although this is perhaps partially reversible after the dramatic falls experienced in all stock exchanges in recent years. It remains to be seen. The introduction of the euro can only be expected to accelerate the trend towards non-intermediated finance, thus adding to pressures for creating the legal and institutional conditions for the development of a truly European capital market.

The European Commission has set a target for full integration of financial services market by 2005, and in February 2002 the Parliament gave the go-ahead for a new programme intended to speed up the legislative procedures in this area: detailed regulation by committees consisting of national representatives, combined with the traditional Community method of decision-making, albeit restricted to the adoption of general principles. The EU is thus experimenting with new methods to reconcile democratic accountability with rule by experts, in a sector where speed in adjusting rules to a changing environment is of the essence. It should, however, be recognized that we are not dealing just with technical issues that can be safely left in the hands of experts. On the contrary, these are issues that can have a major impact on the real economy and hence on general welfare, as well as on the distribution of economic power. This therefore calls for direct political control and democratic accountability of those taking the decisions.

114

Speed in ending the fragmentation of the European market and in adjusting rules to rapidly changing conditions in global markets may be one thing—and a very important thing indeed; the quality and nature of regulation is, however, another—and at least equally important. How will European regulation deal with the inherent instability of the financial sector, defining and redefining constantly the trade-off between efficiency and stability? How does one prevent and/or deal with financial crises, the likelihood of which has substantially increased in today's more deregulated environment? If and when they come, who will pay the costs: the finance industry, consumers, or taxpayers? This has always been a hot political issue, and it will remain so in the future. How does one prevent the emergence of new cases like Long-Term Capital Management, the large hedge fund that went bankrupt while exhibiting strong signs of crony capitalism *à l'américaine?* How does one deal with money laundering, and (why not?) with tax evasion through offshore centres? And is there much room for regulatory competition among national systems in an increasingly integrated European market characterized by so many of our economist's favourite externalities? Where does one draw the line for hopeful free riders?

Regulatory committees should not be expected to monopolize the answers to such questions; parliaments have an important role to play. At the same time, we should expect a trend towards closer coordination among national regulators, coupled with more powers for the European Parliament, as the pace of regional integration gathers momentum. Several European countries have already moved to a single regulatory body for banks, insurers, and securities. What about a single European regulator? We are certainly not there yet, although the pressures are likely to grow in this direction.

The Maastricht Treaty already made provision for a future role of the ECB with respect to the prudential supervision of financial institutions, but this will have to be authorized eventually by the Council. Some national central banks strongly resist such a move. Nevertheless, the question remains whether the present highly decentralized set of national institutions could deal effectively with a systemic crisis. It will prove increasingly difficult to keep the ECB out of it for long. Differences about the kind of regulation and the division of powers between national and EU institutions are, of course, a reflection of different historical experiences, concrete realities, and even ideological preferences. They are also directly linked to the ongoing struggle for market share. Different sets of institutions and rules will affect in different ways the opportunities of the City of London, Frankfurt, or Paris, not to mention their smaller brothers and sisters, to attract business in the future. And it is big business: no need to pretend therefore that it is all about an innocent search for the optimum regulation.

Given the rapidly global character of the finance industry, EU regulatory institutions will need to manoeuvre themselves between their national and global counterparts. It will usually be a difficult manoeuvre. Global problems will require global solutions, which in practice will depend on close cooperation with the Americans (and also the Japanese), multilateral organizations being what they are. The Europeans will have to speak with a single voice, on the assumption that they sincerely want to influence outcomes. The policies adopted by the IMF or the World Bank, for example, have consistently and strongly reflected the preferences of their host country—and not simply out of politeness to the host. The same applies to the whole process of globalization in the financial sector: a process essentially driven by technology and American political power. The large difference in the relative weight Europe carries in international trade as compared with financial matters is a very telling indicator of the difference a common external policy makes. If the Europeans want to have an impact—even more so, if they want to defend a distinct European model of mixed economy (or, to be more precise, their national variations of that model)—they will have to adopt a common policy: perhaps a utopian dream, at least for some time.

The way the Union handles financial integration in the future will be crucial for the whole process of regional integration. This is a strategic sector of the economy characterized by a rapid process of deregulation, globalization, and concentration, with the accompanying growth of systemic risk. The Europeans will be faced with difficult trade-offs. More market integration will require closer coordination and the development of European regulatory networks; in some cases at least, it will also require a further transfer of powers to Union institutions. Regulation should be transparent and open to democratic control. This general conclusion about more Europeanization (or centralization) of regulatory power in the future is different from the one drawn with respect to an old common policy, namely, the CAP, where we may expect movement in the opposite direction. Today, there is no single recipe for European economic governance in different sectors or policy areas, and the starting points also vary enormously.

☆ . . . and No Single Social Model

Social policy has generated more political discussion and controversy than any other policy, including EMU; and, unlike with EMU, there is relatively little to show for the thousands of hours spent in often acrimonious debates in Council and other meetings at the European level. But it is quite understandable. The term 'social policy' covers a very wide area, the boundaries of which are usually left undefined. It includes the regulation of the labour market where state intervention has always been extensive, and where conditions in general bear little resemblance to the standard perfect competition model of traditional economic theory. The labour market is qualitatively different from the market for detergents, although economists would hasten to add that some economic laws still apply (and they would be right to do so). Regulation is mainly about guaranteeing a certain minimum of conditions for the protection of employees. This extends to social security, which has both an insurance and a redistributive dimension. Social policy also includes education and training, housing, and health.

There is, of course, hardly any agreement as to where government intervention should begin and where it should end. Concern about equity and industrial democracy is meshed with the pursuit of economic efficiency. For some, all three are complementary, while others talk in terms of trade-offs, which need to be decided at the political level. Although different kinds of market failure can justify government regulation of labour markets, such regulation and social policy more generally usually have a strong market-correcting and redistributive dimension. Social policy has been traditionally about nation-building and statecraft. It is where politics most directly interacts with the market in modern democracies, and it has therefore been at the centre of the old political divide between right and left.

The development of welfare states marked the period after the end of the Second World War in Western Europe. Social policies were largely aimed at incorporating the working class into the political and economic system as well as securing a wider consensus for the growth policies of the Golden Age. They were, of course, national welfare states. European integration left them virtually untouched for many years. True, the founding European treaties referred to the free movement of workers and the freedom of establishment; and there were also provisions for social policy, although they were limited in nature and mostly non-binding.

In practice, free movement has proved to be a very difficult affair, since it requires much more than the elimination of frontier controls and working permits. In contemporary Europe, labour mobility across frontiers also requires recognition of professional qualifications, transferability of social security and pension rights, and many other things. There are also huge

117

cultural and linguistic barriers, which cannot be simply legislated away. The Europeans are much less mobile than the Americans, even within their national borders, while the difference between intra-country and inter-country labour mobility in Europe remains large. Nowadays, only about 1.5 per cent of EU citizens are resident in a member country other than their country of origin. Cross-border labour mobility inside the Union is concentrated mostly among the young and professionals. Unlike earlier migratory movements, these flows are usually two-way and also less permanent. Given low mobility and the persisting wide diversity of national regulatory systems, it is therefore impossible to talk of a European labour market; it is, in fact, the least integrated market of all. Fragmentation is manifested in very different wage and productivity levels. On the other hand, while citizens of the Union have been very reluctant to cross frontiers in search of better employment opportunities, this has not been true of those outside. Migrants from non-EU countries, both legal and illegal, are much more numerous than those from EU partners. Strong migratory pressures from outside the frontiers of the Union reflect large differences in standards of living and employment, not to mention the frequent need to escape from oppressive regimes.

One area where Europe produced 'hard' legislation early on, making a real difference in many member countries, is gender equality; and the European Court was highly instrumental in bringing this about. Another, more recent, example is legislation concerning health and safety conditions at work. They are both examples of the Union raising standards through concrete legislation, in contrast with virtually all other areas of social policy, where the Union has had to remain content with 'soft' versions of coordination and relatively little impact on the ground. Since this has not been for lack of collective effort, some explanation is required.

The big push came during the second half of the 1980s, and it had a strong Delorsian touch. The former President of the Commission played at the time a key role in shaping the European agenda. The creation of a 'European social space' ('space' being a sufficiently vague term which also implies some kind of elevation from earthly matters) was meant to complement the internal market, thus adding a human dimension to what was perceived to be a project addressed mainly to businesspeople. The more economically developed countries, with strong trade unions, high labour costs, and advanced social legislation, provided the main political support. They were mostly driven by fears of 'social dumping': intensified competition through the elimination of the remaining barriers might force them to lower labour costs and standards.

The creation of a 'European social space', implying among other things the upwards harmonization of standards, also received support from socialist and social democratic parties across frontiers. It was consistent with ideology, although not necessarily compatible with the interests of the less-developed members of the Union, always keen on improving their competitiveness and attracting foreign investment. Thus, socialists from the south of Europe often spoke with forked tongues, and this is at least part of the explanation why there has been such a gap between rhetoric and action in this policy area.

Adopted in 1989, the Community Charter of the Fundamental Rights of Workers formed part of that rhetoric. It has so far produced relatively little in terms of concrete measures at the Union level. The main explanation is, of course, to be found in the wide diversity of national regulatory frameworks, wages, and productivity, since these make common legislation on such matters as part-time employment, working time, or minimum wages close to impossible, unless it is reduced to vague principles and objectives or the lowest common denominator. The large diversity in productivity levels among different members of the Union also helps to explain why there is little concrete evidence of 'social dumping' leading to lower social standards. Countries with higher labour costs, including non-wage costs, usually have many things in addition to higher productivity to offer potential investors, including more efficient administration, better infrastructure, and better training possibilities. Social dumping inside the Union has usually been grossly exaggerated; is it likely to become a real issue with the accession of new members bringing with them much lower wages and social standards?

The ideologically loaded debate on European social policy also led to the demonization of the UK. Margaret Thatcher seemed to relish this role, although British isolation was often more apparent than real; others usually found it convenient to hide behind the threat of British vetoes. The Charter, later incorporated in the Amsterdam Treaty, has been one area where the British ended their opt-out after the arrival of the Labour Party in power in 1997. It has not, in fact, made much difference one way or the other, since little common legislation has come out of it. The famous words of the Alexandrian poet Cavafy could apply here: 'And now what shall become of us without any barbarians? Those people were some kind of solution!'

One of the key characteristics of the European approach, with minority views expressed by conservative parties in the UK and Spain, has been the emphasis on institutionalized dialogue involving social partners, as well as workers' participation in decision-making within firms. It is consistent with the consensual dimension of democratic politics in many European countries and the acceptance of industrial democracy as an objective in itself, and not necessarily incompatible with economic efficiency. The Commission has wholeheartedly adopted this kind of logic. Although the results have not been spectacular, European directives have espoused works councils for multinational companies. Furthermore, at least part of the admittedly meagre European legislation in the social policy area in recent years has been the product of dialogue between business representatives and trade unions at the European level. The first signs of Euro-corporatism, making Thatcherite nightmares come true? Hardly. Some years ago, I described, somewhat uncharitably, the dialogue proposed by Delors between UNICE and the ETUC, the loose European confederations of employers and workers, as a dialogue of the unwilling and the unable. Since then, there has been little visible willingness on the part of industrialists, although distinctly greater ability on the part of the European trade unions, with strong backing from the powerful German IG-Metall and others, as well as from the Commission.

A few modest European directives jointly agreed by the social partners at the European level should not be seen as a precursor to European collective bargaining or social pacts. Both continue to play a very important role in several European countries. If anything, national governments have frequently resorted in recent years to social pacts as a way of gaining wider support for structural reform and/or budgetary consolidation on the road to EMU and after. The Netherlands and Ireland are good examples. However, the crucial point is that the nation-state, not the EU, remains the relevant reference point, even though some coordination, implicit or otherwise, among trade unions seems to have already been happening, with German trade unions usually leading the way.

While the Union has been deliberating a great deal and delivering relatively little in terms of common measures, national policies and welfare states have come under increasing pressure for reform. There are many factors accounting for this pressure: growing international competition, rapid technological changes, the large increase in women's participation in the labour market, the steep rise in unemployment, ageing populations, and low growth, among others. While most European countries have apparently hit the ceiling of social tolerance in terms of tax burdens, the need for budgetary consolidation in at least some of them, with or without EMU, has left little room for deficit financing; hence the talk about reform, including measures to facilitate the entry of those unemployed into the labour market as well as changes in social security systems and state pensions. This has meant tackling old taboos in European welfare states.

Some countries have moved faster than others in this reform process; and they have also followed different roads, not always converging. In addition, the Union has increasingly served as a framework for the exchange of ideas and policies among representatives of member countries, be they ministers, state officials, employers, trade unionists, or just experts. In other words, there has been a proliferation of different kinds of 'soft' coordination, nowadays better known as the 'open method of coordination', covering a very wide range of social, employment, and welfare policies.

Greater reliance on best practice and peer pressure, rather than more directly binding forms of coordination and common legislation, is supposed to suit better the wide diversity of social and welfare systems inside the EU. The optimists, including the Commission, which has learned some hard lessons from earlier experience in trying to impose greater uniformity through common legislation, seem to have high expectations of this more supple form of coordination and the ability of member states and societies to learn from each other.

It is clear that several national political leaders are often and quite explicitly using the EU as a kind of external catalyst and scapegoat for unpopular decisions at home, whether these aim at more flexibility in labour markets or at pension reform. The Lisbon process is precisely used for such a purpose, namely, to provide at least some national political elites with European (peer) support and legitimacy and thus strengthen their hand against domestic resistance to change; some might prefer to view it as the latest phase of modernization. This is quite a familiar story in European integration, although it risks being repeated once too many times, especially when the permissive consensus for integration can no longer be taken for granted. There is surely a limit as to how much the Union can be used as a promoter of economic rationality; and this could boomerang if the EU becomes more and more identified with unpopular reforms, economically justified or otherwise.

The proliferation of meetings at the European level, accompanied by numerous national plans and reports, common guidelines, and a whole set of indicators manufactured by the Commission to monitor progress and to 'name and shame' the laggards on a very wide range of issues and policies, does not always constitute a positive contribution to regional integration or even convergence. True, a growing number of national representatives are being socialized in the European way of doing things; but how much impact does it have on national policies? The cynics would point to sections of national ministries, specializing in EU affairs and regularly meeting and exchanging papers with their counterparts in other member countries, while having little contact with and influence on decision-making at home: a picture of national reports written for European consumption only, while national decision-making goes on regardless of what is being talked about in Brussels? This description would not always be far from the truth, especially for countries where the European departments of national ministries tend to lead independent lives of their own.

On the other hand, European peer pressure could become more effective if it helped draw attention within member countries to the policy failures and inconsistencies of those in power, thereby strengthening the hand of political opposition forces in their control of government. After all, the Union has developed into a sophisticated system of mutual interference. The more this becomes politically accepted within member countries, the easier it will be to translate European peer pressure and benchmarking into domestic political pressure and control.

The above discussion leads to some general conclusions about the role the EU can realistically and legitimately play in the social and welfare field. In view of the persisting wide diversity of institutions and policies, it is difficult to talk of a single 'European social model'; under poetic (or political) licence perhaps, and only when general comparisons are made with the rest of the world. It is common values rather than common policies that unite the members of the EU, even allowing for British exceptionalism, rhetorical or otherwise. The emphasis on social solidarity and justice has been and remains much stronger in this part of the world than in other advanced democratic societies. This is exemplified, among other things, in the amounts spent on social protection.

Figure 5.1 shows the very wide range of public social expenditure as a percentage of GDP inside EU-15, with the Scandinavians, together with France, Germany, and Austria, leading the way, and the cohesion countries, plus Luxembourg, still some distance behind. In some cases, the changes which have occurred during the last two decades are quite remarkable, like the reduction of the share of public social expenditure in the Netherlands and the large increases in all southern European countries but also in France, Germany, and the UK. Last but not least, Figure 5.1 (more recent comparable data are not available) shows the large difference in public social expenditure between most EU members on the one hand, and the United States and Japan on the other; even the poorest EU members spend more as a percentage of GDP. The European social model arguably exists only in contrast with the American model, not to mention the Japanese one, within the club of rich democracies. And an important difference also exists in the regulation of labour markets: this is true of the large majority of European countries. In general, the difference with the

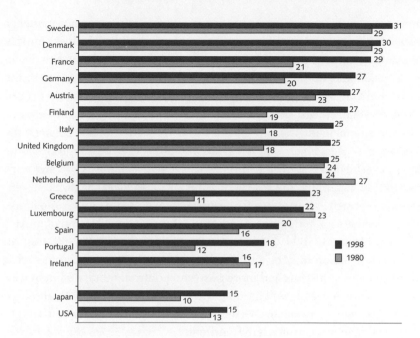

Figure 5.1. Public social expenditure in EU-15, USA, and Japan, 1980 and 1998 (as a percentage of GDP)

Source: OECD.

United States is manifested in terms of smaller risk and uncertainty in economic life and reduced income inequalities and social exclusion—but also in terms of higher unemployment and, arguably, a less dynamic economic system in Europe.

Within this broad context, national systems and preferences in Europe will continue to diverge, thus making subsidiarity the name of the game in social and welfare policies. While the EU may pride itself on having raised the basic floor of social rights in some areas, such as non-discrimination against women and health and safety conditions at work, in other areas of social regulation even minimum conditions may have relatively little practical meaning. European rhetoric therefore needs to adjust to economic and political reality, and hence to recognize the relative autonomy of the nation-state.

National autonomy is, of course, a relative term, and it by no means implies autonomy from real constraints imposed by globalization, demography, or EMU. Pension reform, for example, has become necessary in most European countries because of rapidly ageing populations, unless we assume that future

123

generations should carry the extra burden of financing. It is largely a matter of inter-generational distribution. On the other hand, EMU does impose constraints in terms of deficit financing; but do we seriously believe that generous pension and welfare systems can be financed through deficits in the medium and long terms? Continuing on the path of hard realism, we also need to recognize that, at least in some cases, there is, indeed, a trade-off between equity and employment, meaning that a choice needs to be made between the protection of those who already have jobs and of the outsiders who would be willing to seek employment for lower wages and/or standards: an awkward choice indeed, especially for those with left-wing ideological baggage.

Despite repeated exhortations from international organizations, most professional economists, and others, regulatory reform in the direction of greater flexibility of labour markets has moved very slowly indeed in most European countries. The reason may be simple: those who expect to lose from such a reform are more numerous and more powerful politically than potential winners. The choice, however, will become more painful if slow growth and high levels of unemployment persist. Generous welfare systems will be difficult to sustain in a stagnant economic environment.

Free movement is one of the fundamental freedoms of the EU, although relatively few Europeans are ready to exercise it when it comes to employment. There is, of course, room for further legislative action to facilitate mobility, covering a very wide area from education and health to social security. It will, however, remain an uphill struggle. Legislative action will have to rely mostly on the old recipe of common basic requirements and mutual recognition, and it will usually need to go beyond 'soft' coordination. Much of the popular scepticism about further enlargement is explained by the fear of large waves of immigrants from the new members, which start with significantly lower standards of living and, in some cases, with high levels of unemployment. This has led to long transitional periods for the free movement of labour following accession, which is a particularly ungenerous way of dealing with future partners.

The experience with southern enlargement suggests that expectations concerning the 'push' factors in labour migration from central and eastern Europe may have been exaggerated, although this will surely depend on economic conditions prevailing in those countries in the foreseeable future and the speed of convergence with the European core. The countries most directly affected on the EU side will be those sharing borders with future or aspiring members, namely, Germany, Austria, Greece, and Italy.

124

Migratory pressure from outside EU borders has already become a major political problem in all member countries—and it is increasingly perceived as a common problem because immigrants cross borders with even greater ease inside the Schengen area. Of course, immigration should not necessarily be treated as a problem. On the contrary, it could provide a window of opportunity for the rich and ageing societies of EU-15, a stimulant for economic growth, and a welcome boost for pension systems cracking under the pressure of demography—if only economic rationality were the guiding principle. But this is not so. In times of high unemployment, growing uncertainty, and inequalities in Western Europe, populist and xenophobic reactions have become, if anything, stronger. And several EU countries already host large numbers of immigrants, while being able so far to boast of very slow progress at best in integrating them into their societies.

Can the privileged ones stem the tide from the non-privileged areas? Not at all easy, when the 'push' factors in many of the Union's close and more distant neighbours are so strong. Often, as the figures for legal immigration go down, estimates of illegal immigration go up. The richer countries of the European continent, those lucky enough to find themselves on the good side of the divide after the Second World War, need to combine education at home explaining the benefits of controlled immigration with an explicit recognition of the existence of social constraints. Political correctness can go dangerously far in democracies, as the Dutch, for example, have discovered. There will be need for more effective controls at the border and policies designed to promote economic development in Europe's outer periphery. It will certainly not be easy. Members of the EU have also begun to realize, faster than generally anticipated, that they need a common policy on immigration. However, translating this realization into concrete measures requires difficult political decisions, including decisions on European border guards and burden sharing among countries. A common immigration policy will constitute a crucial component of the Union's policy towards the rest of the world. It will become even more important after the next round of enlargement, when the Union will share common borders with countries such as Ukraine and Belarus.

When the 'open method of coordination' serves as the appropriate framework for the gradual convergence of different national systems, the use of select financial instruments through the EU budget could make such coordination more effective by providing the extra incentive for unpopular domestic reforms. The European Social Fund could be provided with such financial instruments. It could also undertake a more active role, financially and

125

otherwise, in the fight against poverty and social exclusion. This is a dimension of European solidarity which may need to be strengthened in the future, even though the main responsibility will remain with member governments for many years to come. As the number of losers tends to grow inside member countries, such an increased role for the Union could have both a real and a symbolic value. Admittedly, there is also what economists refer to as moral hazard in a more active involvement of the Union in the fight against poverty and social exclusion, namely, that it may end up rewarding countries for their bad economic policies. EU transfers and redistribution would therefore have to come with strict conditionality.

Further enlargement will significantly add to the diversity of institutions, policies, and productivity levels, not to mention the large number of unemployed. There are in fact legitimate doubts about the ability of the new members to implement some of the hard legislation in this policy area. Strengthening their institutional capacity should be a key priority. New members will also bring with them weak and, in some cases, extremely fragile welfare systems, which have, consciously or otherwise, already sacrificed one generation to the altar of economic transition. Did they really have a choice? But can they afford another painful transition following accession, thus adding to the number of losers? There is a serious social problem in many candidate countries, and it could get worse in the next few years. Redistribution in favour of the new poorer members could be given a stronger social dimension. This would require a shift in EU strategies and priorities, arguably a necessary shift in recognition of the new economic and social reality in the enlarged EU.

Common action in select policy areas does not crucially change the main emphasis on continued diversity and decentralization in the Union in terms of social and welfare policies. We have argued that competitive deregulation is not an immediate problem, at least in relation to European integration. There is, however, a more fundamental long-term problem usually hidden behind rather simplistic arguments about social dumping. In the context of mixed economies—post-war European economies are such economies par excellence—the distribution of the national pie between capital and labour (or between different economic and social groups, to use more politically neutral terminology) has been the joint product of market processes and power relations. With the rapid opening of economic frontiers, and with no regional (or global) political authority to compensate for the loss of power of the nation-state, this distribution tends to shift against those who are less mobile internationally.

☆ Taxes and Free Rides

Taxes are another issue on which the Union has spent an inordinate amount of time with rather little to show for it. Tax harmonization had already been envisaged in the Treaty of Rome to the extent that national taxes could create distortions in the free movement of goods, services, persons, and capital; the emphasis on indirect taxes reflected the assumption that, at least in the early stages of integration, goods were more mobile across frontiers. The main achievement in this area has been the adoption of a uniform system of turnover taxes based on the French value added tax (VAT), which does not create distortions in international trade. Yet the introduction of a common system of turnover taxes back in the 1960s was not accompanied by harmonization either of the tax base or of tax rates. Considerable diversity of VAT rates has therefore persisted. But it does not create serious distortions in intra-EU trade so long as taxes are levied at the point of consumption and not of production, and the necessary tax adjustments take place at the border.

A new problem arose with the internal market programme and the desire to eliminate all remaining forms of border controls inside the EU, including fiscal controls. This would have necessitated the harmonization of tax rates and the tax base, a politically impossible task at the time. The result was therefore a typical European compromise: an agreement on minimum rates with a long list of exceptions, coupled with the adoption of a complicated system with a subcategory of goods subject to excise taxes. This has allowed the dismantling of formal fiscal barriers, although there is still an administrative burden imposed on firms engaged in cross-border transactions. The new system was meant to be temporary, but temporary things sometimes last for ever in the EU. This may prove to be one of those cases, given the strong resistance to a more far-reaching harmonization of rates.

At the same time, the decision to liberalize capital movements brought to the fore the link between capital mobility and taxes on capital. This issue extends beyond EU frontiers. As capital becomes more mobile across borders, different national taxation systems and rates are bound to become an important factor in investment decisions. This is surely a factor behind the shift in the overall tax burden in OECD countries towards the more immobile factors of production.

127

There are, of course, major differences between different kinds of capital: foreign direct investment is one thing and portfolio investment or bank deposits are another. The persistent wide diversity of corporate taxes inside the Union, even with a noticeable downward trend in rates but not in the total amounts collected, suggests that different rates are not the only determining factor in investment decisions; and there may be benefits to businesses that compensate for higher taxes. The argument is similar to that applying to high social standards and indirect labour costs; and it is a valid one, although with qualifications. Can we, for example, credibly argue that low taxes did not play an important role in the Irish economic miracle? And why not, others may retort.

We are back once again with the argument about level playing fields; taxes being yet another, albeit important, form of unevenness (unfairness?) in international and intra-Union competition. There has so far been very little progress in the harmonization of corporate taxes; in fact, there is not even an agreement on minimum rates. The deadlock stems from the wide diversity of national systems and rates, combined with the treaty requirement for unanimity on taxation issues in the Council. Does it matter much? After all, we have not witnessed, so far at least, a massive shift of direct investment to lower-tax locations within the EU. This has been, however, true of other, more liquid forms of investment, such as portfolio investment and bank deposits. Successive attempts by countries such as Germany to impose a withholding tax on investment income on their residents have led to massive outflows of capital to other countries, neighbouring Luxembourg being the main beneficiary.

The liberalization of portfolio capital flows was bound to turn tax avoidance into a cottage industry: a trend that can only be further strengthened inside the eurozone after the adoption of the single currency. Since not all member countries have reconciled themselves to a market-induced harmonization of taxes on interest towards zero, there has been strong pressure for the adoption of a minimum withholding tax on all investment income in the EU, backed by a Commission proposal to that effect.

At the time of writing, the EU was very close to an agreement based on a delicate compromise among very different interests. After several years of hard-fought battles in the Council, where the UK and Luxembourg put up strong resistance against any kind of harmonization or even the adoption of minimum rates of withholding tax, the Union has agreed in principle to a system of information exchange among national tax authorities with a long transitional period; as well, exceptions would be granted to Austria, Belgium, and Luxembourg which would levy instead withholding taxes on investment held by non-residents. This compromise package is contingent upon an agreement to cooperate by large financial centres outside the EU, most notably Switzerland. If and when this system of information exchange becomes applicable, it would mark the end of long-established bank secrecy rules in several member countries.

Will this eventually render tax avoidance (or evasion) more difficult, or will it simply recognize, de facto if not de jure, the inability of governments to tax internationally mobile capital? The EU border is in fact a non-border as far as capital flows are concerned, since liberalization applies to third countries as well. Will EU attempts to capture investment income cause capital flight to places still offering less qualified hospitality to foreign capital? This is precisely the argument employed by those defending the interests of the City of London against any kind of EU regime aiming at more effective taxation of investment income; hence the importance of reaching an agreement with competitors outside the EU.

It is indeed a global problem. As representative of the developed world, the OECD has tried in recent years to deal with 'harmful tax competition' from various tax havens and offshore centres offering many opportunities for tax avoidance (and evasion) in a world of globalized capital. More recently, and especially after the attacks of 11 September 2001, money laundering has become an even more important issue than the loss of tax revenue in the list of concerns of OECD countries vis-à-vis the various tax havens. Several of them have already agreed to cooperate in the name of greater financial transparency, although the jury is still out as to the real effects of this collective effort.

There is so much double-talk and hypocrisy on this subject, even by the standards of international diplomacy. Free riding has been the name of the game, and many countries have tried to hide behind highfalutin language about freedom and privacy or behind the effective veto of other countries, all engaged in a fierce competition, with few rules, for larger shares of increasingly footloose capital. The provisional black lists of the OECD included several dependencies of EU member states, supposedly beyond their control, while it remained unclear all along whether all members of the OECD were prepared to abide by the rules that the same organization was trying to impose on the so-called tax havens. The Americans had earlier shown very clearly what happens when the balance of power collides with bank secrecy rules and sacred notions of national sovereignty; they have never shied away from extraterritorial application of their national taxation policies, while showing precious little willingness to reciprocate. Swiss banks have been for some years now acting as tax collectors on behalf of US authorities for investments held with them by US residents.

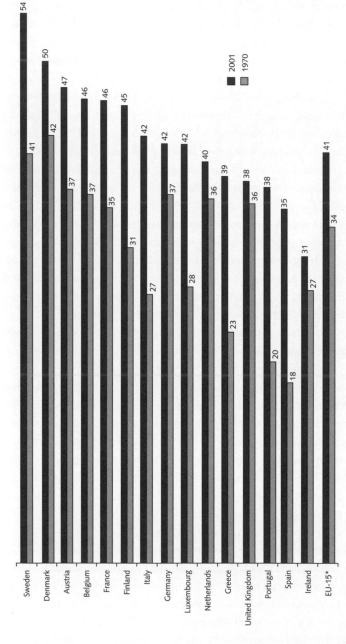

Figure 5.2. Total tax revenue in EU-15, 1970 and 2001 (as a percentage of GDP)

*1970: EU-15 excluding Luxembourg.

Source: European Commission.

Trying to keep taxation out of bounds in the context of the single market and the single currency makes little sense, and so therefore does the preservation of the national veto. This does not, of course, imply that the Union should rush headlong towards harmonization of all kinds of taxes. The argument of level playing fields arises only when cross-border mobility is high, and there is still considerable margin for national manoeuvre and differentiation. The tax-raising capacity of member states does not seem to have been seriously impaired; if anything, total tax revenue kept on rising until recently. Figure 5.2 shows the very large increase in tax revenue as a percentage of GDP in EU-15 between 1970 and 2001. The most dramatic increase has occurred in southern European countries, which have thus narrowed the gap with other continental countries. The European welfare state is still going strong in the face of global-ization, although differences among members of the Union are also quite sig-nificant. In terms of both total tax revenue and public social expenditure (Figures 5.1 and 5.2), Ireland appears as the European outlier. It is likely to find more competition among the new members, who should also be among the less enthusiastic for tax harmonization in general.

The above figures suggest that tax harmonization (and cooperation) will remain a slow process, although the pressures in this direction from those countries with higher levels of taxation are bound to grow as economic inter-dependence also grows. When there is a problem of level playing fields, advanced cooperation within a smaller group of countries makes no sense at all, because it would simply legitimize free riding by those left out. Can the same argument apply to the EU in relation to the rest of the world? In other words, is the objective of a Union tax regime completely futile in the context of global capital markets? Surely there are serious limitations in the absence of international cooperation. Yet the EU is hardly the typical small country forced to take the rest of the world as given. This holds only as long as the Union is determined to make use of its collective power; but this is not always the case.

☆ A Small Budget—and What Else?

Harmonization of taxes is one thing, fiscal federalism and solidarity are another. A crucial issue all along has been how much the Union should spend in differ-ent policy areas and how this expenditure should be financed: the EU budget, in other words. It was bound to become a hot issue sooner rather than later. Although the budgetary effects still represent a small part of the overall eco-nomic effects of EU membership, they have always attracted disproportionate

131

attention from politicians and journalists. They directly affect public finances and they can also be presented in simple figures, which make good headlines; and they have made a great many headlines, especially during the 1970s and 1980s.

The EU budget still has very little to do with a typical European country's national budget; and as long as defence and welfare policies remain essentially a national prerogative, this will continue to be so. The first characteristic of the EU budget is its small size, operating under the ceiling of 1.27 per cent of the Union GNP, although subject to treaty revision; hence it has virtually no macro-economic significance for the Union as a whole. For the sake of comparison, the national budget of the average EU member is nowadays more than 40 per cent of the corresponding GDP. There is also a legal requirement for a balanced budget, which sometimes leads to minor accounting acrobatics. Since 1988, the Union has operated on the basis of multi-annual package deals on the budget, involving the Commission, the Council, and the Parliament; the so-called financial perspectives are meant to ensure budgetary peace over a relatively long period. The negotiation of such package deals clearly constitutes a major political event in Union affairs. The next one should deliver the financial per-spectives for the period between 2007 and 2013. It therefore promises to be a difficult and crucial negotiation, with the participation of the new members, who will be testing their newly acquired negotiating power with seats around the Council table.

On the revenue side, customs duties and agricultural levies on imports, being the product of common policies, naturally belong to the Union system of own resources, although they now represent only a small fraction of total rev-enue. The rest has been filled by VAT and, increasingly, national financial con-tributions on a GNP key. With the growth of the latter, the financing of the Union budget has therefore become more directly related to the national abil-ity to pay, and it has also become more flexible. However, growing dependence on national contributions has been hard to swallow for traditional federalists keen on creating independent EU sources of finance.

On the expenditure side, the EU budget is even more atypical by the stand-ards of nation-states or international organizations. The CAP still represents approximately 45 per cent of total expenditure, having significantly come down in recent years, at least in proportional terms. Structural Funds, together with the Cohesion Fund, add another 35 per cent, and external aid close to 10 per cent, rising steadily. The remaining 10 per cent or so covers research and technological development, administration costs, and the rest, which in fact amounts to little. As with Union policies, expenditure through the EU budget is also highly decentralized: more than three-quarters of it is spent through member states.

The EU budget is small, albeit with a pronounced redistributive dimension in both of its two major items of expenditure. The CAP represents essentially a transfer from taxpayers (and also consumers through higher prices) to farmers, working mostly in favour of big farmers. It also involves large inter-country transfers as a function of the relative size of agricultural production in each country. Thus, in terms of cohesion, which is the official term for the objective of narrowing the gap between rich and poor inside the Union, the CAP continues to produce mixed results.

It is not so with the other major item of EU expenditure. Structural policies are an instrument of development operating through matching grants for investment purposes, although applying a wide definition of investment. The three Structural Funds, together with the Cohesion Fund, also constitute now the main instrument of redistribution on an inter-country and inter-regional basis; and their rapid growth since 1988 testifies to the direct link established between liberalization and redistribution ('structural action' is the preferred official term). The bulk of resources have been directed so far at those areas which are below the 75 per cent mark of the Union average in terms of GDP per capita. The net result has been significant transfers of resources in favour of the poorer countries of the Union, notably Greece, Portugal, and, to a lesser extent, Spain. The Republic of Ireland used to be the biggest beneficiary on a per capita basis, but this has been changing gradually as the Gaelic Tiger climbed up the income ladder: this is the price of economic success. With the exception of Portugal, these countries have also been net beneficiaries from the CAP in budgetary terms, thus adding to net inflows from the Structural Funds. Figure 5.3 shows net budgetary receipts for all member countries in 1998 and 2000.

Alas, the budget cannot be a positive-sum game among member countries: net beneficiaries have to be matched with net contributors. In fact, it is by definition a negative-sum game, since almost 15 per cent of total expenditure goes to external aid and administration, and so does not end up in national coffers or pockets. In recent years, some countries have consistently topped the list of net contributors to the EU budget, when net contributions are measured as a percentage of GNP. They include Germany, the Netherlands, Sweden, and sometimes Luxembourg (Figure 5.3). They all have per capita incomes higher than the EU average, although there is far from perfect correlation between net

133

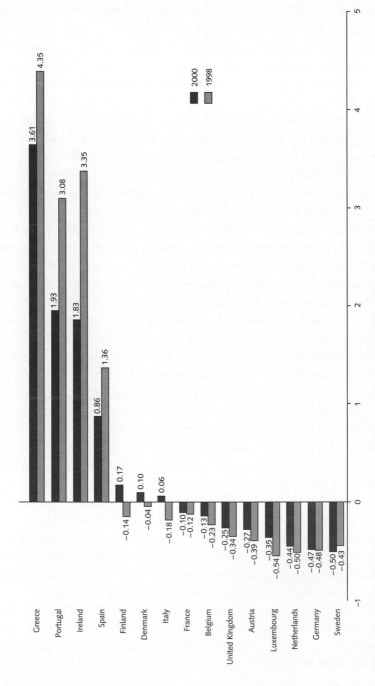

Figure 5.3. Net budgetary receipts, 2000 and 1998 (as a percentage of GDP)

Source: European Commission.

national contributions to the EU budget and the relative position of a country in the EU income league. Some of the rich EU members still get away with murder. The highest annual net contributions have been around 0.5 per cent of the respective GNP; not a very large figure, although in absolute amounts Germany has been, of course, by far the biggest contributor.

The next crucial negotiation on the budget will have to reconcile increasing demands for funds, associated mainly but not exclusively with the accession of new and much poorer members, with the growing unhappiness of net contributors. Further enlargement certainly points to more funds, assuming that the Union continues to include economic and social cohesion among its main policy priorities. Since the richest among the prospective members has about the same per capita income as the poorest member of EU-15, the challenge appears to be enormous; and few people pin their hopes entirely on the market mechanism as an instrument of convergence (and modernization).

The key question is whether the new members will be able to repeat the successful experience of the southern Europeans who joined back in the 1980s. All signs point to a distinctly less favourable environment for the new members. Will the EU miss this historic opportunity of creating the conditions for a wider European area of peace and prosperity? We should, of course, add the cost of stabilization and reconstruction in Europe's outer periphery, including the countries of south-east Europe, which will have to wait much longer as prospective members; the financing of new common policies; and the budgetary implications of EMU.

On the demand side, a growing list of items clamours for more funds. At the same time, the supply constraints are, indeed, more than obvious. The times we live in are not propitious for material expressions of social solidarity, and much less so on an inter-country basis even inside the Union. Solidarity requires a highly developed sense of collective identity, and we are still not there with European integration. Furthermore, German generosity seems to have reached its limits, largely because of the high cost of unification.

It is dangerous, however, when people confuse short-sightedness with realism. Can we imagine a Union of 25 members, with a common currency and an increasingly common market, large income disparities, a problematic outer periphery, and the ambition to play an international role operating with a budget ceiling of slightly more than 1 per cent of combined GNP? The present ceiling should not be treated as sacrosanct. True, the EU budget will continue to be very different, both quantitatively and qualitatively, from national budgets, and this will continue as long as key state functions are mainly performed by national governments. That said, the existing budgetary ceiling is simply unrealistic and inconsistent with officially stated objectives. A modest budgetary increase will therefore prove necessary in the future. And it would become politically more feasible if a number of conditions were to be fulfilled, including a further clarification of the main common priorities, a more equitable distribution of the burden, and, last but not least, a more effective and transparent use of resources.

To take the last point first, the annual reports of the European Court of Auditors, for example, make depressing reading, because they refer to numerous cases of wastage, if not corruption. The popular image of the European gravy train cannot lend support to arguments for European taxes and bigger budgets. It will thus have to be corrected, not only through public relations exercises but also through a radical administrative reform of the Commission and more effective accountability.

On the other hand, since the Union now prints its own money, it should no longer be unthinkable to levy a European tax as well in order to finance its modest expenditure, thus replacing both VAT and national contributions. It would have an important symbolic value, although admittedly taxes rarely add to popularity. Yet, in the case of the EU, the old maxim could be reversed: 'no representation without taxation'. It would add political salience to common policies and the budget, which would certainly not be a bad thing if the objective were to help bring European citizens closer to the workings and policies of the EU. A European tax surely assumes a certain degree of political maturity among citizens, instead of relying on the kind of permissive consensus which characterized the earlier phases of integration.

The European Commission and others have often toyed with the idea of a 'green' tax for the Union as a whole, which would be consistent with environmental considerations. A better alternative would be a small tax on personal income, preferably with a progressive element; that is, with the percentage of tax rising in proportion to the level of income (say, a range between 1 and 2 per cent). It would be a tax on European citizens, replacing national contributions, and hence to be fiercely resisted by national sovereignty diehards who would treat it as an important new step towards a European superstate. Such a tax would introduce an automatic mechanism of inter-personal redistribution on the revenue side of the budget. Once the general principle were accepted— admittedly a long shot politically, given current attitudes—several practical problems would then need to be dealt with, including the wide variety of traditions of tax avoidance (and size of the underground economy) in different member countries. It is time to put the issue of a European tax on the agenda.

As for expenditure, the further shift from price support to income subsidies in the CAP should allow for a partial renationalization of agricultural expenditure, thus releasing resources for other policies at the Union level. It makes no sense at all for the CAP to continue to absorb almost half of the EU budget, and the need for reform acquires further urgency with enlargement, which will add large numbers of potential beneficiaries to the CAP. Furthermore, the heavy subsidization of big farmers by the European taxpayer has become more and more of a political scandal. Income subsidies need to be divorced from production, thus turning the CAP into a more efficient instrument of redistribution from rich to poor, not the other way round. A release of resources from the CAP, even though tempered by the extra costs resulting from enlargement, would allow over time more room for the financing of other common policies.

A key item in the negotiation over the new financial perspectives will be the future of EU structural policies, including most notably the overall amount of money to be allocated to the three Structural Funds and the Cohesion Fund for the next seven-year period, and the list of main priorities and guidelines concerning distribution among beneficiaries. It will be hard to disentangle one from the other. The size of disparities and development needs in the enlarged EU calls for a real and significant increase in the overall amounts to be spent, on the assumption, of course, that the link still holds between market integration and development assistance for the less developed countries and regions of the Union.

After enlargement, the bulk of financial transfers through the Structural Funds and the Cohesion Fund must be directed to the new members of the Union. They should serve as an instrument of economic development as well as a lubricant for structural reform and modernization. The more seasoned beneficiaries, belonging to the old group of cohesion countries, will have to gradually adjust to smaller amounts of aid, thus following the earlier example of Ireland. It will not be easy politically, and the period of adjustment may last several years in order to accommodate the interests of those already in, and probably also because of practical constraints in the new members.

A ceiling for annual transfers through the Structural Funds has been introduced, which now stands at 4 per cent of GDP for beneficiaries. It was imposed with the new members in mind officially on the grounds that those countries would have neither the administrative capacity to make effective use of larger amounts nor the financial capacity to match more EU grants. There is, of course, nothing sacred about the 4 per cent figure: it is, not by accident, very close to the figure representing earlier transfers to Ireland and Greece. And if we are to judge from the difficulties experienced in absorbing the much smaller amounts of pre-accession aid by future members, even the 4 per cent ceiling may prove to be an optimistic target in the early years following accession.

There is already a discernible trend of a reduced Commission role in the choice of priorities for Structural Funds, the implementation procedures, and contacts with regional authorities that deliberately bypassed national governments. The days when the Commission and a few others entertained illusions about developing genuine multi-level governance in Europe through the operation of the Structural Funds are over; and national governments are trying to reassert control. Is it another example of partial renationalization? After all, why should the Commission pretend to know better the development needs and priorities of individual member countries and also try to impose models of governance on them? Delivery systems surely need to be simplified, and, to go further perhaps, the Commission needs to concentrate on more effective control of policy outputs instead of each item of expenditure where there is co-financing from the EU. But this is not the same as doing away with controls in general. Compared with some national or regional administrations, even the Commission appears to be a model of efficiency and transparency; and this will become more true after enlargement. Rightly so, EU structural aid includes an important chunk for institution building. After all, underdevelopment rarely has only an economic dimension. Furthermore, conditionality should, if anything, be strengthened in order to ensure a more efficient use of resources; and conditionality implies control by the Commission.

Some reordering of priorities may prove desirable. In the new economic and social environment, an enlarged Union may need to do more in the fight against poverty and social exclusion, thus adding a supplementary European dimension to existing national policies. It may also need to provide financial support for weak social protection systems in some of the new members. Such new initiatives, combined with a European personal tax on a progressive scale, would bolster the redistributive dimension of the Union budget. They would also partially shift redistribution from an inter-country to an inter-personal basis, thus dealing more adequately with changing economic realities in Europe and possibly also with growing discontent and Euroscepticism among losers, who tend to identify (the threat of) economic change with European integration.

It is also high time that the Union began to put real money behind some of the so-called common policies, be they the old CFSP or the new immigration policy. Surely, the main financial and other responsibility for traditional foreign policy and the security of borders will remain at the national level. But, even for those who think only along intergovernmental lines, it should have become obvious that common actions usually require some common funds. The CFSP has repeatedly suffered from a lack of such funds. In the present international environment, and especially in the Union's near abroad, safeguarding common interests will be a costly business. It will have to be more efficiently managed in the future. This, of course, should also apply to external aid, which already represents a growing item of expenditure in the common budget. It is arguably the price that civilian powers, albeit frustrated ones, need to pay.

☆ It Is All Highly Political

Economic integration is as much about markets as it is about different modes of governance. This is particularly true of Europe's mixed economies. And the choice between different modes of governance, including the distribution of power between different levels of authority as well as between elected representatives and experts, is not politically neutral. It is therefore not something to be left in the hands of experts. There are different traditions, institutions and interests at stake; and prevailing ideas also change with time. To put it differently: integration is not a game played in the name of efficiency only. The choices and compromises to be reached at the European level are fundamentally political—and they should be perceived as such. There is therefore work to be done in terms of public information and education.

The progressive elimination of national barriers in markets for goods, services, and capital, markets that have become increasingly European and to a lesser extent global, has not so far produced a rapid convergence of economic governance models in different member countries. National systems compete in open markets, as do goods, services, and capital. In other words, nationality still counts in production and trade in a variety of ways, although surely less so than it did some decades earlier. The rules governing this competition are therefore absolutely crucial. In some cases, regulatory powers are already centralized at the Union level, the best example, perhaps, being competition policy. At the other extreme, we find European regulation being limited to non-binding forms of coordination of national regulatory systems, and often producing meagre results. Many aspects of social and welfare policies fall into this category.

A good deal of intra-European negotiation on regulatory matters is presented as a matter of creating conditions of 'fair competition' and 'level playing fields'. There are no easy and generally accepted definitions of such terms, and sometimes the negotiations can go on for ever, with different sides genuinely convinced that the others are cheating. If only they recognized that national models of capitalism are not all the same, and each of them is not generally accepted as being the model for others to follow. Such recognition would render debates on the liberalization of financial markets or the harmonization of social standards, for example, more sober and perhaps also better informed or less hypocritical.

Labour markets are still at a very low level of integration for a wide variety of reasons, the most important of which is that Europeans, still very much attached to their national, if not local, culture and enjoying the protection of usually quite generous welfare systems, show little willingness to cross borders in search of better job opportunities. As long as this remains so, and as long as social and welfare systems retain their strong national characteristics and hence their diversity, there will be limited scope for harmonization, not to mention centralization, of social standards. Furthermore, this means that issues of high political salience, such as health, education, and welfare, will remain essentially the prerogatives of the nation-state for a long time to come. This should be comforting to those fearing the dilution of national sovereignty and identity; and why not? European integration is not, and should not be, sweeping nation-states out of existence. There are, however, many other policy areas where the EU makes a big difference: they form the core of the *acquis*, the term used to refer to the ever-growing body of EU legislation.

Financial markets present a different kind of problem: cross-border mobility is already very high, and this in turn calls for more effective coordination or even centralization of rules. However, national approaches to financial regulation, and the whole institutional structure linking banks and financial markets to the real economy, still differ a great deal. Compromises at the European level have therefore been difficult to reach. We should not pretend it is just a question of eliminating protective barriers, although it is that as well. And because these are markets driven by global forces, the difficulties experienced in reaching agreements at the European level on new forms of joint regulation have been translated into a correspondingly small European influence in international forums.

The application of the principle of subsidiarity cannot therefore be divorced from the nature and degree of market integration, actual or desirable, and the degree of convergence of national regulatory systems. The policy conclusions to be drawn with respect to agriculture are not necessarily identical with those applying to the environment or competition policy. On the other hand, diversity comes at a price, and sometimes it may indeed be a price that the politically responsible are prepared to pay, defending the 'national interest' or just very specific interests.

European integration has distributional consequences. For many years, these were mainly absorbed within member states, which also proved adept in neutralizing or, perhaps better, in compensating their losers. This is proving increasingly difficult in times of economic adversity and rapid change. In the more recent phase, characterized by continuous deepening of integration through the single market programme and later through EMU, the redistributive dimension of EU policies and the common budget has been strengthened. Further enlargement will present a serious challenge in this respect.

Taxation promises to have a privileged position on the European agenda in the foreseeable future; how could it be otherwise? As with economic regulation, the more integrated the market (and the greater the cross-border mobility), the more relevant will be the question of the harmonization of taxes or, more realistically, of the adoption of minimum rates. Taxation can no longer remain out of bounds in European councils. We have already gone far enough in terms of economic integration. We are also approaching the point where some kind of European tax would become a realistic proposition; a European tax to help finance a still small European budget.

Several ideas have been roughly sketched above concerning the future of the EU budget. It would still be a small budget, although, one hopes, more efficient in the use of scarce resources, more equitable in terms of the financial burden undertaken by the rich, and with a stronger redistributive impact in favour of the poor. It should also provide a more effective backing for common policies and common actions. Last but not least, it would represent a decisive step in the direction of a more mature political system. Is the Union ready to take such a step?

6

☆☆☆☆☆

EMU: A Unifying Factor

The unthinkable has indeed happened. Twelve European countries have already replaced their national currencies with a new single currency, the euro. And in doing so they have also transferred a big chunk of their sovereignty, and the symbols that go with it, to the EU. Money is at the heart of national sovereignty: the currency has always been seen as a key symbol of nationhood, while monetary policy and the exchange rate constitute major instruments of economic policy. Economic and monetary union is therefore the most important thing that has happened in Europe since the fall of the Berlin Wall; and there is surely nothing in its fifty-year history of integration comparable to EMU in terms of political and economic significance.

Few people would have dared to predict such a development as late as 1993, when bilateral exchange rates in the EMS came under massive attack in international markets, while European societies greeted the Maastricht Treaty with remarkably little enthusiasm. EMU has, in fact, a long and turbulent history of ups and downs. Many people repeatedly dismissed it as both unreal and unserious, although few as graphically as John Major, the former Prime Minister of the UK, who said that support for it had 'all the quaintness of a rain dance and about the same potency'. EMU was born at the same time as European political cooperation, the predecessor of the CFSP; and both were meant as bold attempts to venture beyond low politics. Their trajectories have been very different so far: while EMU has already reached the final (irreversible?) stage, the CFSP still has a long road to travel.

EMU provides a real-world laboratory for economists and other social scientists, an unprecedented opportunity to test their theories, while history has little to teach us in this respect since currency unions in the past were formed in very different political, social, and economic contexts. Economists and lesser mortals have risen to the challenge. There is already a vast literature on the subject, from the very theoretical and even visionary down to the most pedestrian. Since EMU opens uncharted territory, academic writings have often influenced policy; yet, interestingly enough, the big political decision to go ahead with EMU had relatively little backing among professional economists.

☆ Driving Forces

So important a project deserves an explanation. How is it, after all, that a slow and conservative system—an apt description of the European political system—operating under extremely complicated rules and requiring very large majorities, has produced such a revolutionary decision followed by remarkable political commitment?

It all started from zero. The Treaty of Rome contained very little in terms of binding constraints in the field of macroeconomic policy: some wishful thinking about the coordination of policies; provisions for balance of payments assistance; and considerable caution with regard to the elimination of exchange controls. There was clearly no intention to set up a regional currency bloc. The Bretton Woods system provided the international framework, and the US dollar the undisputed monetary standard. Moreover, Keynesianism was at its peak. This meant that national governments were zealous in retaining the independence of their monetary and fiscal policies in the pursuit of domestic economic objectives, and a heavy armoury of capital controls was considered an acceptable price to pay for this independence.

Interest in monetary integration grew during the 1960s, largely in response to the increasing instability of the international system and the perceived need to insulate Europe from the vagaries of the US dollar. The French were more sensitive to those problems than the other members of the EEC, who were not keen on a confrontation with the United States. This complicated matters and helped to confine notions of a shared European interest to a general debate which remained far short of any kind of serious common action.

The situation seemed to change in December 1969, when the political leaders of the Six adopted for the first time the target of a complete EMU. It was a political decision reached at the highest level, and it was directly linked to the first enlargement of the Community and the further deepening of integration; in other words, it was an integral part of the overall package deal to combine widening with deepening. It was also the first major example of a Franco-German initiative. But solemn decisions taken at the highest level did not prove strong enough to survive the adverse conditions of the 1970s; divergent economic policies combined with an unstable economic environment to make nonsense of fixed intra-EC exchange rates. EMU thus became the biggest non-event of the decade. After 1974, what was left of the ambitious plan for EMU was a limited exchange rate arrangement, closer to a Deutschmark (DM) bloc, from which the majority of EC currencies stayed out.

However, interest in developing a regional currency bloc never disappeared. The 'snake', as the system of bilateral exchange rates came to be known, was generally considered only a temporary arrangement, to be improved and extended when economic conditions became more favourable. The next step was taken in March 1979 with the establishment of the EMS, the product of another Franco-German initiative, from which only the British decided to abstain. It was a renewed attempt to establish a system of fixed, though periodically adjustable, exchange rates between EC currencies. Concern about the proper functioning of the common market was combined with the desire to preserve common agricultural prices. Exchange rate stability was to be backed by increased convergence between national economies, with the emphasis clearly placed on inflation rates. The EMS was considered an important instrument in the fight against inflation, and its creation meant an implicit acceptance by other European governments of German policy priorities. The experience of the 1970s was seen as validating Germany's anti-inflationary stance combined with a strong currency option. The EMS was also intended as a defensive mechanism against US '(un)benign neglect' towards the dollar, especially at a time when no serious reform of the international monetary system was in sight, and hence there was no prospect of a return to some form of exchange rate stability. Last but not least, European monetary integration was seen as a means of strengthening Europe economically and politically; in other words, the EMS was used, in a somewhat vague manner, as an instrument for political ends.

The EMS was built on the existing snake, but with some important novel features intended to foster the enlargement of its membership as well as the smoother functioning of the Exchange Rate Mechanism (ERM). The period between 1979 and 1992 was characterized by an increasing stability of exchange rates, until hell broke loose in exchange markets. Greater stability in bilateral exchange rates was achieved largely through an accelerating convergence of inflation rates downwards. The early years were marked by high inflation and persistent divergence between member countries, which explains the frequent realignments of exchange rates and the tension experienced during this early phase. The turning point came in 1983, when the French socialist government finally opted for a *franc fort* policy, seeking competitiveness through disinflation. For countries such as France and Italy, participation in the ERM acted as an important constraint on domestic monetary policies. Price convergence and intra-ERM exchange rate stability relied basically on monetary policies and the almost exclusive use of short-term interest rates. Price convergence, coupled with the growing credibility of stability-oriented policies, in turn brought about the gradual convergence of nominal long-term interest rates. The success of the ERM also led to an extension of its membership to the peseta, sterling, and the escudo, although the outbreak of the crisis in 1992 made their participation in the old-style ERM rather short-lived.

Until then, the ERM operated as a system of fixed but adjustable exchange rates. Adjustments, soon the product of collective decisions, became smaller and less frequent as prices converged. Central banks made use of different instruments whenever bilateral exchange rates came under attack. Those instruments included changes in short-term interest rates, foreign exchange interventions, and capital controls, which later had to be abandoned as a result of capital liberalization, itself part of the internal market programme. The everyday management of the system was left to central bankers, who relied as much on informal networks as on established EC institutions and committees.

Monetary stability was, however, also directly linked to the asymmetric nature of the EMS. Asymmetry in a system of fixed (even if periodically adjustable) exchange rates is manifested by the unequal distribution of the burden of intervention and adjustment and of influence in the setting of policy priorities. Despite special provisions intended precisely to prevent this, the EMS operated all along in an asymmetric fashion, thus following the earlier example of the snake. And this asymmetry had a very specific character, with the DM acting as the anchor of the system and the Bundesbank setting the monetary standard for the others.

Asymmetry is not always bad, at least in economic terms. The EMS enabled countries such as Italy, with a poor record of monetary stability, to borrow credibility by pegging their currencies to the DM. Participation in the ERM thus provided a convenient external constraint and strengthened the hand of institutions and interest groups inside countries fighting for less inflationary policies. This largely explains the popularity of the system with most central bankers, contrary to their earlier expectations. On the other hand, the asymmetry of the EMS became less acceptable in times of recession and growing unemployment, especially when German policy priorities diverged from those of the other partners. This is precisely what happened in the early 1990s, when the unification of Germany and the large budgetary deficits which ensued forced the Bundesbank to keep interest rates high while recession hit the European economies. This was a major reason for the exchange crisis of 1992–3; the other was the overvaluation of certain currencies following a period without realignments. Markets no longer believed in the sustainability of bilateral exchange rates, and they finally turned their belief into reality by forcing European governments to succumb to speculative pressure.

In the meantime, EMU had returned to the European agenda. It was initially linked to the internal market, exchange rates being an important non-tariff barrier yet to be eliminated. On the other hand, the liberalization of capital movements presented European governments with a completely new situation: either fixed exchange rates or independent monetary policies would have to give way. In the late 1980s, the EMS was still remarkably stable (and also asymmetric), while Europe's virtuous circle, linked to the internal market programme, was at its peak; hence the urgency felt in some European circles to win political commitment for the next stage of integration while conditions remained favourable.

Monetary union would be the final and irrevocable confirmation of the reality of the single European market and of a unified European economy. A common currency was seen as the means of welding national economies together, but also, very importantly, the means of accelerating the movement towards political union. This was familiar stuff to the integrationist lobby; but, arguably, nothing much would have come of it had it not been for the fall of the Berlin Wall and German unification, which provided the unexpected catalyst. The pressure came again from the French, with valuable support from the Commission. Initially, the Germans showed very little enthusiasm: the government and the central bank were happy with the status quo and any move towards monetary union was perceived, quite rightly, as leading to the erosion of Germany's independence in the monetary field. In purely economic terms, monetary union offered the Germans precious little, on the assumption, of course, that some kind of regional currency arrangement which helped to contain the overvaluation of the DM could be taken for granted. There is no doubt that an EMS in which Germany set the monetary standard was infinitely better for the Germans than a monetary union in which they would have to share with others the power to run monetary policy.

What finally tipped the balance was the perceived need to reaffirm the country's commitment to European integration in the wake of German unification. This is how the matter was presented in Paris. Chancellor Kohl spoke of economic and monetary union as a matter 'of war and peace in the twenty-first century'. The economic weight of the country, its strong reputation for monetary stability, and its preference for the status quo enormously strengthened the negotiating power of Germany, thus enabling it in most cases to impose its own terms for the transition and the contents of the final stage of EMU. The Germans set a high price for signing the contract. Once a Franco-German agreement had been reached, the process appeared almost unstoppable, thus repeating earlier patterns of European decision-making. Italy was supportive, and it also provided much of the intellectual input. The Dutch shared much of the economic scepticism of the Germans, but their margin of manoeuvre was extremely limited. Belgium and Luxembourg were fervent supporters, although Belgium was at the same time extremely concerned in case a strict application of the admission criteria to the final stage of EMU kept it outside the privileged group, because of its very high level of public debt. Denmark felt almost like a natural member of the European currency area, but its politicians were not at all sure that they would be able to carry the population with them into a monetary union; hence the 'opt-out' protocol.

The main concern of the other southern countries was to link EMU to more substantial budgetary transfers and to avoid an institutionalization of two or more tiers in the Community. As for Ireland, it benefited from the transfers and felt more confident than its southern brethren that it would be among the first to obtain an entry ticket into the final stage. It would, however, have preferred the island separating it from the continent to join also, since so much of its trade is still with Britain.

Britain remained the only country whose government, itself internally divided, expressed grave doubts about the desirability and feasibility of EMU on both economic and political grounds. The situation had apparently changed little since the establishment of the EMS. Realizing its isolation, the Conservative government made a conscious effort to remain at the negotiating table, and sacrificed Margaret Thatcher in the process. It made alternative proposals as a diversionary tactic, which failed to make much of an impression on the other partners. In the end, it reconciled itself to an 'opt-out' provision in the treaty.

As already mentioned, the Maastricht Treaty met with little applause from European societies and international markets alike. What proved to be an agonizing process of ratification of the Treaty coincided with turmoil in the exchange markets, and the two became mutually reinforcing. Governments finally won the battle of ratification, but they were forced to concede defeat to the markets by widening the margins of fluctuation of the ERM from 2.25 to 15 per cent in 1993, not exactly the most auspicious way of displaying their intention to move to irrevocably fixed exchange rates. Yet, only five years later, this irrevocable fixity of exchange rates, together with the creation of the euro, was officially proclaimed for eleven currencies, thus confirming the entry into the final stage of EMU from 1 January 1999. The twelfth currency joined two years later.

During the intervening period, most member governments, acting separately or through European institutions, showed remarkable commitment to the goal of EMU. A number of important decisions were taken by successive European Councils, dealing also with the host of practical measures needed for the introduction of the new single currency, thus adding real flesh to more general treaty provisions. At the same time, national macroeconomic policies were adjusted to the convergence criteria in order to secure admission to EMU. The cost was, however, almost a decade of deflationary policies contributing to low growth and a further rise in unemployment in Europe—or so non-monetarist economists would argue. Europe's macroeconomic performance in the 1990s was far from spectacular, indeed, quite depressing when compared with the performance of the US economy. Growth rates were very low, even by the standards of the 1980s, while unemployment reached new peaks (Figure 6.1). But how much of this poor macroeconomic performance can be attributed to the stabilization policies linked to EMU? This is a hot issue on which economists disagree.

Being apparently more interested in monetary stability than growth, markets gradually began to believe in EMU. Thus, the decline in inflation and budget deficits was soon followed by exchange rate stability and a convergence downwards of nominal and real interest rates, both short-term and long-term. This in turn helped to reduce the cost of servicing the public debt and hence also budget deficits. This was a major factor, especially for heavily indebted countries such as Italy. Societies followed: public support for EMU increased as the day of entry into the final stage approached. This is indeed an interesting case study of governments leading and markets and societies following.

(a) Economic growth (annual percentage change)

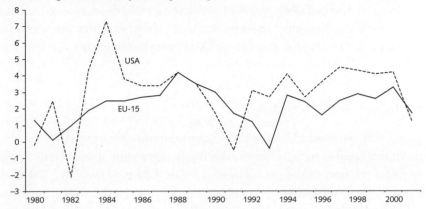

(b) Unemployment rate (%)

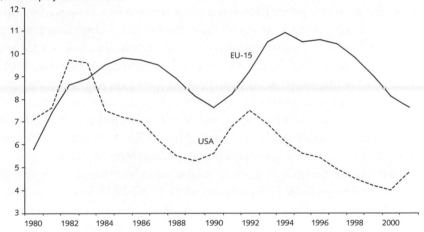

Figure 6.1. Macroeconomic performance in EU-15 and USA, 1980–2001

Source: European Commission.

This brief history helps to explain how EMU came about. As Europe entered the last decade of the twentieth century, an unusual set of events provided an additional and powerful impulse. Yet the main driving forces for European monetary integration had not changed much over the years; and there was already much accumulated experience to build upon. Those driving forces included the perceived need for exchange rate stability as a precondition for the proper functioning of the large European market; the search for symmetry, both inside the Union and vis-à-vis the rest of the world (a diplomatic way of referring to the US dollar); and the now familiar reliance on economic instruments for the achievement of wider political objectives. There was some consistency after all, which opponents of EMU failed to recognize.

☆ An Incomplete Constitution

Maastricht delivered EMU: the articles added in this most important of treaty revisions, together with the accompanying protocols, contained detailed provisions for the transitional period as well as for the functioning of EMU in the so-called final stage. Arguably, there is too much detail for a constitutional text, yet also many glaring omissions. Economics is an inexact science, and politics the art of the possible; hence the very imperfect product of Maastricht. Responsibility for monetary policy has been transferred to a new federal institution, while fiscal policy remains highly decentralized and the European political system even more so. This combination has no precedent in history, at least none that passed the test of time. EMU looks like a construction defying the laws of gravity, but perhaps anything is possible with postmodern architecture.

The admission ticket to the final stage of EMU, otherwise known as convergence criteria, sets explicit conditions in terms of inflation rates, budget deficits and public debt, exchange rate stability inside the ERM, and long-term interest rates. They had to be met, and were indeed met by all countries which entered EMU, although with the help of some creative accounting for national budgets and a very loose interpretation of the public debt criterion. For some countries, this meant a remarkable and largely unexpected process of macroeconomic adjustment in the years following Maastricht, although arguably at some cost in terms of output and employment. The three countries still outside—Denmark, Sweden, and the UK—have chosen to remain so; and it should not come as a surprise that public opinion in those countries includes large groups of Eurosceptics. Public opinion has, however, been highly volatile on the subject of EMU. According to recent polls, it appears that a majority of people in both Denmark and Sweden may now be in favour of the euro. The most stubborn opposition to EMU remains in the UK (Figure 6.2). The three countries that have stayed out thus belong to the category of 'able but unwilling'—ability here being defined in relation to the convergence criteria.

The national currencies of participating countries have been replaced by the new single currency, following a transitional period (1999–2001) during which

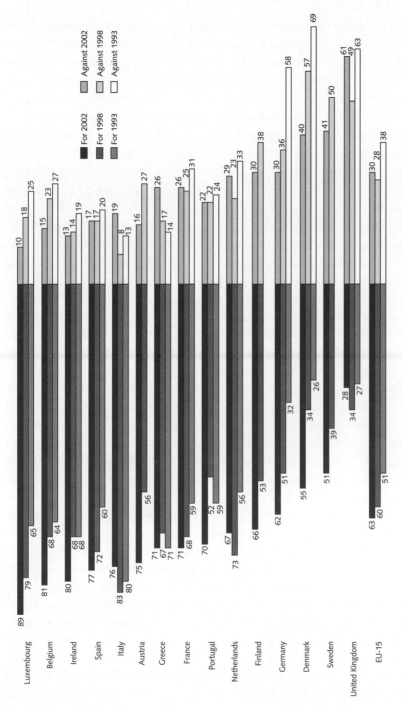

Figure 6.2. Popular support for the single currency, 1993, 1998, 2002 (percentage for and against)

Source: Eurobarometer 1993 (October–November 1993), 1998 (April–May 1998), 2002 (Autumn 2002).

they had been tied to the euro, still a virtual currency, and also between themselves with irrevocably fixed exchange rates. The European Central Bank (ECB), located in Frankfurt, has been given exclusive responsibility for the conduct of European monetary policy, including foreign exchange operations and the management of foreign reserves. Its primary objective is the maintenance of price stability, while other objectives, such as growth and high employment, are clearly meant to be secondary. The ECB is independent and strongly protected from political interference; it is also, in practice, largely unaccountable. It follows closely the German central-bank model, even more so because of the lack of a corresponding political authority at the European level. It is governed by a six-member Executive Board consisting of the President, the Vice-President, and four other members appointed by the European Council for an eight-year non-renewable term; and the Governing Council in which the members of the Executive Board and the governors of the twelve participating national central banks take part.

The Governing Council is the main decision-making body, deciding by simple majority on interest rates, reserve requirements, and the provision of liquidity in the system. The simple majority rule clearly gives excessive weight to the small members, but the principle is that governors of national central banks do not represent national interests; and this principle applies even more so to the members of the Executive Board. The refusal to publish minutes of the proceedings and the way members of the Governing Council have voted is also meant to protect members from political pressure. National legislation has also been changed to ensure the independence of national central banks. European monetary policy has been very consciously entrusted to the experts. Thus, EMU implies not only the transfer of power from the national to the European level but, for most countries, also the transfer of power from elected representatives to technocrats. At the centre of the system are the six members of the Executive Board, setting the policy agenda and implementing decisions by giving instructions to the national central banks. The decision-making system of EMU is the closest to a federal structure that can be found in the Union.

The ECB has the exclusive right to authorize the issue of money. It is not permitted to lend to governments: any form of 'monetary financing' is prohibited and so is any 'bailing out' of indebted governments and other public institutions. Provision has also been made for a future role of the ECB with respect to the prudential supervision of financial institutions, although this will have to be authorized eventually by the Council. Until then, supervision as well as the role of the lender of last resort will remain the responsibility of national central banks. On the other hand, the Treaty allows the Council of Economics and Finance Ministers (ECOFIN) a role in the exchange rate policy of the Union, notably in the negotiation of international agreements and the formulation of 'general orientations'. This leaves the formulation of exchange rate policy and the division of responsibilities between the ECB and ECOFIN somewhat unclear.

The Maastricht Treaty did not create any new institution for the conduct of fiscal policies, which remain a national responsibility, nor is there any mention of fiscal federalism leading to the creation of a bigger EU budget. It did, however, provide for the strengthening of existing mechanisms of multilateral surveillance, while also attempting to define in some detail what constitutes 'economically correct' behaviour. On the basis of a recommendation by the Commission, ECOFIN drafts each year 'the broad guidelines of the economic policies of the Member States and of the Community', although those guidelines are still generally seen as a kind of 'soft' coordination of national policies. In fact, 'soft' coordination has been gradually extended to other areas of economic policy.

There are, however, much stricter provisions for profligate members, introduced at Maastricht through the so-called excessive deficit procedure and subsequently made more stringent through the adoption of the Growth and Stability Pact in 1997 (the word 'growth' was apparently added for mostly decorative purposes). The Pact was the product of strong German pressure; it aimed at budgetary balance for participating countries, and provided for sanctions in the form of fines of up to 0.5 per cent of GDP to be levied on countries whose budget deficits exceeded 3 per cent of GDP, making allowance only for exceptional circumstances. Thus, the 3 per cent limit on budget deficits became more strictly enforceable, while balanced budgets were adopted as the norm for the medium-term. This has also led to the adoption of medium-term stability programmes by each member country. In one of those unexpected turns that history sometimes takes, Germany was destined to become in 2002 the second country, after Portugal, to exceed the 3 per cent limit.

The monthly meetings of ECOFIN are now preceded by meetings of the Euro Group, consisting of the ministers of the countries participating in the euro-zone. Although it so far has no legal status, the Euro Group has acquired growing importance as the only forum in which national ministers can exchange views on developments concerning the eurozone and also engage in a privileged dialogue with the ECB. This may contribute to a more effective coordination of national policies through peer pressure and benchmarking, although there are clear limits to such an approach. Turning the Euro Group into a proper institution with real powers would lead to a much clearer separation between 'ins' and 'outs' with wider political implications, given the importance of EMU.

EMU was supposed to be backed by political union—or so the Germans and some others argued during the negotiations leading to the Maastricht Treaty. What the supporters of political union usually had in mind was the further strengthening of European institutions and especially measures to tackle the democratic deficit. Little came out of Maastricht in this respect, and even less from subsequent treaty revisions. So, if anything, the gap between economics and politics has widened considerably with EMU.

The constitution of EMU is incomplete, but it is very much the product of its time in terms of political feasibility and economic ideas. The negotiations leading to the Maastricht Treaty, and subsequent negotiations which added important pieces to the EMU construction, were, of course, conducted by human beings: not entirely rational, at least in the economic sense of the term; each carrying his or her ideological baggage, the contents of which change with economic and political fashion; and taking decisions on the basis of imperfect information, although knowing full well that EMU was part and parcel of a much wider ongoing negotiation on the future of Europe. In intergovernmental conferences, which lead to EU treaty revisions, all countries are theoretically equal and all have the right of veto. But some surely are more equal than others. The EMU construction which came out of the Maastricht Treaty and subsequent negotiations reflects essentially the strong interest of France in EMU, Germany's ability to set the terms of reference, the prevalence of monetarist ideas, and the lack of sufficient support for tackling the political deficit of the Community, now metamorphosed as Union.

The economics of EMU has been much debated by economists. There is certainly no consensus that the economic advantages of a single European currency outweigh the disadvantages resulting from the loss of important policy instruments at the national level. Of course, the balance sheet for Belgium would be substantially different from that for the UK. It has to do with the openness of the national economy, among other things. The EU is not an optimal currency area, far from it, though such an optimum currency area could be created *ex post*. The European economy is not yet sufficiently homogeneous, which means that different countries and regions can be subject to asymmetric shocks. And there are no adequate adjustment mechanisms, such as flexible labour markets, high labour mobility, or large budgetary transfers, to act as effective substitutes for the exchange rate. But how effective is the exchange rate as a policy instrument in a world characterized by highly mobile international capital and highly unstable financial markets? And can there be a true European market with constantly fluctuating exchange rates linking its national components? The economics profession gives no decisive answer. With EMU, the broad answer was given at the highest political level and mostly on the basis of political arguments; then it was left to the experts to negotiate the technical arrangements. It had been different with the internal market programme, which enjoyed wide support among the economics profession.

The strong emphasis on price stability as the primary, if not single, objective of the ECB in the conduct of monetary policy, coupled with the provisions for the political independence of the bank, reflects mainly the preoccupations of the Germans and their desire to export their successful (at least until recently) national model as well the prevalence of monetarist thinking, not to mention the influence of the 'brotherhood of central bankers' who did most of the drafting of the statutes of the ECB. Monetary policy is not supposed to have an impact on real economic variables in the long term, but only in the short term and at a high price in terms of inflation. Furthermore, the independence of central banks is meant to protect monetary policy from political interference and thus becoming a victim of the electoral cycle; and since the ECB has no history behind it, legal provisions were meant to be even stronger in order to ensure its credibility in the markets.

Given the shortage of adjustment mechanisms in EMU, it would make sense to strengthen the flexibility of national fiscal policies as a way of dealing with asymmetric shocks or simply with the insufficient synchronization of economic cycles. But there is also the risk of free-riding by national, or even regional, governments operating under the shield of the Union, on the assumption, of course, that markets cannot be relied upon to provide an effective restraint on government overspending (and under-taxing). In the end, fear of this risk prevailed over the attractions of fiscal flexibility, because of German doubts about the fiscal rectitude of some of their partners, while budgetary consolidation constituted an integral part of economic correctness; hence the straightjacket imposed by the Stability and Growth Pact. Rigid rules were meant to act as a substitute for the lack of institutional history in EMU. Keynesianism was also supposed to be dead and buried. A similar combination of factors applied to fiscal federalism in the context of EMU. The MacDougall report back in 1977 had argued in favour of a substantial increase in the Community budget with an important stabilization function as a precondition for the proper functioning of EMU. No longer in the early 1990s: the Germans were not prepared to pay and the very idea of stabilization was unfashionable.

So the architects of EMU rejected intra-EU budgetary transfers as an automatic adjustment mechanism, while imposing heavy constraints on national fiscal policy. In so doing, they have implicitly assumed one of two things: either that economic convergence will be very fast, including convergence in wage bargaining in different European countries, thus reducing the need for adjustment instruments; or that labour markets will become much more flexible and thus be able to absorb asymmetric shocks. Prevailing economic orthodoxy would clearly put the emphasis on labour market flexibility; and in recent years, there has been indeed considerable pressure from international organizations, some governments, and the great majority of the economics profession to move in this direction. But are the Germans, for example, ready to replace their corporatist model of industrial relations with the model of flexible labour markets, following the American example? Whatever success the Bundesbank had in the past in securing low inflation cannot be understood in isolation from the way in which the German political system functioned and continues to function, including relations between government, business, and organized labour. And this may be precisely one of the main problems with the ECB: the rest of that successful package is not there.

The convergence criteria were something totally new in European integration. It was the first time that preconditions were set for a country to be able to participate in a common policy. They have been criticized on many grounds. They are mechanistic, some of them are arbitrary and superfluous, they ignore real convergence, and they are also arguably deflationary. They can be viewed at best as a rough (and also ephemeral) indicator of the stability orientation of countries before they enter EMU, although this could admittedly strengthen the credibility of EMU and the ECB. In purely economic terms, it would have made sense to go for a much shorter transition period with easier conditions for entry and better (and perhaps stricter) rules for the final stage of EMU; but this was not politically possible. The convergence criteria were also meant to restrict, at least for some time, the number of countries allowed into the final stage, although that is a dangerous political precedent. Who could have guessed that as many as eleven countries would slip through the net on the basis of 1997 data; two years earlier, only Luxembourg would have qualified. This is what it means to live in a world of limited information and even more limited predictability. Presumably, many economists inhabit a special world of their own.

EMU is compatible with the strong tradition of elitism and depoliticization in European integration. The key decisions were taken at the very top behind closed doors, the texts were drafted by central bankers and diplomats making of the ECB a fortress for the *cognoscenti*, big business was allowed a say in later stages, while the wider public was simply expected to acquiesce. There was very little public debate on the pros and cons of EMU and its wider implications, or on alternative ways of managing the new single currency, prior to the signing of the Treaty; the exceptions were those countries, notably the UK, which had a large number of sceptics from the beginning. The unenthusiastic response accorded to the Treaty came as a nasty surprise to European political elites. If other countries, especially Germany, had followed the example of the Danes, the Irish, and the French in holding referendums the project might have sunk for good. Apart from the usual Eurosceptic suspects in Scandinavia and the UK, even the Germans showed precious little enthusiasm for EMU in the beginning (Figure 6.2). In their case, however, political leadership paid off: public support for EMU grew steadily during the transitional period. The highest levels of popular support have been consistently recorded in Italy, the Benelux countries, and the cohesion countries; the lowest in the UK.

Big questions have remained unanswered concerning the long-term implications or the links with other policy domains—and, in some cases, apparently deliberately. For those who thrive on conspiracy theories, EMU is therefore justifiably the most dreaded example of economic integration leading to political integration and the creation of a European superstate. After all, is it not true that European integration has relied heavily until now on a sequence of spillovers, generally moving from the economic to the political?

☆ Democracy and Economic Orthodoxy

We have created a European single currency with a weak and unbalanced institutional structure, and rigid rules to compensate for those faults. This is what was politically feasible at the time, and the architects of EMU went for it, postponing several difficult decisions—only half-consciously perhaps, since their design closely reflected current economic fashion. Furthermore, market integration has always proved easier than political and institutional integration. The weak institutional structure of EMU, coupled with its unbalanced nature, is, however, likely to entail economic costs in terms of lost output and employment and of a weak currency. Politics and economics are inseparable: poor economic results on the one hand, and fragile popular acceptance of the project and low levels of legitimacy of common institutions on the other, may be closely linked and mutually reinforcing. Experience seems to suggest that the safest way to the hearts of European citizens has been through their pockets: popular support for integration is closely related to the associated material benefits, while European identity has remained weak all along. Is this likely to be repeated with EMU? There are major issues of economic governance and democratic legitimacy at stake.

It did not help much that the new single currency reached the pockets of European citizens at a time of low growth and high unemployment. Decision-makers prayed (as they should, in any case) that the first recession after the introduction of the euro would arrive as late as possible, thus allowing the ECB and other European institutions time to establish their credibility and legitimacy with markets and societies alike. Their prayers were apparently not heard at higher levels, and they were therefore forced to learn how to manage the new currency under adverse conditions. The issue of legitimacy may prove particularly important in times when popular support for integration has reached historically low levels, while the economic benefits from EMU may not prove to be that great, may be slow to materialize, and may be unevenly distributed. Predictions are, of course, very risky, especially when they relate to a highly uncertain future and with precious little relevant experience to back them up. For the time being, millions of European citizens are experiencing the tangible effects of the euro in their everyday lives.

Our starting point is that the stabilization function of EMU should involve a continuous dialogue between the central bank and a European political institution responsible for economic policy at the Union level and accountable to the European Parliament. This should also, albeit slowly, encourage Europe-wide debates on the direction and key policy priorities for European economic policy, as the constraints on national choices become tighter (and are perceived as such) as a result of treaty obligations and market integration. The europhobes are, indeed, right about the political conclusion they draw from EMU: it is bound to have a centralizing effect on economic policies, although this is likely to take a long time.

To compensate for the lack of history, the authors of the Maastricht Treaty tried to strengthen the credibility of the ECB through strict rules guaranteeing its political independence and its attachment to the goal of price stability. They seemed to be less concerned about its popular acceptance, presumably assuming that the new institution would gain legitimacy as it was seen to deliver the goods. In other words, credibility in the markets was given precedence over credibility in European societies in general. The existing arrangements are based on certain assumptions about the role of monetary policy and its divorce from majoritarian democracy. For some, EMU forms part of the 'Golden Straitjacket' made famous by the US journalist Thomas Friedman (the 'Golden Straitjacket' is meant to transform the democratic game in advanced societies into a competition among more and less efficient managers of the capitalist system). It will not necessarily survive the test of time, at least in Europe.

Within the national context, an independent central bank is accountable to democratic institutions and can draw its decisions from the reservoir of legitimacy of the nation-state. There is no equivalent at the EU level. This has prompted outside observers to develop catastrophe scenarios for EMU, in which economic orthodoxy meets political reality in times of recession. Although such scenarios may stretch the point too far, there is clearly a problem of legitimacy with European institutions in general and the ECB in particular.

The ECB will therefore need a political counterpart for EMU to function properly and also for the Bank itself to strengthen its own credibility and legitimacy. An independent central bank, without a credible political interlocutor to which it is answerable and which in turn enjoys democratic legitimacy, is essentially a weak central bank. The markets clearly perceived this, especially in times of crisis. This analysis seems to be corroborated by experience: the weakness of the euro in exchange markets during the first years was at least partially a function of the institutional and political weakness of EMU.

The ECB was designed as a conservative bank in conformity with German preferences and the prevailing economic orthodoxy. It behaved accordingly during its first four years of operation, putting the emphasis virtually exclusively on price stability, defined by the ECB as an average eurozone annual inflation rate within the range 0–2 per cent, at the expense of other considerations such as growth, employment, or financial stability. This inflation target has been too restrictive, especially at a time when deflation has ceased to be a matter of concern exclusively for historians; hence, European interest rates have sometimes been kept at too high a level. And the ECB has shown little inclination to pursue a proactive monetary policy, the comparison with the US Federal Reserve under Mr Greenspan being more than indicative. The straitjacket imposed on the European economy seems to have been made of copper, not gold, thus adding insult to injury; but this is more true of Germany than, say, Italy.

Greater self-confidence, which can be acquired only through experience, and a stronger political interlocutor in the form of a European institution for economic policy should (one hopes) lead the ECB to become less conservative, and also more accountable to the democratically elected representatives of European citizens; the sooner the better for all concerned. Independence does not mean lack of accountability, and accountability needs to be strengthened in the case of the ECB. Testing the boundaries between orthodoxy and heresy (as others have already done), one could in fact go even further and argue that there is nothing in the holy books of central banking which requires that setting the inflation target should be the prerogative of an independent central bank. Independence can be defined in terms of the policy instruments employed to meet the target set by political authorities.

With time, we are likely to witness further centralization in the implementation of monetary policy and a reduced role for the governors of national central banks in decision-making. The latter will become almost inevitable with the addition of new members to EMU, which should lead to a corresponding increase in the number of national governors with the right to vote in the Governing Council of the ECB, unless the present rules are changed. Most likely, they will change. Thus, the Bank will be forced to shift from the principle of 'one governor, one vote' to some kind of regional constituencies or vote by rotation, following the example of the IMF or the US Federal Reserve. It will not be a simple operation. In the future, the ECB should also be expected to acquire more powers of banking supervision and regulation, ending up probably as the lender of last resort for the Union as a whole. But this may prove to be a long process that encounters much resistance from national banking and financial regulators. With rapid financial integration, and with EMU acting as an important catalyst in this respect, it will be increasingly difficult to continue with the practice of the twelve or more national subsidiaries of the ECB acting independently as banking supervisors, thus pretending that national markets are much less interdependent than they actually are.

On the economic side of EMU, there is, of course, the immediate problem of reforming the Stability and Growth Pact, which has manifestly failed in the main task assigned to it, namely, to impose effective limits on fiscal laxity in the context of EMU. Rules are, indeed, needed in order to deal with free riders: large budget deficits run by individual governments can undermine the credibility of the single currency and thus force the central bank to raise interest rates by way of compensation. But the rules adopted have proved too rigid, especially in an adverse economic environment, and hence unenforceable.

Combined with a restrictive monetary policy pursued by the ECB, they have unnecessarily reduced the freedom enjoyed by national governments in the conduct of fiscal policy. There is nothing sacred about the 3 per cent rule for budgetary deficits in times of low growth; and since even the Germans cannot keep to this 'stupid' rule (a description of the pact that was first introduced by the President of the European Commission, Mr Prodi), there has been growing acceptance of the obvious, namely, that restrictions on national budget deficits should be interpreted more flexibly and should also take into account cyclical factors, debt sustainability, and the distinction between expenditure on consumption and investment. At the time of writing, the pact was ready for reform.

But we should go further. The 'E' in EMU will need to be more precisely defined and also given the appropriate institutional structure, while the persistent reality of nation-states, including the fact that the bulk of public money will continue to be spent by national governments, should of course be recognized. A monetary union needs a more effective coordination of fiscal policies, going beyond the restrictions imposed on national budget deficits and the broad economic policy guidelines, which are usually too broad to have a real effect on national policies. It needs a more effective coordination and also a more symmetrical approach to fiscal policies, thus not only responding to the need for fiscal consolidation in several countries but also being able to deal more effectively with recession. The same observation concerning the need for symmetry of course applies to monetary policy. Otherwise, we risk continuing to fight the battles of the past.

The Union will need a policy institution that takes a global view of the European economy as a whole and can collectively agree on the main macroeconomic policy priorities, thus allowing for a more proactive policy for the Union. At present, the policy mix emerges mostly by default and not as a result of explicit coordination; and it is also biased in one direction. Such a development would, of course, be very much enhanced by the existence of a stabilization fund at the EU level and the operation of automatic stabilizers in an expanded EU budget. Alas, the political conditions are not yet ripe for such a development.

EMU needs a more effective coordination of economic policies in the wider sense, thus introducing a minimum of coherence to the multitude of coordination procedures introduced in the Union in an almost absent-minded fashion, ranging from employment guidelines to structural reform. In a monetary union with weak internal adjustment mechanisms, the emphasis has been laid on greater flexibility of labour markets as a means of absorbing asymmetric shocks. The Lisbon process was meant to provide the external catalyst and ideological justification for painful domestic reforms. Yet it was not sufficiently realized that such reforms create losers, and hence strong resistance from those who have an interest in defending the status quo; they are the majority, and also the best organized. Earlier experience with European integration suggests that internal adjustments were made possible in a dynamic macroeconomic environment and with the aid of redistributive instruments. As long as we fail to create similar conditions today, economists' calls for structural reform will fall on the usually deaf ears of politicians and their electorates. Macroeconomic policy can play a positive role in this respect, creating conditions more conducive to growth, although many in Europe have tended to play down this role for years.

Monetary union requires a European economic government, with clearly defined powers and a still decentralized structure. In that context, a clearer role would also have to be mapped out for the European Commission, including the provision of technical back-up and the monitoring of policy agreements. The Commission seems to have done a good job with the narrow mandate accorded to it by the Maastricht Treaty.

The term 'economic government' was first introduced by the French Socialists, but it was never properly defined, perhaps wisely so because the Union may not yet be politically ready for such a step. But support for it is likely to grow out of frustration with EMU's weak institutional structure, which in turn causes economic weakness. Yet the closer coordination of national economic policies is much easier said than implemented. It is bound to be a gradual learning process. The trouble is that macroeconomic policy needs more discretion than fixed rules, and the Union is ill-equipped, historically and politically, to act in a discretionary manner.

Important issues of sovereignty are at stake which were conveniently swept under the carpet during the negotiations leading to the Maastricht Treaty, but which are unlikely to remain there for long. Then we shall discover that many of those who have been instrumental in setting up EMU may not be ready to accept the institutional and political consequences. The existing mechanisms of soft coordination could be strengthened and thus become more effective. But in some cases this would imply further constraints on national sovereignty, more specifically on national governments and parliaments, in terms of economic policy. For example, an agreement on the general European macroeconomic policy stance would have to set limits within which national budgetary policies could be determined, while national ministers sitting in a European economic policy council, yet to be created, would have to act increasingly as intermediaries or transmission belts between the European and the national levels, in the process gaining in power vis-à-vis their national cabinet colleagues. It does not look at all easy.

In the case of the reprimand of Irish fiscal policy issued by ECOFIN in 2001 (the first in the application of rules for multilateral surveillance), at stake was not only the right of the Irish parliament to decide on the magnitude of the budgetary surplus in an inflationary period but also the ability of the government to sustain a long-standing agreement with the trade unions, an agreement which had provided the foundation for the Irish economic miracle during the last decade and more. How much room can European economic policy coordination allow for national idiosyncrasies? Can binding rules and majority voting replace benchmarking and peer pressure? The transition may indeed be slow and often painful. Yet it would be ridiculous to pretend that national budgetary policies or decisions on structural reform can continue as if EMU did not exist.

The effects of EMU will surely not be limited to macroeconomic policy. The single currency is expected to act as a major unifying factor mainly through greater price transparency and the elimination of exchange-rate uncertainty, thus leading to more intensified competition across borders. This is by far the most important step for the creation of a truly internal market, leading to even greater economic interdependence between national economies and further restructuring with more cross-border mergers and acquisitions. Most economists expect a substantial further increase in trade and FDI flows within the eurozone. Deeper market integration will in turn exert pressure for further Europeanization of a wide range of policy issues, thus raising new questions about the division of powers between European and national institutions as well as the distribution of gains and losses among countries or economic and social groups. EMU will place an even greater premium on mobility and size. Thus, EMU will not be politically neutral; only the most naive of technocrats would believe so.

The regulation of financial markets is one of those issues which have already acquired prominence on the European policy agenda. Deeper market integration and more restructuring across borders will also have important effects on competition policy. Questions of tax harmonization, more precisely the prevention of harmful tax competition, have been a hot issue for some time. The political temperature is unlikely to fall in the future; if anything, it should be expected to rise further. How does one reconcile national fiscal autonomy with increasingly European and global markets and a single European currency? On the other hand, while other adjustment mechanisms remain weak, the emphasis will continue to be placed almost exclusively on labour market flexibility as a shock absorber inside EMU. In a stagnant economic environment, this will continue to cause much frustration.

There is another very sensitive question concerning the institution to be entrusted with the coordination role at the European level. ECOFIN with extended powers would be the obvious candidate. Yet there is a serious snag: ECOFIN cannot perform such a role while some EU members stay out of EMU, thus leaving the upgrading of the Euro Group, with proper legislative and even more importantly executive powers in economic policy, as the only practical option. This is likely to be postponed until those countries voluntarily remaining out of EMU take their final decision whether to join or not. But it cannot be postponed for ever. The institutionalization of the Euro Group would in turn have major political implications for the Union as a whole, with EMU acting as the basis for further differentiation between categories of members. As long as EMU remains the most important manifestation of European integration, it seems inevitable that membership of it will crucially affect the value of membership of the Union more generally. In this sense, EMU would act as a divisive factor.

Denmark, Sweden, and the UK will decide by popular referendum whether or not to join. Such decisions are rarely taken on the basis of rational calculation of costs and benefits. After all, when the Danish voters rejected their country's membership of EMU in a referendum in September 2000, they did not vote for an independent monetary policy and all that it implies. An independent monetary policy had been voluntarily abandoned many years before, without much political fuss. The krone will continue to be tied closely to the euro (replacing the DM) through its continued membership of the new ERM. Thus, Denmark endures many of the constraints of monetary union without enjoying all of the benefits of participation. After all, Danish voters were deciding on much wider issues—or so they thought. If the three countries continue to stay out of EMU for long, the conditions for an inner and an outer core of EU members will be there. Those in the outer core risk becoming second-class members, unless there are spectacular developments in foreign policy and defence, which may in turn produce a different constellation of power in the Union. Mr Blair seems to understand this particular point only too well.

The risk of EMU creating different classes of members inside the Union will become even greater with enlargement. Some of the prospective members of the EU are not expected to be able soon to meet the convergence criteria on inflation, budget deficits, and interest rates. And even if they did so, the price could be high in terms of growth forgone. Many economists are ready to accept that, at least for developing countries—most transition economies belong to this category—some inflation is a necessary lubricant for growth. On the other hand, a strict application of the exchange-rate criterion would imply that new members would have to pass the test of exchange rate stability for a minimum of two years as members of the ERM before they qualify for EMU. They will most probably need that experience, at least those countries that have not already abandoned the exchange rate as a policy instrument through the adoption of currency boards. After all, for transition economies facing large current account deficits and so relying on capital flows to balance them, the risks of exchange rate instability are considerable.

Decisions will also need to be taken on the external representation of the Union. It makes little sense to continue with separate national representations of EU countries in international financial organizations, such as the IMF, or even with separate membership of the Big Four in the Group of Seven (or Eight, when Russia takes part) when international economic issues are being discussed. Governors of national central banks have already formally lost the right to act on monetary policy or even to discuss it independently. How long will it be before European ministers agree that the President of the ECB needs a political counterpart (a Mr or Ms EMU) to represent the Union in international forums? And should they follow the example of the common commercial policy, where the Commission acts as the single representative and negotiator on behalf of the Union, or alternatively that of the CFSP so far? Perhaps, Mr/Ms EMU should have a seat on both Council and Commission. Without a common external representation, EMU will continue to suffer from the cacophony of uncoordinated voices which has so far characterized it, with obvious negative consequences for negotiating power and the value of the new single currency in financial markets.

Do Europeans have common views and interests to defend with respect to the role of international financial institutions and the rules governing the financial system? Experience again suggests that, as long as European views and interests on such issues are represented separately, they will continue to have only a small impact on global economic governance, not commensurate with the relative weight of the Union. Such considerations have historically provided one of the main driving forces behind EMU in an international system still characterized by US hegemony. It remains to be seen whether the

Europeans will be able collectively to rise to the challenge of the euro growing into a major international currency, and thus assume the responsibilities that go with it.

The list of questions in search of answers is still very long. The general message is, however, straightforward: EMU is indeed a high-risk strategy. There is a serious economic risk in the irrevocable fixing of exchange rates and 'one-size-fits-all' monetary policy, while other adjustment mechanisms are still very weak and economic divergence persists. The 'misfits' are likely to pay a heavy price. If managed badly, EMU could have a negative effect in terms of output and employment for the Union as a whole, with more losers than winners. Arguably, the instability of currency markets, combined with the wide openness of individual EU economies, left European policy-makers with little choice; but this a debatable proposition. There is also a political risk linked to the legitimacy deficit of the Union and the weakness of the institutional structure, which is not adequately equipped to cope with crises. And there is no easy exit option, if things go wrong. This is very important.

On the other hand, for EMU to work it will need a stronger and more integrated EU in both political and economic terms. It will also require some painful structural reforms. This is not a project for the faint-hearted. After all, the history of European integration has been marked by bold initiatives, which seemed to provide easy targets for various categories of Eurosceptics. On most occasions, it was the Eurosceptics who had to adjust to the ever-changing European reality. It remains to be seen whether EMU will prove to be a step too far for several European governments and societies. Of course, between open crisis and deeper integration there are variations of the muddling-through option, often popular at the EU level. In the case of the euro, muddling through is likely to entail a high cost if it were to continue for long.

7

☆☆☆☆☆

Extending *Pax Europea*

It is a commonplace that the Union looks bigger from outside than from inside, although this very much depends on the eye of the beholder. Other Europeans tend to treat it with respect, usually combined with strong doses of desire. In the rest of the world, however attitudes vary: from admiration in Africa and Latin America, where the EU is seen as an impossible model to follow, to incomprehension in most of south-east Asia, whose economic tigers apparently have little time to spare for supranationality, democratic pluralism, and the costly social model associated with Europe. The Union is universally regarded as a powerful economic bloc with an extremely complex system of decision-making, which makes it a difficult partner to negotiate with. On the other hand, foreigners rarely fail to notice the limitations of the European civilian power. They have learned from experience that, when the guns begin to speak, the Union usually has precious little to say. Strangely enough, its difference from a real superpower became more obvious after the end of the cold war, which ushered in a new phase of undisputed US hegemony.

The Union exerts its strongest influence on other countries through the prospect of membership. This is the most effective way of extending *Pax Europea*, which carries with it peace, democracy, welfare, and a highly advanced form of joint management of interdependence. Membership of the Union comes with several preconditions; these have become increasingly difficult over time and, once a country has joined, socialization (and Europeanization) becomes an ongoing process. Sharing sovereignty can be learned only the hard way, not through the texts prescribed for candidates. With repeated rounds of enlargement, the Community and now the Union has been spreading its gospel (we may need to use another term, since not all candidates share Christian values) to an increasing number of European countries; and it has been gradually transformed as a result of new accessions. This time, the challenge is greater than ever before.

The frontiers have been constantly shifting, but there is always a 'near abroad'—the term used by the Russians after the breakdown of the Soviet Union to denote proximity and also special interest in the former members of the empire—which deserves special attention from the EU. A narrow definition of the near abroad would include only European countries, and hence also potential members of the Union: that is, if only we knew how far to the east the boundaries of Europe extend. And, assuming we define Europe more broadly, is the Caucasus more or less vital to the interests of the Union than the southern shores of the Mediterranean? For a continental power, the perspectives of individual countries and regions are bound to differ.

In trade matters, the Union has been for a long time a major international actor. Repeating this success in other policy areas has, however, proved difficult. In some respects, the Union already seeks to exert influence in the rest of the world and in so doing tries to defend collective interests and export common values. The weapons it employs to achieve its objectives do not constitute the armoury of a traditional power; and, increasingly realizing their limitations, the Union has been trying, albeit with limited success so far, to endow itself with the more conventional weapons of diplomacy and war. In the world of today, the EU needs to define and defend its collective identity in the context of globalization and also vis-à-vis the only remaining superpower: those two objectives are hardly separable. Whatever the Union does on the external front, it will have repercussions on the model of integration and the internal configuration of power.

☆ (Almost) All Want to Join

There have so far been three rounds of enlargement, with three new members joining in each round: the first group of Eftans, led by the UK, in the 1970s; the southerners in the 1980s; and the second group of neutral Eftans in the 1990s. Three, therefore, has so far appeared to be the magic number, although, as with everything else magic, it has emerged from some sleight of hand. To be more precise, the southern enlargement took place in two instalments, since Greece joined on its own—an event highly unlikely to be repeated; and there is also the very important enlargement of 1990, when the eastern *Länder* joined Germany and the Community, although this does not officially count as enlargement but only as an internal German affair.

The numbers are now very different. At the European Council of Copenhagen in December 2002, the historic decision was taken to admit ten new members. Thus, barring any accidents in the ratification process, the European Union of Twenty-Five will become a reality on 1 May 2004. The ten new members include Poland, Hungary, the Czech Republic, and Slovakia, the central European countries which, to all intents and purposes, constitute the core group of the new enlargement; Estonia, Latvia, and Lithuania, the three Baltic republics, which until 1990 were part of the USSR; Slovenia, the only one among the former republics of socialist Yugoslavia; and the two Mediterranean islands of Cyprus and Malta, which have been treated almost as an adjunct to the eastern enlargement of the Union.

There are already two more official candidates from the Balkans, namely Bulgaria and Romania, which have been engaged in accession negotiations since 2000. Because of slow progress (also in terms of domestic reforms), these two countries have been excluded from the first wave of entrants; they now pin their hopes on accession in 2007, the officially proclaimed target date. And there is a thirteenth candidate, namely Turkey, the only one not to have yet started accession negotiations with the EU. Size is one among several reasons why Turkey constitutes a category of its own in this new enlargement. If anything, the company in the waiting room is expected to grow, thus possibly opening the way for a never-ending process of enlargement. In February 2003, Croatia was the first among the unofficial hopefuls to make the next move by lodging an application for membership.

The reasons that so many countries want to join the EU are obvious: they want to secure access to European markets, access to private and public funds, access to a reliable insurance policy for security and democracy, and also their share of influence and prestige associated with membership of the most important club in town. It is to be hoped that they also want to play an active role in the construction of the still unfinished common European home.

Access to markets is crucial, because the candidates are already as dependent on trade with the EU as are existing members. Much of the liberalization has already taken place, with only a few exceptions, most notably in agriculture. In the process, candidate countries have discovered that trade liberalization involves reciprocity, and this has in turn led to the widening of current account deficits with the Union. The bulk of FDI in candidate countries already comes from the EU, while the prospect of membership surely helps to reduce the risk factor for foreign investors, Europeans and others alike. On the other hand, accession is expected to lead to transfers of funds to the new members through the EU budget. The new members' low level of economic development will ensure that they become net beneficiaries from the Structural Funds and the Cohesion Fund, and most of them should also expect to receive net transfers from the CAP. However, transfers from EU Funds will require patience because of the transitional arrangements following accession; and the new members will also hope that policy reforms in the future will not seriously dilute the redistributive dimension of the EU budget. On the negative side, membership entails the adoption of costly standards, such as social or environmental, considered by many as an expensive luxury for countries which find themselves at a lower level of economic development. It will impose a heavy premium on scarce administrative resources and it will most likely produce an exodus of some of the best brains.

Most important of all, membership of the Union is perceived as a highly political choice linked to the consolidation of democracy, the preservation of peace and security, and full participation in common European institutions. And there is another, usually unspoken factor: as happened before, EU membership will be unavoidably linked to the process of modernization and Europeanization in the new members—and such a process creates both winners and losers. The trouble with the new members in central and eastern Europe is that the losers from the process of adjustment to the EU will join the ranks of those who have already been sacrificed on the altar of transition from communism. In several countries, real GDP is still significantly lower than pre-1989 levels.

According to opinion polls, there is clear majority support for EU membership in the ten new members, although there are sizeable Eurosceptic minorities in some of them. Public support has been declining in recent years—as it has in existing members—although it is generally expected that, in the referendums on accession, voters in all the applicant countries will deliver a 'yes'. Has public support for EU membership declined in candidate countries because of frustration with long-drawn-out negotiations and an apparent lack of generosity and flexibility shown by the Union side? There is, of course, some truth in this: the handling of candidates has hardly been the kind of edifying experience that could generate a wave of Euro-enthusiasm in those countries.

On the other hand, comparison of levels of public support in prospective members suggests that the more distant the prospect of membership, the more popular it is. Thus, the highest levels of support are usually recorded in

Bulgaria, Romania, and Turkey, which do not expect to become members for some time. This may suggest that the Union, as an object of desire, loses its shine as the suitors get closer to it: a rather depressing conclusion—could it be age? For some of the prospective members at least, it is also unlikely that EU membership can serve as the powerful external mechanism and means of justification for unpopular measures at home. 'Joining Europe' may therefore not prove such a strong mobilizing force as with southern European countries earlier. Estonia has a very different history from Greece or Spain.

As with many other issues, there has been a wide gap between official rhetoric and action in the EU with respect to enlargement. It is extremely difficult to refuse an application for membership when it comes from a European country that fulfils the basic political and economic criteria. This has been confirmed again and again. The EU cannot say 'no', but it is very good at procrastinating. It comes naturally because of the slow system of decision-making. With the new enlargement, there has been an additional and highly powerful reason for not hastening: while the benefits of enlargement for the Union are mostly long-term and intangible, the costs are perceived to be more immediate and concrete. This is hardly the combination to mobilize politicians in a democracy, let alone in the highly complex system of the EU.

Surely enlargement means, first and foremost, an investment in democracy, security, and prosperity, in other words an extension of *Pax Europea* to the whole of the European continent. This is what is really at stake and little less than that. But for the immediate future, enlargement will cost money in times of financial stringency; it will threaten vested interests, be they farmers or net beneficiaries from EU Funds; it will make decisions and the running of the EU much more difficult; and it will require painful internal reforms. Numbers are, of course, very important. A Union of 25, and one day even more, members is bound to be different in many respects from what we have known so far. But it is not just a question of numbers. The new candidates are characterized by low levels of economic development and limited experience of democratic governance. Thus, the accession of the three southern European countries in the 1980s becomes the appropriate reference point and standard for comparison. With the benefit of hindsight, however, that may look like a small and relatively easy operation. Who would have guessed some twenty years ago that much more difficult challenges were lying ahead? Adding insult to injury, the majority of prospective members often appear less enthusiastic about further European integration. This should, of course, make them more attractive to British and Scandinavian Eurosceptics—which it does.

The potential economic gains have often been exaggerated. The prospective members are supposed to provide rapidly growing market outlets and investment opportunities for economic agents in the existing members of the EU. This is true, although expectations need to be cut down to size. The applicants have in fact more potential than reality in economic terms, and much of what they can offer at present in terms of market and investment opportunities has already been seized by companies in the West. The ten countries expected to join in 2004 represent 23 per cent of the area and 20 per cent of the population of EU-15, while their GDP per capita, measured by purchasing power standards, ranges from 80 per cent for the small island of Cyprus to 33 per cent for Latvia—and it is even lower for the three candidates remaining in the waiting room (Table 7.1). In economic terms, the ten new members are together smaller than the Netherlands: not insignificant, but hardly enough on its own to add new dynamism to the European economy. As for growth prospects, they surely depend on a host of economic and political factors: economic convergence is not an automatic or indeed inevitable process. The economic performance of several among the future members has been anything but spectacular in the more recent years.

Enlargement has therefore been a difficult product for politicians to sell to their electorates in the member countries. Most of them did not even make the effort at least until recently, limiting themselves to occasional expressions of general support, usually in the name of political correctness. These are not, after all, times of political vision and statesmanship; most politicians slavishly follow the latest opinion poll—the waging of war against Iraq apparently being an exception, at least in some countries, and arguably for the wrong reasons. In the meantime, the number of populists trying to make political capital out of public fears has been steadily on the increase. There is widespread fear (mostly exaggerated) among Union citizens that enlargement will lead to large new flows of immigrants. Immigration has already become a major political issue, and is often linked in the public mind to the increase in criminality. It is therefore not surprising that justice and home affairs ministers have been meeting all too frequently, and it is also not surprising that existing members have insisted on—and obtained—long transitional periods before allowing free movement of people for the new members. On the other hand, there is concern (again exaggerated) about possible social dumping and the budgetary cost of accepting much poorer countries as members.

Public support for enlargement in EU-15 has not been strong; it is hardly an issue that can generate popular enthusiasm. If it weakens further in the future, it could endanger the whole process, especially subsequent rounds of

Table 7.1. Enlargement: main economic indicators (2001)

	Area (1,000 km²)	Population (million inhabitants)	GDP per capita as % of EU-15 average	Agriculture % of employment	GDP real growth p.a. (average 1999–2001)	Inflation (average 1999–2001)	Unemployment (average 1999–2001)	Budget deficit as % of GDP (average 1999–2001)
EU-15	**3,191**	**379.0**	100	4.3	2.5	1.9	8.2	−0.1
Cyprus	9	0.8	80	4.9	4.6	2.7	4.9	−3.1
Czech Rep.	79	10.3	57	4.6	2.4	3.4	8.4	−4.0
Estonia	45	1.4	42	7.1	3.8	4.2	12.4	−1.4
Hungary	93	10.2	51	6.1	4.4	9.7	6.4	−4.1
Latvia	65	2.4	33	15.1	5.8	2.4	13.7	−3.2
Lithuania	65	3.5	38	16.5	1.9	1.0	14.1	−3.4
Malta	0.3	0.4	55[a]	2.2	2.9	2.6	6.3	−7.4
Poland	313	38.6	40	19.2	3.1	7.5	15.7	−2.4
Slovakia	49	5.4	48	26.7[b]	2.3	11.3	18.1	−8.3
Slovenia	20	2.0	69	9.9	4.3	7.9	6.6	−2.6
Candidates-10	**739**	**74.8**	—	—	—	—	—	—
Bulgaria	111	7.9	28	6.3	3.9	6.8	16.8	0.4
Romania	238	22.4	25	44.4	2.0	42.0	6.6	−4.1
Turkey	775	68.6	22	35.4	−1.7	58.1	7.6	−17.7
Candidates-3	**1,124**	**98.9**	—	—	—	—	—	—

[a] data refer to 1999. [b] data refer to 2000.

Source: Commission & Eurostat

enlargement. There is a serious risk that the EU of 25 will become an unmanage-able affair, at least in the early years after the accession of the ten new members. Will the Union then be able to sustain the momentum of further enlargement, and if so for how long? After all, national parliaments in member countries, as well as the European Parliament, need to ratify the treaties of accession.

☆ An Unmanageable Affair?

It should come as no surprise that the Union took a long time to develop a coherent policy vis-à-vis the new candidates and, having done so, it has contin-ued to proceed at a slow pace. Admittedly, the end of the cold war and the breakdown of the communist order in central and eastern Europe and the for-mer Soviet Union caught the other side of the old Iron Curtain totally unpre-pared. The Union's first response was to employ the policy instruments with which it had been most familiar, namely trade and aid. Only gradually—and with considerable reluctance—did it accept the inevitability of a new enlarge-ment, thus going beyond preferential agreements and their political embell-ishments. Here again, the Germans were highly instrumental in pushing forward the whole process of enlargement. They received support mainly from the British and the Scandinavians as well as from the Commission. The United States also provided both encouragement and pressure.

Since the prospect of the new enlargement became—unavoidably—linked once again to internal reforms and the deepening of integration, the attitudes adopted by member countries on the nature of this link differed widely. For some, institutional reform and further deepening were seen as a precondition for enlargement; for others the link appeared to be more tenuous, and they seemed not to mind much if the arrival of many more members were to lead to a more loose and intergovernmental structure. Ideas about free trade areas die hard. The battle is certainly still going on, most notably inside the European Convention.

First, admission criteria were made explicit, and they were followed by what came to be called the 'accession process'. The criteria adopted at the European Council in Copenhagen in 1993 refer to stable and democratic institutions, the rule of law, and the protection of human rights and minority rights; a func-tioning market economy with the capacity to cope with competitive pressures; and the ability to adopt the Union *acquis*, including EMU and political union, however the latter is to be defined. In other words, the Copenhagen criteria refer to Western democracy, governability, and economic competitiveness. Once they are fulfilled, with the Commission and the Council acting as judges, a candidate country can begin accession negotiations. Regular monitoring and annual progress reports on each of the candidate countries then follow; and they are expected to continue until the day of accession.

The prospect of membership therefore serves as both carrot and stick in shaping the political and economic status quo in those countries aspiring to join. Carrots and sticks are, indeed, popular in international and, even more so, intra-European relations, but they surely cannot always work miracles on recalcitrant domestic actors—they have to believe in miracles too. Union conditionality has already contributed to the strengthening of democracy and a market economy in several former communist countries. It may also have produced better treatment of minorities and improved neighbourly relations. However, it failed to stop the war in Yugoslavia or the vicious circle of weak states and criminality in much of the Balkans; and, at the time of writing, it looked rather unlikely that the prospect of EU membership would lead to an internal political settlement and the accession of the whole island of Cyprus. Will it be different with democracy in Turkey? This is the principal reason why accession negotiations have not yet begun with Turkey, which submitted its application for membership back in 1987, since that country is not yet deemed to fulfil the political criteria.

Once started, accession negotiations are conducted on a purely bilateral basis. Each candidate negotiates with the Commission, which therefore assumes a central role—very similar to what happens with external trade negotiations. When accession negotiations start, the enlargement train thus shifts down to bureaucratic gear. The body of legislation that accompanies EU membership, the so-called *acquis communautaire*, amounting to tens of thousands of pages, is non-negotiable. Therefore, accession negotiations are mainly about ways and means by which new members adopt and implement the *acquis*. The bulk of the *acquis* is meant to be adopted before accession, although there is also provision for transitional periods of normally up to five years after accession to allow more time for adjustment; permanent derogations are treated as the exception.

Because of the continuous deepening of integration, new members face a much more difficult adjustment task than those who joined earlier. In the context of the accession negotiations, this adjustment is also by definition highly asymmetrical: it is the new members who need to adjust to the EU, not the other way round. It should follow that transitional periods are essentially intended as a means of smoothing the process of adjustment for the new members. This is not necessarily so in practice, since the Commission and the Council have not hesitated to impose long transitional periods in policy areas where future members are expected to benefit, most notably with respect to the CAP, the Structural Funds, and labour mobility. They should have known better. Carthaginian terms of entry are likely to backfire in the future. It has happened before, and the British could surely explain how.

There is, undoubtedly, a big asymmetry between the candidates and the Union, which will disappear only when candidates become members with guaranteed seats around the table. Until then, they have to reconcile themselves to the uncomfortable role of supplicant, often faced with a policy of 'take it or leave it' from the other side. They have been learning this lesson the hard way; hence their willingness often to make concessions in order to shorten the time they need to spend as candidates, but such willingness has limits imposed by their own public opinion. To go beyond the narrow context of accession negotiations, it is generally recognized that enlargement, especially of such a scale and nature, requires a two-way adjustment process. However, this is easier said than done. Early on, it was agreed that this new enlargement would necessitate important internal reforms for the Union, in terms of both institutions and policies. Two intergovernmental conferences have already taken place, concentrating mainly on institutional reform. The Amsterdam and Nice treaties are the products of those two exercises, and they are generally deemed to be highly inadequate for the task they had been set. The Union is now preparing for a third intergovernmental conference in a space of ten years and, one hopes, this time it will prove more successful. Meanwhile, the most important form of deepening has already happened through the introduction of the single currency. Thus, the European political system now faces the double challenge of having to adjust both to EMU and further enlargement. In many respects, the two point in different directions.

The European Convention, under the Presidency of Valéry Giscard d'Estaing, a former President of France, began its work in early 2002. It comprises representatives of governments and national parliaments from all member countries and candidate countries as well as from European institutions (a total of 105 members from 28 countries). It was given a wide-ranging mandate at the Laeken Council, together with a long list of questions concerning the future of the Union; and this time the fifteen heads of state and government plucked up enough courage to spell out politically awkward questions. The members of the Convention have been asked to think about the desirability or otherwise of a proper European constitution, the direct election of the President of the Commission, and a truly common European foreign policy, among other things. The Convention is a novel experiment intended to introduce an element of democracy in the process of treaty reform, which so far has been a strictly diplomatic exercise conducted by government representatives behind closed doors. It is also intended to help generate a wider debate on the future of Europe.

The Convention will prepare the ground for the new intergovernmental conference and eventually for a Union of 25 and more members. The new constitutional treaty, as it is generally expected to be called, will be different from old-fashioned international treaties—a fine distinction for European professionals, although unlikely to generate much enthusiasm among the wider public. It should come into operation at best shortly after the new round of enlargement. On the other hand, not everything in the Union depends on constitutional revisions. As a live political system, the EU produces a steady flow of policy outputs on an everyday basis. Thus, reform becomes an ongoing affair, and very probably the catalyst of enlargement will begin to have a much stronger effect as the big day approaches, and even more so after the new members have joined.

There is a host of institutional and policy issues to be tackled; most of them are not new at all, although with enlargement they will acquire much greater urgency. Let us briefly consider a few representative ones. There will be, first of all, a problem with numbers, which will directly affect the functioning of common institutions and the whole process of decision-making in the enlarged Union. The European political system is already very slow and complex; it is also cut off from the large majority of European citizens. Can it cope with many more members without changes in the basic rules of the game? The extension of qualified majority voting in the Council is an important issue on the agenda, unanimity being increasingly tantamount to gridlock. On the other hand, small countries have always been overrepresented in European institutions, since the principle of equality of states still takes precedence over that of equality of citizens. With the continuous widening and deepening of integration, some re-balancing between big and small countries in terms of votes and representation in different European institutions has become necessary. It has also been directly linked to the extension of qualified majority voting. Why should countries with large populations accept being outvoted by coalitions of their smaller brethren because of their disproportionate weight in decision-making? Some changes will be introduced when the Nice Treaty comes into effect. The next (constitutional) treaty may go further.

The next round of enlargement will bring in a large number of small and medium-sized countries, with one exception: Poland. Thus, re-balancing becomes more urgent. It could also be seen as part of a gradual shift from diplomacy to democracy in the European political system, as long as change is not reduced to a mere re-weighting of votes in the Council and additions to or subtractions from the number of national representatives in the European Parliament, or even membership of the Commission. It is all linked to the old question of legitimacy: to what extent should European institutions rely more on direct forms of legitimization, and can a European demos be created from above? We shall return to those issues in the final chapter.

New members will have to go through a long and difficult process of socialization, likely to prove even more difficult because of the communist legacy, the traumas of transition, and sensitivities concerning national sovereignty. After all, these countries long suffered under foreign domination; and they may now attach themselves with religious zeal to some of the formal attributes of sovereignty, having already relinquished many of their real powers especially in the economic field. The combination is likely to produce repeated hiccups, if not crises, in European councils, arguably an inevitable price to pay since *Pax Europea* is not (luckily) spread through the sword. There is a serious risk of a further rise of populism in some of the new members, bringing to power unsavoury politicians; and this would clearly have repercussions on the functioning of the EU. But are the old members completely immune from this political disease?

Many observers have chosen to approach the transition to pluralist democracy and a market economy as some kind of modern plastic surgery that can quickly and radically transform the way the patient looks. They seem to have grossly exaggerated expectations of political and economic engineering and, like those devoted to plastic surgery, they care little about what goes on below the skin. The traces of several decades of communism will not easily disappear from political and social behaviour, and the economic and social costs of transition have been significant and very unevenly distributed. Europeanization, directly linked to membership of the EU, is therefore likely to prove a slow and painful process, which also means that the consensual nature of EU decision-making will be stretched further, perhaps beyond its limits. Interestingly enough, there is little synchronization of political cycles on the east and the west of the European continent. While the pendulum has in recent years been shifting to the right in several EU members, exactly the opposite has been happening in transition countries waiting to join.

Enlargement will cause problems in EU decision-making; it will, however, cause even greater problems in the implementation of whatever decisions are reached. Most of the new members have weak administrative and judicial structures and no strong tradition of the rule of law. They have already adopted a large part of the *acquis communautaire* as internal law, but there are serious doubts about their ability to implement and enforce it. Thus, the implementation deficit of the EU, a direct product of its highly decentralized structure, will be magnified after enlargement. The Union will have to spend considerable time and money in technical aid to the new members, thus helping to lubricate the process of Europeanization. It will also have to show a great deal of patience.

The future development of EMU will be decisive. A strict application of existing rules means that the new members will have to spend at least two years after accession in the purgatory of the new EMS, thus providing concrete proof of their capacity to ensure exchange rate stability. Furthermore, only very few among the Ten presently fulfil the inflation or budget deficit criteria for admission to EMU (Table 7.1). What happens with the other countries still outside—Denmark, Sweden, and the UK—will be absolutely crucial: if several countries stay out of EMU for a long period, this will have major consequences for the whole process of integration. After all, EMU is not like any other policy. It is now the main policy of the Union and likely to remain so for the foreseeable future, unless there are dramatic developments in the areas of foreign policy and defence. Long-term exclusion from EMU, because of lack of will or of ability, is therefore likely to create some kind of second-class membership of the Union, and further enlargement could only strengthen such a tendency.

It will be a larger and more diverse Union, with much wider income disparities, both between and within countries. Only Cyprus and Slovenia have income levels close to those of the three poorest members of EU-15; the rest are trailing behind, and some of them very far behind indeed (Table 7.1). Will the new members be able to repeat the successful experience of the Cohesion Four and, if so, who are more likely to follow the Irish and who the Greek example? Most of them start from much lower levels. On the other hand, wide income disparities within the enlarged Union are bound to raise difficult questions concerning the link between liberalization, regulation, and redistribution. Some renegotiation of the overall European package deal will be unavoidable. Trying to repeat the successful experience of southern European countries will require money, among other things to act as a catalyst for modernization and as compensation for losers, mostly within countries. Meanwhile, net contributors to the EU budget have for some time been sending a very different message; cross-border generosity is conspicuously declining.

A very difficult negotiation is therefore looming to reach agreement on the new financial perspectives of the enlarged Union. It promises to be more difficult than the negotiation on the budgetary aspects of enlargement as part of the accession negotiations. The agenda of the next big negotiation should include reform of the CAP, changes in the Structural Funds, support for the poor, and new sources of EU financing. The enlarged EU will need some reordering of priorities, policy reforms, more money, and a more efficient and better targeted use of scarce resources. It is all about trying to reconcile effectiveness, legitimacy, and diversity on a much bigger scale than ever before. Does the Union have the stomach for that, especially those countries that have traditionally acted as big providers of ideas and money? This combination is usually referred to as leadership.

It will be a big challenge to integrate successfully a large number of much poorer countries, with weak administrative and regulatory structures, not to mention a relatively short experience of markets and democracy. Surely, there will be longer delays in decision-making and more internal crises and introspection. There will also be more opt-outs (like the British opt-out from EMU) and differentiation, as well as more instances of the willing and able going ahead while the others remain behind. Last but not least, it will make the prospects for the CFSP even more difficult, especially if the Americans resort to divide-and-rule tactics.

European integration has never been a neat picture with straight lines; it has become more complex as a result of continuous deepening and widening, and it will become ever more so in a Union of 25 and more members. But, taken too far, differentiation and variable coalitions of the willing and able could seriously undermine the whole project of European integration as something, so far, qualitatively very different from a collection of ad hoc forms of cooperation with a loose institutional backup.

This in turn leads to the politically awkward, if not incorrect, question: how much diversity (and how many more new members) can the EU take before it becomes totally unrecognizable and unable to deliver the goods? This is the kind of question that most European politicians have so far avoided asking (at least in public), for obvious reasons. Asking the question unavoidably leads to a discussion about the final objective and the ultimate boundaries of this ever-enlarging Union—and we all know that there is no agreement on either of them, and that a discussion on boundaries is guaranteed to insult some of our more or less distant neighbours. True, it will be politically awkward and divisive, but it cannot be swept under the carpet for ever. The fact that a public debate on these issues is only just beginning provides yet another illustration of the democratic deficit of the Union. It is most likely to gather momentum with further enlargement.

Does the extension of *Pax Europea* necessarily go through EU membership? If so, where does it stop: on the eastern frontier of Turkey, in Vladivostok perhaps, or can it also include Israel or Morocco? In an ever-enlarging Union, will there be different categories of members? Those who have not yet secured their entry ticket to the EU may painfully discover that these questions creep into the European public debate as the Union tries, with difficulty, to digest the next enlargement. And there will be no easy or clear answers. At some stage, those inside will have to face the awkward choice between inclusion and commonality of values and interests. It would be perfectly legitimate to do so. After all, US policy-makers have not usually considered the option of offering full membership of the United States of America to Mexico or Nicaragua as part of their stabilization policy of the American continent.

☆ Europe's Near Abroad

The immediate neighbourhood of the enlarged Union will consist of a small number of rich democracies, which will continue to deny themselves (for how long?) the privileges and constraints of EU membership; the troubled region of the Balkans, including the two official candidates, Bulgaria and Romania, as well as likely future candidates in the Western Balkans; Turkey as the southeastern outpost of Europe and the West; former Soviet republics, with Russia figuring most prominently among them; and, last but not least, a host of countries on the southern and eastern shores of the Mediterranean, themselves with no prospect of EU membership in the foreseeable future because they hardly fit any definition of Europe. With very few exceptions, they represent a difficult neighbourhood. While handling accession negotiations with those who are already candidates and others who strive to join the ranks, the enlarged EU will have a strong interest in establishing close relations with all countries in its neighbourhood. It will also have an interest in extending at least some elements of *Pax Europea* beyond its immediate borders, irrespective of whether the countries concerned are expected to join as members sooner or later—and in some cases later may last very long indeed.

The number of European countries willingly remaining outside the Union fold has diminished rapidly over the years. Interestingly enough, this has happened while the exigencies of membership have continued to grow. Is this an irrefutable sign of the growing attraction of EU membership (opinion polls may suggest otherwise) or a sign of the rising cost of staying out? It hardly matters. Norway is such a country, having already gone through two extremely painful referendums on EU membership with negative results; Switzerland is another, situated in the heart of Europe; and so is far-away Iceland—plus minuscule remnants of the old medieval order, such as Liechtenstein. Except for the latter group (the Middle Ages had a different concept of democracy), these are prosperous democratic countries, and they would be very welcome in the EU; Norway and Switzerland invariably top the popularity polls of potential candidates. They have decided to stay out for a variety of reasons, although bilateral relations with the Union are very close.

Norway hardly presents a problem: it already has one foot inside through participation in the internal market as well as the Schengen agreement on the free movement of persons; and it is also a full member of NATO and other regional organizations. A long history of domination by its Scandinavian brethren—the term 'Union' has very bad connotations in Norwegian—coupled with the trauma of two referendums, which deeply divided an otherwise consensual society, feed into the anti-integrationist current. Oil and fish further strengthen the strong sense of independence of this small and very rich country on the northern edge of Europe.

It is different, and arguably much more difficult, with Switzerland, a country proud of its long history of independence and neutrality, its (con)federal structures, and its separate identity. The Swiss took several decades to agree to membership of the UN. Having now taken the first step, it remains to be seen whether they take as long to decide to go further by joining a much more ambitious regional organization. If so, who knows how the European Union will look after so many years? It is, however, possible that recent developments, which in many ways have shattered widely held notions of Swiss invulnerability (political as well as economic), may precipitate a change in popular attitudes in Switzerland towards European integration.

In the meantime, bilateral relations with the EU will continue to be influenced by sensitive issues on which perceptions and indeed interests differ. Being a key transit country for much intra-EU transport, licences and quotas for lorries have always been a point of contention. On the other hand, with rapid liberalization of capital and financial services, followed by growing pressures for tax coordination/harmonization inside the EU as a response to tax evasion, the role of Switzerland as the world's leading banker for offshore capital, backed by strong legal provisions safeguarding bank secrecy, has attracted more and more attention. Switzerland is often treated as a free rider by European politicians who resent the loss of tax revenue resulting from the flight of their citizens' capital held in search of tax havens and anonymity. Pressure on Switzerland to cooperate with EU countries has therefore been steadily growing.

Relations with Norway and Switzerland are, indeed, a luxury for the Union when compared with the problems faced in dealing with other countries in its neighbourhood. Turkey stands out in this respect. Relations with that country have a long and turbulent history, going back to an Association agreement with the Six signed in 1963, followed by a customs union agreement. The application for full membership was lodged in 1987, thus arriving long before the wave of applications from former communist countries in central and eastern Europe. Nevertheless, Turkey's accession to the EU still looks uncertain: if anything, it is a project unlikely to come to fruition before sometime during the next decade. What we know for now is that the European Council of the enlarged EU will decide in December 2004 whether Turkey meets the criteria for accession negotiations to begin. No wonder Turkey's Europhiles—and there are significant numbers of them—experience a strong sense of frustration directed both at member countries of the EU and at many of their own political class.

Turkey has presented the ever-growing Community/Union with an almost impossible problem. A large country, with a predominantly Muslim population, yet secular and closer to the Western democratic model than any other country in the Islamic world, Turkey has a strategic position vis-à-vis large chunks of the former Soviet empire, major oil producers, and the Middle East. It is a valued member of NATO, with the second largest army after the United States, and is also a member of most other regional organizations in Europe, barring the most important one, the EU. Since the end of the cold war, Turkey's strategic importance for the Atlantic alliance has shifted considerably: from a front-line state in the long confrontation with the USSR to a valued ally and a staging post in the battle for influence in the central Asian region, encompassing the fight against terrorism as well as control of oil production and oil routes. All along, Turkey has basked in almost unqualified American favour, which has also been translated into US pressure on the EU to hasten to accept Turkey as a member. American diplomats and politicians have been the strongest advocates of Turkey's membership of the European Union. But they usually fail to understand (or simply do not care about) the subtle distinction between a military alliance, such as NATO, and an emerging political system founded on democratic principles. And they were in for a shock when they discovered that Turkish support for the war in Iraq was not to be taken for granted.

Turkey's overtures to the EU could not, therefore, be met with indifference, not to mention outright rejection, even though there are plenty of reasons why Turkey in its traditional garb would not make a very suitable member of the Union. Geography surely matters: the Union is hardly keen or politically ready to extend common borders to the eastern borders of Turkey. A large country with a rapidly growing population, Turkey is expected to outgrow Germany, the country with the largest population in the EU. This rapid growth in population has not permitted a significant improvement in living standards, despite usually high rates of economic growth, which turned negative during the recent crisis (Table 7.1). It is still a poor country with a per capita income 22 per cent of the EU-15 average, the largest income inequalities among European OECD members, and a long history of macroeconomic instability. Had it not been for its strategic importance, which helped mobilize American and IMF support on a very large scale, Turkey would have most probably suffered a similar fate to Argentina when faced with financial crisis in 2001.

The state of the economy is, of course, intimately linked to the political system. Although a market economy, the state in Turkey has traditionally had a pervasive economic role, only recently curtailed as a result of the customs union agreement with the EU and, even more importantly, following the latest financial crisis and the conditionality attached to the IMF rescue package. And although Turkey is a parliamentary democracy of a kind, interrupted by periods of direct military rule, *raison d'état* has almost always prevailed over the development of civil society, human rights, and the rule of law more generally. All-pervasive and still inefficient and corrupt: this appears to be an apt description of the Turkish state, and also of much of the political class summarily voted out of office in the 2002 elections. These brought to power new politicians, many of them with a moderate Islamic background, who are now being asked to transform the country in preparation for its European marriage at a time still to be determined. In the process, the Turkish military will also have to relinquish many of its powers and privileges as guardian of the legacy of Kemal Atatürk, the founder of the modern Turkish state.

It may be a paradox that more democracy in Turkey could mean more power for Islamist parties in the foreseeable future, which is precisely what the self-appointed guardians of secularism greatly fear. This should not necessarily constitute a paradox so long as Islamist parties respect the fundamental principles of democracy. But will they? Those in Turkey who look to the EU as a powerful instrument of modernization and Europeanization of their country could be faced with some awkward dilemmas as this process unfolds.

Size, level of development, and degree of difference have combined to make the prospect of Turkey's membership of the Union a threatening one for many Europeans: too big, too poor and unstable, and also too much different for the EU to be able to accommodate. Since it is not particularly diplomatic to refer publicly to cultural and religious differences as an obstacle to membership—a privilege usually, but not always, reserved for populist politicians—European leaders have been desperately looking for ways of handling the Turkish problem. For years, Greece obligingly provided the fig leaf: bilateral disputes and the continuing problem of divided Cyprus led to Greek vetoes inside the EU concerning relations with Turkey. This, however, ended with the recognition of Turkey as an official candidate for membership at the Helsinki Council in December 1999. Since then, and in the midst of deep economic crisis and political instability (at least until the elections of 2002), important legislation has been introduced in an attempt to meet the political criteria set by the Union. It remains to be seen whether this represents a serious (and irreversible?) step towards the establishment of a proper democratic system.

If the Union does succeed in extending *Pax Europea* to Turkey, helping it to transform itself into a modern, stable, and democratic country with rising levels of prosperity, it will have achieved a great deal indeed. But, if Turkey continues on the democratic road, the EU will be faced very soon with extremely difficult decisions. Does it really want Turkey in, even some years down the road, or not? The ideal solution for many European political leaders, given also that public opinion polls show weak support for Turkey's membership of the Union, would have been a close, indeed special, relationship with Turkey, falling short of full membership. Yet it has proved impossible so far to devise a satisfactory formula, that is, a formula that is acceptable to the Turks as well.

The ambiguity of EU policy towards Turkey is also reflected in the way the Union has been perceived so far by the Turkish public: very high levels of support for membership coupled with low levels of trust for European institutions. The accession of Cyprus, without an internal settlement, could further complicate an already difficult relationship. A European Union with Turkey as a member would be a very different Union from what we have so far known. Equally, Turkey will have to become a very different country unless the EU dilutes itself in the future into some kind of free trade area and/or traditional alliance. Either scenario is likely to take some time to materialize, if at all. One thing is, however, certain: it is too late for Europeans to renege on the commitments repeatedly offered to Turkey as a member of the European family. Instead, they should insist on fundamental political, economic, and social conditions and rights, and forget about religious differences.

It will surely not be easier with the other descendants of the Ottoman empire in the Balkans, a region which has suffered from bloody wars, spreading criminality, and progressive fragmentation following the collapse of communist regimes. The continuing trouble in the Balkans brought back to the collective Western mind all the stereotypes about the region: backward, violent, and torn by ethnic strife. Many people in the more fortunate western part of Europe would dearly have liked to forget all about the Balkans—too much trouble, little concrete interest, and no easy solutions—and they still do. Of course, those EU countries closer to the region, namely Greece, Italy, and Austria, cannot even contemplate such a luxury. As for the others, they may sometimes need to be reminded that Europe cannot afford a big black hole in its flank—or in its midst, depending on where you stand. There are humanitarian considerations, and they have indeed played an important role in external involvement in the Balkans in recent years. At the same time, Europeans have learned from bitter experience that instability, poverty, and criminality are not easily confined within national boundaries. They tend to spill over: people in need cross frontiers in search of jobs, and criminals usually do so even more easily. Trafficking of human beings and drugs has become an extremely lucrative activity in the region, and a major export industry as well.

The Union has become deeply involved in the Balkans. But it is still short of a coherent policy for the region as a whole; EU involvement is not backed by a global vision or an effective coordination of the numerous ways in which it attempts to influence developments. The Balkans should in fact be a litmus test for the CFSP: if the Union cannot have a common foreign policy in the Balkans, which is also perceived as such by outsiders, it is most unlikely that it will be able to develop one with respect to central Asia or the Pacific. It was muddled and often divided at first, facing the progressive disintegration of socialist Yugoslavia, which turned more and more bloody. It then ceded the driver's seat to the Americans (or was it pushed away from it?), who masterminded the Dayton accords which created the complex entity of Bosnia and Herzegovina, and later led the negotiations and the bombing campaign for Kosovo. Although individual European countries tried, with variable success, to play second fiddle to the United States at this later stage, the role of the EU was truly marginal, if noticeable at all at times. Characteristically, at the peak of NATO bombing of Yugoslavia, the European Council refused even to discuss the matter, presumably in the true spirit of the common foreign and security policy of the Union. The Yugoslav tragedy in the 1990s showed the severe limitations of European civilian power, which had no effective means of persuasion when the other parties decide to resort to arms, and often produced a cacophony of national voices.

The situation has changed considerably since the last NATO bomb fell on Yugoslavia. Milošević and Tudjman are gone. Political leaders in the successor republics of Yugoslavia now negotiate, even with difficulty, different forms of cooperation instead of shooting at each other. The Americans are rapidly losing interest in the region, while the Europeans, bilaterally or multilaterally and often with the aid of the so-called international community, try to bring peace and stability to the region. The EU High Representative is learning how to draft constitutions for individual countries, and in doing so he has been backed by greater capacity to provide peacekeeping forces. The Union—and its member countries—are by far the biggest providers of aid; and, last but not least, it also offers the perspective of a step-by-step integration into the European political system. This is a powerful weapon, since 'joining Europe' means much more in the troubled region of the Balkans than anywhere else on the continent, where peace, security, and a minimum level of welfare have not been in such short supply in recent years.

The region consists today of a collection of weak at best, failed, or virtual states or entities. Some are literally run by the international community (Bosnia and Herzegovina, as well as Kosovo) as protectorates or semi-protectorates, while in others the state is only able to perform minimal functions; and in most of them the fall of communist regimes has led to a straight switch from autocracy to kleptocracy. Governments are bankrupt and aid-dependent, while much economic activity takes place in the so-called informal economy: unregulated, untaxed, and often outright criminal. Citizens suffer from a strong sense of insecurity since the state fails to perform its traditional function of providing law and order; and they also feel frustrated and disempowered since the democratic process is perceived as offering hardly any real choices.

This is not just a description of large parts of former Yugoslavia or Albania; it also applies to a large extent to Bulgaria and Romania, which have already been accepted as candidate countries for EU membership. Not surprisingly, people are voting with their feet as much as they can, while they keep voting governments out of power always hoping that the next ones will act as *dei ex machina* in a tragedy with no end in sight. The Bulgarians' election of a former king and a former communist as prime minister and president respectively and in very quick succession is a characteristic recent example.

The Union's commitment to the Balkans will require consistency and patience: stabilization, democracy, and economic development will need time to establish roots. The EU should act as leader and agenda-setter, in close collaboration with international or regional organizations and interested parties, including most notably the USA and also Russia, and of course with the active participation of the people directly involved. There is, no doubt, a need for active external involvement in the stabilization and reconstruction of the Balkans, and none other than the EU can provide the lead; all other potential candidates for this role are either too weak or too uninterested. We are still short of a final settlement following the disintegration of Yugoslavia, and the ambiguity concerning the political status (and also borders?) of successor republics or entities may last for some time. Bosnia and Herzegovina, Kosovo, Montenegro and its link with Serbia, which remains a crucial part of the Balkan puzzle. Possibly also what is still internationally referred to as the Former Yugoslav Republic of Macedonia? For the time being, that country is enjoying the benefits of the first-ever peacekeeping force waving the Union flag.

As long as there remains the ambiguity about political status and borders— usually associated with poorly functioning political entities under international tutelage—the necessary conditions for long-term stability, democracy, and development will not be there. But many people believe that it is still too early to go for a final settlement; blood is still fresh on the ground. What is arguably worse is that we may be nurturing some non-viable entities in the process, products of the kind of adhockery that has mostly marked international and European involvement in the region since the fall of the communist regimes. Even in the best of possible scenarios, a strong external presence will be needed in the region for several years to come.

Peacekeeping and peace-enforcement should provide the minimum conditions for the long process of nation building in some cases and state rebuilding for the region as a whole. The Union will be asked to commit financial and human resources for training judges and policemen, paying for customs officials and border guards, helping with legislation, and promoting civil society. If the EU is to play a leading role in the stabilization and reconstruction of the Balkans, it will require a very different kind of flexibility and efficiency in management from what it has been able to deliver until now. Admittedly, the structure of the organization does not lend itself to effective coordination and the efficient use of resources. The High Representative and different commissioners have been regularly stepping on each other's toes in the Balkans, while Commission services have been dispensing (and often wasting) EU aid in the region.

Can the EU deliver something better in the future, with a more efficient organization of Commission services and more effective coordination among the Council, the Commission, and the Parliament? The problem is more general: the proliferation of aid donors in the region has led to enormous wastage of both money and the time of the few qualified local officials acting as interlocutors for foreign donors. One practical step would be for the Union to take over the Stability Pact for South East Europe, inaugurated with much fanfare in 1999, and run it differently from now on. So far, it has been a depressing let-down. Yet there is surely only so much that outsiders can do. The danger of excessive aid-dependency, and dependency more generally, is a very real danger in large parts of the Balkans today.

The Union's long-term policy for the Balkans will have to combine the regional and the bilateral. True to its mission, the EU has tried to promote regional cooperation in the Balkans, as in other parts of the world, but so far with very limited results. The limitations of regional cooperation in a region where there are few factors conducive to it should be recognized; but it seems to be worth pursuing for economic as well as political reasons. Infrastructure investment, for instance, would be a means of promoting such cooperation, while creating the conditions for development and reducing the region's distance from the rest of Europe. Better roads, rail routes, and telecommunications can perform these functions. This is generally recognized, although rarely translated into concrete measures. Is there not a key role to be taken on by the European Investment Bank?

The bilateral dimension in relations with Balkan countries will also need to remain strong. The two countries already engaged in accession negotiations with the Union have always been extremely suspicious of any regional approach adopted by the EU, fearing that this would handicap them in the race for membership or that regional cooperation was being offered as a poor substitute. The same is true of Croatia, which hopes to join soon the ranks of official candidates. Conditionality is an integral part of the policy of carrot and stick employed by the Union, and this means that each country is judged individually and rewarded accordingly. This should continue applying all the way down the pyramid of institutional relations which the Union has constructed regarding candidates or potential candidates. For much of the western Balkans, at least, EU membership remains a distant prospect. Thus, the pyramid is likely to continue to act as the reference point for a relatively long time, and the EU will be hard-pressed to invent more attractive forms of virtual membership. This should, of course, become easier if, with successive rounds of enlargement, European integration begins to take the form of concentric circles. Are we ready for such a development?

The inability of the EU so far to develop a proper relationship with Russia, and before that with the USSR, speaks volumes about its limitations as an independent actor on the international stage. Until recently, Russian leaders had shown little understanding and interest in the intricacies of low politics and the refined diplomacy of postmodern civilian powers, choosing instead to behave in the fashion of a traditional great power. They did not comprehend the world of Brussels and, in perfect reciprocity, EU institutions showed themselves incapable of dealing with a big country and former empire which was not duly impressed by offers of diluted versions of association agreements, including some technical assistance. The Union also took some time to realize, having already invested money in it, that the Commonwealth of Independent States (CIS), created after the disintegration of the Soviet empire, had very little in common with regional integration EU-style and even less content. For all those reasons, Russian leaders continued to deal with the individual countries of the EU, and they seemed happy to go along with it. EU-Russian relations were for years a case of mutual neglect.

Things have begun to change recently, although both sides still experience serious difficulties in translating official rhetoric about a privileged relationship into action. Meanwhile, a few Russians have begun to talk of membership of the EU, although even the most optimistic are ready to admit that this would be at best a very long-term prospect. Even without the other former Soviet republics, Russia is a continental power on its own, big and extremely diverse, still strong militarily although weak economically—the very opposite of the EU. It is also a long way from meeting European standards of democratic governance and market economy. Thus, the traditional instruments employed by the EU in its external relations have only limited applicability in the case of Russia.

Further enlargement will bring the EU closer to Russia and its own near abroad. The accession of the Baltic republics will mean, among other things, that sizeable Russian minorities, including many stateless people, will be living in EU (and Schengen) territory. Furthermore, the Russian enclave of Kaliningrad will be surrounded by EU states. There are concrete issues to discuss and resolve with Moscow, including of course visas, the movement of people across borders, and organized crime. An agreement has already been reached concerning the movement of people between Kaliningrad and the rest of the Russian Federation after the enlargement of the EU; many other issues still need to be tackled.

The stability of countries situated between the enlarged EU and Russia should be a matter of concern for both, and, one hopes, an opportunity for close cooperation rather than providing fuel for a wasteful and dangerous competition for spheres of influence. This borderland consists of extremely weak states, most of them internally divided, with one part of the country looking eastwards and the other westwards. This is very much true of Ukraine, an important and highly unstable neighbour of the enlarged EU. It is also true of Georgia and Moldova, although less so of Belarus, which has gradually approached the status of a Russian satellite. Admittedly, the Union does not presently have much to offer those countries, and it remains unsure about how to handle relations with them. Membership of the EU is not on offer, even as a long-term prospect. For the time being at least, the frontiers of uniting Europe stop before those countries. They will become, however, part of Europe's near abroad after the next enlargement, as they are already of Russia, which has frequently resorted more to muscular power than to diplomacy in order to make its presence felt in the region. Imperial habits always last longer than empires.

If NATO has been able—admittedly with difficulty—to define a new special relationship with Russia in the post-cold war era, it is perhaps not beyond the realms of possibility that the European Union, with a slowly maturing CFSP, will also prove able to do so eventually. In that context, the two sides could begin to discuss security and trade as well as energy and pipelines. When this happens, we will know that the EU is at last developing into a credible actor in a new multipolar world. This process of maturing may, however, prove both long and painful. In the meantime, it will help when Russia becomes a member of the WTO and when the Union acquires a true common market in energy.

The European policy of the Union looks like a mosaic of parts of different colour and size. The central elements of *Pax Europea* provide the unifying theme. Yet the European policy of the EU still relies mostly on bilateral relations. Any attempts at multilateralism have so far produced limited results, whether in the form of the European Economic Area (EEA) or the regional approach towards the countries of the western Balkans. Would it make sense to try to create a pan-European forum in which the EU provides the driving force, thus adding a truly multilateral dimension to its relations with other European countries while waiting for subsequent rounds of enlargement? President Mitterrand came up with the idea of a European Confederation. Can there be any substance in the idea that could attract a very disparate group of countries, including Albania and Switzerland, not to mention Russia, and thus create real added value in a European context where there is already a surfeit of regional organizations? The idea is perhaps worth exploring as the political map of Europe begins to take final shape after the collapse of the cold war order.

EU membership, even as a long-term prospect, has served as a powerful instrument for democracy, peace, and stability, and also as a catalyst for economic and political modernization in new or aspiring members. This instrument is clearly not as yet available in relations with non-European countries in the Mediterranean, which is another very important part of the Union's near abroad. The European Community before, and now the EU, has invested a great deal of money, ideas, and energy in different incarnations of a 'global' Mediterranean policy, with generally poor results. Its ability to influence this very sensitive region for Europe has been extremely limited, in relation to both the Arab–Israeli conflict and the domestic factors inhibiting development in most of the Arab world.

The further deterioration of the Middle East conflict, coupled with the tragic events of 11 September 2001, have only made matters worse, while European and American perceptions have increasingly diverged. The countries of the EU could soon be faced with developments that once again test their already fragile unity, thus probing further the limits of the European civilian power. The Mediterranean and the Middle East have been the source of much frustration for the Europeans, and they are likely to continue being so in the future. Frustration is in turn closely linked to persistent instability in this neighbouring region, growing fears about trade and oil links, and new waves of immigrants adding to the already large and politically highly sensitive presence of minorities, mostly from the Maghreb and also Turkey, in European countries. A more active European engagement in the region may be required; but can we agree on its form and shape?

☆ Globalization, Hegemony, and Civilian Power

For many years, European integration was mostly about the joint management of increasingly interdependent mixed economies. In the process, Europeans developed a complicated package consisting of liberalization and regulation, with some elements of redistribution, which has no parallel in any other part of the world. Regional integration may indeed have influenced the relationship between the state and the market in Europe. It has not, however, fundamentally changed the mixed character of European capitalism(s). It should not be surprising therefore that for many Europeans globalization, essentially a market- and technology-driven process, raises fundamental questions of governance. It is certainly not the heavenly glow that we can all lie back and enjoy. Together with its undeniable wealth-creating effects, globalization often brings along greater inequalities, social disruption, and environmental damage, the kinds of negative externalities that those benefiting from globalization prefer to ignore.

Their collective experience in regional integration, relying heavily on common rules and institutions, and their long political traditions, in which the mixed economy, public goods, and solidarity occupy a prominent position, has made Europeans naturally much more inclined than the other big power in the international economic system, the United States, to contemplate multilateral rules and institutions for the management of global interdependence. Several examples prove the point, such as the creation of the WTO and its dispute-settlement procedure, a successful European initiative, and the Kyoto Protocol on global warming, which remains on paper because the Bush Administration refuses to endorse it. True, consistency has rarely been the main characteristic of political and social behaviour; this also applies to Europeans, who have sometimes collectively succumbed to the temptation of unilateral action when they felt strong enough to do so. Yet there is a considerable, and apparently widening, gap between the two sides of the Atlantic with respect to multilateralism and global rules, a gap which is even wider in what international relations theorists refer to with awe as 'high politics'.

The Europeans have values as well as goods and services they would like to export. These values include a developed sensitivity for the environment, the rights of workers, and distributional justice. They form part of the European model, if there is to be one. They therefore need to be reflected in common European policies and linked more closely to the objective of further trade liberalization in the context of the WTO and the new multilateral trade round launched in Doha in November 2001, as well as in other international forums. In Doha, as before, the United States talked mostly about free trade and the EU about governance.

More recently, European integration has generally developed in parallel with globalization: witness the liberalization of capital and financial services.

In some cases, the Europeans were simply swept along with the current, while in others they succeeded in developing a collective regional response to globalization. EMU could be seen as an example of the latter, although how consciously so remains to be seen. The Europeans have been learning from experience—some faster than others—that regional cooperation/integration usually enables them to deal more effectively with global interdependence. They have the size and the degree of self-sufficiency that enables them to establish collective forms of management and regulation in place of ineffective national ones. And they also have the collective power to influence international decisions; individually, (most) European countries count for little in international economic affairs. The continuous deepening of regional integration has not always been accompanied by a corresponding transfer of powers to the external policies of the Union, and this has been clearly reflected in European weakness in international negotiations.

The comparison between international trade and international finance is most illuminating. Whereas in trade there has been a multipolar system for some time, in which the European regional bloc carries as much weight as the USA, there is nothing similar in international money and finance. Things may, however, begin to change gradually with the arrival of the euro. This is the area where the EU could be expected to develop in the next few years a collective response to globalization and a unified stance in international institutions and other forums. The Europeans will surely discover in the process that they acquire a very different kind of influence in the IMF and the World Bank, and also in the way in which the international financial system is managed (or mismanaged). Given the importance of Turkey as a close partner and potential member of the Union, is it not strange, for example, that the EU was unable to adopt a common position in the IMF with respect to the financial assistance package offered to Turkey when the crisis erupted?

Relations with developing countries are very important: Europe's colonial past, having left behind accumulated knowledge, some vested interests, and feelings of collective guilt strengthened by traditions of solidarity and social justice in European societies, will probably continue to compensate for the declining economic importance of much of what is still euphemistically called the developing world. The European regional bloc has made repeated, albeit often half-hearted, attempts to establish a new model of North-South economic relations, thus trying to satisfy at least some of the demands made by less developed countries. Admittedly, those attempts are not universally deemed as successful (to put it mildly), but they need to be pursued. Multilateralism in trade is not necessarily incompatible with special concessions to the less developed countries.

There are, however, a number of difficult issues to be tackled. One is surely the much-delayed reform of the CAP. As long as the European agricultural fortress keeps many of the exports of the less developed countries out of European markets, the credibility of the image of Europe as the generous partner of poor countries will continue to be severely tested. The test will become more difficult in the new multilateral trade round. On the other hand, the EU has created its own group of privileged partners in the developing world, and they certainly have not been among the most dynamic—not that this is the Europeans' fault. Some kind of privileged relationship is most likely to continue, with the privilege being progressively shifted from trade to aid. This should also help to further reduce the negative trade discrimination against non-privileged partners in the Third World.

The EU is already a big aid donor; in fact, by far the biggest in the world if we include aid provided by member states. Aid recipients almost invariably prefer multilateral to bilateral aid because the latter usually has political and other strings attached. EU aid is multilateral, yet conditionality need not be confused with political strings. In order to avoid wasting European taxpayers' money, external aid should be given with strict conditions linked to development. And the Europeans now also seem to have fewer qualms about imposing political conditions related to democracy and human rights, although in practice they experience great difficulties in applying them consistently in many parts of the Third World suffering from very low standards of governance. They should find the political courage to do so. Otherwise, redistribution will mostly take place from the European middle classes and workers to the benefit of corrupt rulers in very poor countries—and also a small number of European consultants. It is a question of political courage; it is also a question of coherent policy and efficient management and monitoring of EU external aid. Coherence and efficiency were sorely missing for many years because of Council inconsistencies as well as shortage of staff and poor organization in the Commission. Serious efforts are now being made to tackle this problem.

From trade matters to defence, the relationship with the United States has always been absolutely crucial. It has become even more so after the end of the cold war and the demise of the Soviet empire. In political and military terms, we now live in a world where there is only one superpower; and if anything the distance between the United States and the lesser mortals of the international scene has been growing bigger with time. Thus, any attempt to come closer to the declared objective of a common foreign and security policy for the EU necessarily goes through a definition (or redefinition) of Europe's relationship with the United States. It touches almost on everything, including the re-organization of NATO, relations with Russia, the new division of labour regarding peacekeeping operations in Europe and beyond, the Middle East conflict, and the International Criminal Court. There is no escaping it: Europe's CFSP needs, first and foremost, a strong American dimension if it is to develop beyond anodyne words in communiqués drafted by diplomats. How does the EU want to define its relation with the only superpower, a close ally of the Europeans and, so far, their protector of last resort? Most importantly, can it speak with a single voice? The answer to these questions, of course, depends largely on whether the Europeans have a common perception of external threats and of the role they want to exercise in international affairs.

Transatlantic relations have become much more difficult since the arrival of President George W. Bush, who leads a coalition that contains a strong representation of Christian fundamentalists, neoconservatives, and imperial unilateralists. Is it just a hiccup or a reflection of long-term trends? The unrivalled military might of the United States tends to make of unilateralism a kind of instinctive reaction to international events. Who needs coalitions, not to mention international consensus, when the distribution of power is so unbalanced? And who wants to be tied by rules and the threat of sanctions imposed by international institutions? Multilateral rules are, after all, the ultimate defence of the weak, are they not? True enough, although this has been the way societies have evolved from Hobbesian anarchy to civilization; and this is, hopefully, the way the international system will also evolve, however slowly. If the Europeans usually tend to project their own experience on to the rest of the world, often with a strong dose of wishful thinking (or perhaps simply trying to make a virtue out of their political and military weakness), many Americans find it naturally hard to resist making use of their power in order to obtain desired outcomes. And this situation should not be totally unfamiliar to those Europeans with an imperial past; the British seem to understand it best. On the other hand, power in the United States is often combined with a missionary zeal and strong views about good and evil, which those secular Europeans find extremely awkward to deal with.

The gap in military capabilities between the two sides of the Atlantic has never been bigger. The Americans no longer need their European allies to launch major military operations; they need only bases for their aircraft and troops. They regard political support from allies and friends (and international organizations) as desirable, although apparently dispensable if they were not willing to follow the leader without asking many questions—or so several prominent members of the Bush Administration seem to think. This gap in military capabilities, coupled with the elimination of the old Soviet threat, may be leading NATO towards obsolescence; yet this rarely happens with international institutions, which tend to survive even when the purpose for which they were set up has long disappeared. Successive rounds of enlargement of NATO may only reinforce the trend towards obsolescence. The debate on the new role, if any, of the Atlantic alliance has hardly begun; and there is surely no collective European view on this matter as yet.

If we assume that Europe is most unlikely to want to fight a war against the Americans in the foreseeable future, a plausible assumption by any standards, the Europeans do not need to try to match the fighting power of the United States. This would make no sense. Yet they have also realized from experience that even civilian powers may occasionally need to resort to other means of persuasion in a world which does not consist only of postmodern states. *Pax Europea* has repeatedly shown its limitations even within the boundaries of Europe. The EU has now decided to develop a rapid-reaction force of 60,000 soldiers to be used for peacekeeping and peace-enforcement operations. Such a development would certainly strengthen the credibility of the EU and its stabilization role in the near abroad and beyond.

Far short of an independent European military force which would take collective responsibility for safeguarding the territorial integrity of the enlarged Union (we are still far from that), this rapid-reaction force has encountered many obstacles in trying to define a modus operandi with NATO; and it will also have to be reconciled with the US proposal for the development of a similar force within NATO. In the course of long and difficult negotiations, which often faltered at Turkish objections to the European force having access to NATO facilities, it has also become clear that EU member countries still have very different views (and hopes) about the relationship between Europe's slowly emerging security and defence policy and the Atlantic alliance. From the French and the Germans all the way to the British, not to mention the neutrals and the new members, the distance is very great. Apparently, some people had grossly exaggerated the convergence of views among European countries on this crucial issue.

The new members from central and eastern Europe are likely to occupy a special position in this respect. There is a genuine feeling of gratitude towards the United States for the crucial role it played in their liberation from Soviet rule. And there is also a natural tendency to look to the American superpower for protection against any possible threat from the east. At the same time, these countries are weaker and more vulnerable to pressure from outside, most notably from the US, while they are only just beginning to experience the effects of Europeanization.

The fragility of European unity on important matters of foreign policy was confirmed once again with the war in Iraq. Under strong pressure to follow the American lead, the Europeans were deeply divided. It was in fact worse than ever before. To be precise, it was their leadership that was divided; public opinion appeared to be much less so, and mostly against the war. The war in Iraq and its aftermath could prove to be a major turning point in transatlantic relations as well as in European efforts to develop a true CFSP. Will the Europeans succeed in mending their internal divisions, with or without the Americans? And if not, will some of them try to revive the old idea of the core group? Whatever they do, they will not be able to avoid some awkward questions, and most notably questions about money.

Even if the Europeans want to limit their ESDP to peace operations, thus leaving responsibility for collective defence to NATO while also pretending that there is broad consensus regarding the nature of external threats and the means of handling them, they still need to put some of their money where their mouths are: that is, to increase defence expenditures in order to improve their logistic capabilities among other things. They are unlikely to fight the kind of high-tech wars in which the Americans have increasingly specialized. Nevertheless, they still need much improved transport and intelligence capabilities if Europe's commitment to peacekeeping and peace-enforcement is to become a credible force for stabilization. Soft security does not necessarily come cheap. And it would surely help if the Europeans began to make real progress in the cooperation/integration of their armaments industries and their arms procurement policies, accepting along the way a deeper division of labour in their national defence strategies.

The European defence dimension and, linked to it, Europe's relations with the only remaining superpower will largely depend on how the UK defines its own interests in the near future. In military terms, the UK remains a leading power in Europe, together with France. Will it seek a stronger European defence pillar, complementary to the American one but also implying a more equal relationship between the two sides? Or will it prefer, as it has in the past, to cultivate the role of privileged follower, often trying to mediate between the Americans and the other Europeans? If the UK were to choose the former option, which still appears the less likely, it would also strengthen its position within the European system. The European balance of power, to the extent that this idea is not complete sacrilege in the context of EU Europe, largely depends on what Europe does and does not do.

Mr Blair has understood this, and he has gone so far as opting for a European superpower while insisting he is against a European superstate. There is, of course, a contradiction here. Does Mr Blair honestly believe that a superpower, even of a postmodern variety, can develop without strong institutions and a common European identity to back it up? It is hardly convincing as a proposition. And worst of all perhaps, what happens if the Americans disagree with the policies agreed upon collectively by the Europeans? Will Mr Blair and others be willing to toe the line agreed upon by the majority? The development of a common foreign policy, not to mention a common security policy, will most likely prove to be a slow process. When France and the UK become ready to swap their permanent seats on the Security Council for a seat occupied by the Union, we shall know that a real CFSP is beginning to come into existence.

There is arguably yet another contradiction inherent in this process. At least some Europeans want to project power into the rest of the world through the development of a common foreign and security policy. This is particularly true of the bigger powers, notably France and the UK. Yet not only are they the least willing to accept sacrifices in terms of national sovereignty, but they also often prefer to forget that European integration constitutes in itself an attempt to go beyond power politics. How then does one reconcile internal structure with external ambitions? Perhaps through coalitions of willing and able, thus following the precedent set by EMU. More than any other policy before, the development of the CFSP could indeed lead further away from the old model of integration based on common institutions and rules applying to everyone.

The most likely scenario, however, is that the CFSP will continue to develop slowly—and so will the ESDP, together with all the other abbreviations usually invented by the Europeans in lieu of real policies. If anything, further enlargement will tend to slow it down further. Unless, of course, there are major crises on the way—and crises usually arrive unexpected, as history teaches us. It is remotely possible that President George W. Bush becomes unintentionally the biggest unifier of Europe by pushing aggressive unilateralism to extremes, thus forcing the Europeans into greater unity as a way of constraining American power gone wild; but this will surely take a lot of effort. Europe is not yet ready for it; and it is also a very dangerous scenario.

It would be a safer world if uniting Europe were instead to concentrate on its role as a civilian and mostly regional power, with a civilizing mission and some additional instruments to enforce peace when necessary. This is where its comparative advantage lies; and it would also help Europe to be taken more seriously by the Americans, thus helping to create the conditions for greater complementarity between the two. Surely, being a credible counterpart does not exclude the role of counterweight when necessary. Superpower status will come much later, if at all. In the meantime, it would be good for world peace and stability if this slowly uniting Europe also contributes to the strengthening of international institutions and the development of a multipolar system relying more on rules and equity and less on military might. Hegemonic power can be dangerous, even for those who exercise it.

PART III

☆☆☆☆☆☆☆☆☆☆☆☆

Conclusions

8

☆☆☆☆☆

What Is at Stake?

☆ Real Deficits . . .

More than fifty years after it all began, regional integration in Europe has developed into a complex system, with no precedent in history and no rival in other parts of the contemporary world. Old and new nation-states in Europe have joined in: some still anxiously waiting in the antechamber and only a very few willingly staying out (for how long?). Successive rounds of deepening and widening, meaning in plain English that regional integration becomes ever closer and also extends into new areas of policy while membership continues to grow, constitute the best proof of success. The European Union is very much alive and delivering the goods, perhaps against the odds and contrary to all kinds of doomsday scenarios.

Unlike empires in the past, European integration is centred on democratic systems and the principle of free association. No country has been forced to join or stay against the collective will of its citizens. It must therefore be judged as satisfying real needs, at least for a sufficient number of people, in government, among interest groups, or among simple citizens who have been ready to lend it their active or passive support.

First and foremost, European integration can be seen as a highly developed system for the joint management of interdependence. This interdependence started with trade and steadily extended into many other manifestations of cross-border interaction and exchange in a crowded continent with a long and turbulent history, relatively scarce natural resources, and a wide diversity of cultures, political traditions, and economic systems. Nowadays, the welfare of

European citizens is intimately linked with this system of regional inter-dependence, and so more generally is their quality of life to the extent that it too depends on the freedom to travel, study, or work anywhere inside the Union, and to the extent that it depends on access to a wide variety of goods and services and greater security, among other things. One may be tempted to add the ability to preserve a certain way of life, although this remains a controversial argument for the minority who still prefer to emphasize diversity rather than commonality of values and models of society.

Many aspects of the everyday life of European citizens now depend on decisions taken beyond their national borders, albeit with the participation of their representatives. A key characteristic of European integration has been the attempt to combine liberalization of markets and the elimination of national barriers in general with the establishment of common rules and institutions— a new level of governance, in contemporary parlance. This is, after all, only proper for countries where individualism has been long tamed by considerations of the public good and where government is not necessarily a dirty word; it may also have something to do with Europe being old and crowded.

Interdependence is, of course, not a uniquely European phenomenon. It has increasingly characterized international relations during recent decades, and the accelerated pace of transnational forces has often led to exaggerated notions of a shrinking world and a global village: the sophisticated analyst from New York preaching globalization to the tribesman in the Kalahari desert. Yet globalization is not just a fad; it depicts real forces operating in the world today, striking down many of the barriers carefully and painstakingly built over the years by governments in the name of national autonomy, or simply for the sake of protecting special interests.

In most cases, regional interdependence in Europe today is substantially different from what we find at the global level in at least two important respects— intensity and governance—which are usually mutually reinforcing. The regional concentration of economic exchange is very high indeed in Europe, and this is intimately linked with a system of rules and regulations governing this exchange. This applies to almost all aspects of trade, although arguably less so to financial markets where the regional tends to merge with the global. The extent to which such differences may be due to market fundamentals rather than to man-made rules is not always easy to establish.

Regional integration has served as an instrument of economic development, a catalyst for modernization, and in many ways a kind of convergence machine for the benefit of the less developed countries of the European continent.

This has reduced the geographical (as well the political and cultural) distance between the core and the periphery. And economic development, coupled with modernization, is still helping to strengthen the new democratic institutions in countries emerging from long periods of authoritarian and totalitarian rule. They all constitute integral parts of what is generally referred to as the process of Europeanization. These considerations also help explain why the periphery has a more rosy picture of the European Union, at least the one it has known so far, even though the challenge of adjustment has been much greater for it than for the core.

It has surely helped that a sense of solidarity has gradually developed among participants, which has been translated into, among other things, financial instruments of redistribution through the EU budget. Although limited, given the small size of the common budget, redistribution constitutes today a key element of the overall package deal behind European integration; and this is a highly important distinguishing feature of the EU. Solidarity has been manifested in mutual aid in a wide variety of instances and also explicit burden sharing, be it with respect to asylum policy or the costs of environmental protection. Burden sharing and redistribution of costs are, for example, a major component of the internal EU agreement linked to the Kyoto Protocol. A sense of community has been developing, albeit slowly, inside the EU; of course, it is still far short of the sense of community (*Gemeinschaft*, as the Germans would call it) to be found within old nation-states with a long common history strengthened by close bonds, shared symbols, and myths.

European integration started as a way of laying the foundations of Franco-German reconciliation, hence an instrument for peace and security in the old 'Carolingian core' of Europe. It was functionalism at its best and at its most ambitious. Franco-German cooperation subsequently provided the motor for integration. EMU is the most prominent example of how economic integration can serve as means to high political ends; this is how it was perceived by both French and German political leaders. After all, money and war have always been closely linked in European history.

Yet the main instruments of war remain beyond the control of regional European institutions. Most national governments continue to opt for defence cooperation within the Atlantic alliance rather than the EU. During the cold war, everyone knew full well that the ultimate guarantee for the security of Western Europe lay in American hands, although perhaps less so nowadays since it is no longer clear who or what constitutes the main threat to security for Europeans as a whole. Arguably, this ambiguity is the kind of luxury that can be afforded only by those living a safe distance from trouble spots and the old Soviet border; Belgians and Portuguese, among others, can relax. Citizens of the new Baltic republics would, however, see things differently, and they would naturally turn to Washington for external protection rather than Paris, London, Berlin, or Brussels. Memories of the Russian bear die hard. This may indeed change as perceptions of external threat adjust to the new geopolitical situation and also as internal security tends to merge with external security; but it will surely take time.

Common European policies and common institutions have also served as means of projecting collective power and influence in international affairs. This has certainly been true of trade. Europeans have learned from experience that acting together was the only way of having a real impact in multilateral negotiations. However, not all have yet drawn the conclusion that the lessons learnt from external trade can be easily applied to other areas of policy, even less so as they move along the spectrum from so-called low to high politics. Thus, the shift from economic to political power has proved extremely difficult. Relations with the superpower across the Atlantic have usually acted as a dividing factor. The pursuit of a common foreign policy assumes that members perceive they have more interests in common than with outside countries, and are therefore prepared to sacrifice their independence of action (or simply the illusion of independence) in order to strengthen their collective negotiating power. This has not always been obvious, especially in those areas where regional self-sufficiency has been relatively low—security again being a case in point.

European integration has delivered many concrete benefits; it has also produced huge amounts of rhetoric that have often created exaggerated expectations or fears, depending on one's starting point. Many people have tended to take official rhetoric too seriously, only to be surprised when they later discovered that political union or a genuinely common foreign policy were not simply waiting around the corner. Political leaders meet regularly in European councils, followed by a long train of advisers. When they finish these meetings, long joint communiqués and solemn declarations sometimes serve as substitutes for real decisions. They should not always be read literally, but rather viewed as part of the European ritual. This is one of the first lessons that observers of the European scene are forced to learn.

Too much hard realism, on the other hand, can be equally, if not more, misleading. Behind all the rhetoric, a political vision for a united Europe has been mobilizing a significant number of people in political elites and beyond, and acting as an important driving force in various stages of European integration. And like all visions, it has not been very precise. Those down-to-earth pragmatists who are convinced that visions, when they do appear, only require treatment by specialists have been repeatedly disappointed and left behind by events. They have failed to see the 'vision thing' and the political will it could generate. It happened many times in the past, and more recently with EMU; it could happen again with the Convention.

The institutional framework of the EU, though highly advanced—indeed unique—by international standards, still preserves a central role for participating nation-states and their representatives. Nation-states have not withered away—and they are unlikely to do so in the foreseeable future. On the contrary, they have been strengthened in many respects through the process of regional integration. For some, at least, the threat of internal fragmentation looks much more real than the prospect of being dissolved in some kind of European soup. The symbiotic character of regional integration and the nation-states participating in it may sound contradictory only to those who still approach sovereignty as something absolute that you have or you do not have (like virginity, I suppose).

On the other hand, in this rapidly evolving European system there has been no dominant power imposing its wishes on the others. The lack of a hegemon, remarkable in itself, does not, of course, mean that some countries have not been more equal than others in the influence they have exerted on policy outcomes. It could not have happened otherwise, given the huge differences among participating states in terms of size, economic might, and institutional capacity.

Thus, Germany and France have often played a leading role in European integration, and the UK has also tried doing the same, albeit with less success so far. Italy and Spain have made repeated efforts to join the big league, while the others remain less equal even though they are not always reconciled to this hard reality. This is all true. It is equally true, however, that the so-called Community method of decision-making has given small and medium-sized countries a much greater role and influence in European integration than they would have ever had in a traditional intergovernmental system. The regional construction built after the end of the Second World War is qualitatively very different from a concert of big powers, which is more familiar to students of earlier European history. This is another key and novel feature of European integration.

Surely, the new European political system—and there is, indeed, a political system that has developed over the years, even though diplomacy and intergovernmental negotiations remain more important than democratic politics as we have learned to recognize it within our nation-states—is overly bureaucratic and often inefficient and wasteful. It tends to react to events since it is not the kind of system that can easily produce initiatives or political leadership. It is also conservative in the sense that any change from the status quo requires very large majorities and the need to go through many checks and balances. The EU juggernaut moves slowly and negotiates with difficulty the continuous twists and turns in the road.

Europe has turned into a lucrative business for policy-makers, lobbyists, and the growing number of those benefiting from handouts from European institutions. They are a minority to be reckoned with; yet by necessity only a minority. In the meantime, the European system has become increasingly unappealing to the wider public. Decisions are perceived as taken far away from those directly affected and behind closed doors, mostly by faceless technocrats, with little transparency and even less accountability. It surely does not help that the issues are usually presented in the politically sterilized language of the Brussels bureaucracy. What started as an elitist project par excellence has in the process become also heavily bureaucratic. And the democratic deficit has grown wider as new items have been added to the European agenda.

This deficit is real, and it is very much reflected in the lack of Europe-wide debates on issues that have long ceased to be the exclusive prerogative of nation-states. The result has been a widening gap between perception and reality in national politics, while there is still precious little European (democratic) politics to talk about—and no shortage of European policy. Thus, in an indirect way, European integration has reduced democratic choice for citizens while also strengthening the managerial dimension of politics in Europe. The 'Golden Straitjacket' may be sometimes good for economic efficiency. But in the long term it is certainly bad for democracy and politics, and hence unstable and potentially dangerous, especially if there were a significant number of losers hiding behind the general concept of efficiency. We could be approaching such a point in Europe today.

Different methods of governance have developed for the wide variety of policy areas coming under the umbrella of European integration. They cover the whole spectrum from simple intergovernmental cooperation to outright federalism: federalism that in several countries still dares not speak its name. On the other hand, weak common rules and non-constraining forms of intergovernmental cooperation usually go hand in hand with low levels of integration on the ground and persistent wide diversity. There is nothing necessarily

wrong with that, as long as it is compatible with economic and political fundamentals, and as long as the latter naturally include a conscious choice by a sufficient number of participants. It is up to the Europeans collectively to decide
what they do together and what separately, and consequently what price they
are willing to pay for further integration or continued fragmentation.

Social and welfare issues are among those where diversity is likely to remain
the name of the game for some time to come. It is common values rather than
common policies that sustain what some people prefer to call the European
social model. This persistent diversity of policies continues to allow a considerable degree of autonomy for European nation-states, although this is subject
to the constraints imposed by demography and international capital mobility,
as well as rules on deficit financing in the context of EMU. Social and welfare
policies should be expected to remain for long mostly matters of national
responsibility. This should also mean that the bulk of government expenditure
(and consequently taxation) continues at the national or even sub-national
levels. Health, education, and social security are at the core of politically salient
issues for European citizens; hence, there is little risk of national systems running out of political ammunition in the foreseeable future. But this should still
leave ample room for active political engagement at the European level for
those issues that have long since crossed the boundaries of the nation-state.

☆ . . . and Favourite Myths

The novelty of European integration and the difficulty in accommodating it in
old familiar categories help to explain the birth and survival of various myths
about what this new Europe is or should be. One such myth, popular among
Eurosceptics, is of the European superstate, which is supposed to constitute
already a real threat to national sovereignty. Its proponents argue instead for a
loose association of sovereign states, with the Commission serving at best as a
secretariat, and managing what would be essentially a free trade area (the old
EFTA still has its supporters, and now there is also its younger and more
dynamic sister on the other side of the Atlantic).

There are surely examples of centralizing excesses of the Brussels bureaucracy, often aided by national politicians looking for imported external discipline when the going gets tough at home. Weak states and weak governments
search for an external scapegoat or turn to Brussels as the appropriate
reference point for imported economic rationality and financial orthodoxy.

It becomes dangerous when this is repeated too often, and the consequent pressures for further centralization or harmonization are rightly resented by those who retain more confidence in the ability of their national or sub-national institutions to deliver the goods.

However, the nostalgia for free trade areas usually ignores (or rejects) the reality of mixed economies in Europe and the coexistence of different economic systems. Common rules have been devised not only to regulate markets but also to govern interaction between different national systems. The search for the so-called level playing fields in economic competition and other areas has driven much European regulation and the bureaucracy that goes with it. The criticism is therefore at least partly ideological; market fundamentalism is at the heart of it. There is also, apparently, little understanding (and even less appreciation) of the degree and kind of interdependence already reached in Europe and the management required for it, not to mention the other functions performed by European institutions.

Eurosceptics are, of course, deeply concerned about the loss of national sovereignty resulting from regional integration and the constraints imposed by European rules and institutions. At the same time, they conveniently underestimate the loss of national autonomy resulting from increasingly global markets, while grossly overestimating the capacity of individual European countries for independent action in a world where power is very much asymmetrically distributed and Europe is no longer at the centre of it. Implicitly, Eurosceptics often seem to prefer market regulation made in Washington and applied extraterritorially rather than negotiating common European rules.

Many British Conservatives form a category of their own. They are clearly unhappy at being part of a journey to an unknown destination, as the process of European integration has been so aptly described in the past. They also suspect they know what the destination will look like, and they do not want to get there. To make matters worse, many of them would prefer different fellow passengers, since they feel much closer to Texas or Arizona than to Finland or Greece—and there can be no rational arguments over matters of taste.

The other myth, originating from near the left of the political spectrum, with the French socialists being among its main proponents, is that of social Europe. 'Social Europe' signifies an advanced level of harmonization of social standards and policies as the necessary counterpart to market integration, although it is not always clear whether this proposed harmonization of standards should be coupled with a substantial transfer of the financing of welfare policies to the European level of responsibilities. The better-off countries in Europe would surely not be so keen on such a transfer; and we all know that cross-border solidarity still has its limits, even among socialists. It is surely easier for Greek or Polish socialists to be in favour of cross-border solidarity than their German comrades. After all, the former would usually expect themselves to be on the receiving end and the latter to pay.

Social and welfare systems are indeed an integral part of post-Second World War Western Europe. Proponents of 'social Europe', however, prefer to ignore the persistent wide diversity of national social and welfare systems, which will become even wider after enlargement, and the lack of an integrated European labour market. Thus, trying to build a 'social Europe', some kind of Scandinavia writ large, still looks like trying to build skyscrapers in the sand; it may work as long as you stop after the first floors, which in this particular case means a certain minimum level of common standards as well as carefully selected programmes at the EU level.

The third widely held myth is of Europe as a global power. This is popular on both the right and the left of the political spectrum, although people on the right are usually more inclined to want to operate on power borrowed from the Americans. Europe acting as a global power means that Europeans would collectively recover much (or some) of the power lost by individual nation-states after two disastrous 'civil wars' during the twentieth century: a journey back to history for people who refuse to reconcile themselves to a more modest place in a rapidly changing world order. In fact, contrary to much official rhetoric in public forums, most European countries appear to have only narrow regional concerns and little inclination to pay the price of an active global role, including the role of global policeman in a world where 'soft power' has many limitations. France and the UK are arguably the exception: they still have the ambition (illusion?) and perhaps also the potential for a more active international role, thus not accepting the constraints of a regional civilian power. The trouble is that both countries sometimes seem to assume that the other Europeans would simply be content to follow their lead, with weak common institutions and rules; this has rarely proved to be a realistic assumption.

Relations with the United States have been absolutely crucial, both during the cold war when the USA led the 'free world' and now in the age of what may prove to be the new empire. There has always been a great deal of ambivalence in official US attitudes towards European integration: public support, reiterated on almost every available occasion, was usually offered on the assumption that the balance of power and influence between the two sides of the Atlantic would not change as a result of greater European unity, and consequently that

211

the Europeans would happily continue following the American lead. Was it not Churchill who once said that you certainly need allies, but the trouble is that allies tend to develop opinions of their own? He could perhaps have added that as the allies get stronger their opinions also become louder. This ambivalence in US attitudes has been more than apparent with respect to both the creation of the single currency and the establishment of a common foreign and security policy—scepticism would be a more appropriate term to use in these cases, if not outright opposition. A European global power cannot emerge without, first of all, tackling the awkward problem of its relations with the only superpower.

☆ Treaties, Constitutions, and More

The EU has often been accused of inaction and muddling through. Yet at the turn of the century this Union replaced twelve old national currencies with the euro, and it is now preparing to receive ten new members, having already completed accession negotiations with all of them. It is not a bad record by any standards. True, there have been many delays, half measures, and inadequate preparations. But are they not all characteristic of human societies, including most notably democratic political systems of a large size, with federal or confederal structures?

EMU and further enlargement are the two big projects of the first decade of the new century, and also the main driving forces of change. In many ways, they point in opposite directions. The introduction of the euro has undoubtedly been the biggest step in integration since the Treaty of Rome. It is expected to have a significant impact on markets, production structures, and public policies; and the effect will be long-lasting. The management of the euro raises basic questions about how members of EMU collectively want to define themselves in the context of globalization, and also how they individually handle economic instruments and structural policies that are still available at the national level. EMU could end up having a much stronger effect on the process of convergence of different capitalist models in Europe than anything seen so far.

Currencies are not self-managed. The institutional structure provided for in the Maastricht Treaty is inadequate, but it is all that was politically feasible at the time. Furthermore, it is not just a question of legal provisions. There is also an institutional wisdom that comes with time and experience. Using the same

212

currency from Lapland to the Azores is in itself a revolutionary change. Poor management of it would, however, entail significant economic and political costs.

The ECB will need to go beyond the strictures of narrow financial orthodoxy and acquire the flexibility and self-confidence necessary to manage the new currency in a probably adverse economic environment. It will also need a credible political interlocutor. The new single currency will require a European dimension of macroeconomic policy, which cannot be identified exclusively with monetary policy in the hands of the ECB. It will also require a common stance in international forums and difficult internal adjustments in member countries. Until those things happen, there is real risk of misfits languishing inside the eurozone and conditions developing which are not conducive to growth for members as a whole. EMU may prove in the end the big step that Europeans were not really ready to take. Such an outcome should be avoided at all costs: going back to national currencies is almost inconceivable, while the price of failure looks prohibitive.

The euro needs to be managed; it also needs a solid base of public acceptance and legitimacy. This can develop, at least in part, through a tangible improvement in the welfare of European citizens (it has happened many times before). But EMU will also need more democracy and accountability. Those who have long argued for a close link between monetary union and political union are most probably right; it has not happened yet. In different ways, EMU is likely to act as a powerful unifying factor in the long term, and possibly also as a divisive factor if some countries stay out for a long time. In either case (and possibly both), it is bound to shape the course of European integration.

The next round of enlargement has already been decided. It will happen in May 2004 with ten new members joining (unless something unexpected happens during the ratification process). And there is at least another smaller round of enlargement planned to take place before the end of the decade; more may come later. However, as we move beyond 2004, the political horizon becomes more and more hazy. There is no clear strategic vision of the further enlargement of the Union. For some years, the bureaucratic obsession with the *acquis* served as a poor substitute. But the harmonization of standards for fertilizers should not determine the scale and pace of expansion of the Union's boundaries.

We know, and we usually avoided saying so in public until recently, that the new enlargement will be an extremely difficult affair, which risks turning the Union into a highly diverse and increasingly loose association—in many ways an unmanageable affair. A minority of Europeans in countries that are already members would clearly be happy with such a development; the others are trying to strengthen the Union and its institutions in order to cope with the challenge. A loose association of twenty-five and more states does not easily square with EMU or the other objectives widely shared by Europeans.

We can fairly safely predict that it will take the Union considerable time and effort to digest the effects of the next round of enlargement. After all, it involves taking in mostly young states with weak economic structures and deep scars from long periods of totalitarian rule, followed by incomplete transitions that had highly unequal effects on different strata of society. Trying to digest the effects of the next enlargement, and while doing so most probably turning inwards, the Union may begin to lose even the small appetite it now appears to have for further rounds of enlargement. It is almost certain that the ultimate boundaries of the Union will become in the process a major political issue.

The Convention, and the new intergovernmental conference that follows, are expected to provide the institutional framework for a stronger and more effective Union that will be able to cope with the dual challenge of enlargement and EMU: that is, a Union that succeeds in reconciling effectiveness, democracy, and diversity—not at all an easy combination. There is a need for a stronger European executive, including both the Commission and the Council, that can deliver robust results with greater efficiency and transparency; and this should include, among other things, more qualified majority voting in the Council and further rationalization of the Commission and the tasks it performs. There is also a need for more democracy in the form of greater powers for the European Parliament, closer participation of national parliaments, and more active engagement of citizens in European decision-making.

On the other hand, the Convention should be expected to provide additional safeguards for those who feel threatened by harmonization or centralization freaks in Brussels. More Europe is not always a better Europe. There is room for decentralization and subsidiarity, including most notably the management of some of the sacred cows of integration. A Union with large membership and wide diversity needs to concentrate more on the essentials. This should be a key message for the enlarging Union.

In some cases, greater differentiation and flexibility, combined with more exceptions (opt-outs in the European jargon), may also become unavoidable. Many people have used a wide variety of metaphors to describe this possible evolution of the EU: from variable geometry and multiple tiers to flying geese and magnetic fields, hubs and spokes, and concentric circles. Observers of the European scene have shown remarkable fertility of imagination in the metaphors employed, and less ability to describe more precisely the institutional and other consequences of such arrangements.

No country will want to be relegated to lower tiers, although some may be forced to through domestic popular opposition or economic constraints. It is difficult to imagine that the EU can continue at the pace of the slowest of its members, especially as membership grows and becomes more diverse. Veto rights will thus be difficult to preserve in an enlarged Union, especially in the economic field. Until now, membership of the EU has been treated like marriage under the Catholic Church: no divorce allowed, although affairs on the side have generally been tolerated. This may have to change as veto rights progressively disappear. Divorce could then provide the last resort for countries that may at some point perceive themselves as a beleaguered minority unable to block decisions that consistently go against their perceived interests. Although this is highly unlikely to happen in a Union with twenty-five and more members, still heavily relying on consensus or at least large majorities, provisions for divorce could provide a useful safety valve.

Are we ready for such a step and, even more difficult, are we ready to agree that constitutional changes in the future, except for key provisions, will no longer require unanimity among participating states? In a more mature European political system, in which the equality of citizens should increasingly count more than the equality of states, further development can no longer be hostage to small minorities. After all, this should be one of the key elements distinguishing a constitution from an international treaty; or do we just have a fetish for words?

The Convention can deliver the institutional framework. It should also be expected to provide some of the symbols as well as to endorse the key common values of a uniting Europe. It cannot, however, deliver concrete decisions and policies. This is the stuff of everyday politics. The Maastricht Treaty, for example, declared the birth of a common European foreign and security policy. More than a decade later, the CFSP is still a mirage rather than a reality. To be sure, a new foreign minister for Europe, born out of the Convention and the new intergovernmental conference and backed by additional human and financial resources, could make a real difference in the future. Yet he or she would have to depend on the collective political will as well as the convergence of views of member governments. And this is not given at present. Most probably, the shift towards majority voting in foreign policy matters will be a slow process.

215

The EU has developed mainly into a civilian and regional power. Its most powerful weapon in relation to neighbouring countries is the prospect of membership of the Union. It is not at all unimportant, although this weapon risks turning into a boomerang with successive rounds of enlargement. Trying to do more, especially in situations of armed conflict, has often caused much frustration and no less humiliation. If anything, the EU will continue to be mostly affected by developments in its near abroad. New crises will present new challenges and could eventually act as a catalyst for a more effective CFSP.

A continued deadlock in the Middle East, further sustained by the blatantly partisan involvement of the United States on the side of Sharon's Israel, would cause further frustration for the Europeans and also harm their interests; but it is unlikely to act in a similar fashion as a catalyst for an active common policy in the region. There is very much at stake there, the Europeans have relatively weak instruments of influence at their disposal (or so they think), and going against the United States is not something that many Europeans seem ready to do yet.

A serious rift in transatlantic relations, if confirmed, would, of course, have major consequences for Europe's fledgling foreign policy, but also for European integration in general. Relations with the superpower remain a crucial variable in the formation of Europe's new political landscape. In the age of American supremacy, greater European unity is bound to have an anti-American element, at least in the sense that a stronger European power would tend to act not only as a counterpart but also sometimes as a counterweight to the United States. Those who abhor the idea of a multipolar world would therefore tend to equate the emergence of a European pole with anti-Americanism; luckily for them, they are likely to have to wait longer for such a development. The majority of European citizens, however, seem more willing nowadays to move in this direction than some of their political leaders. Foreign and security policy arguably lends itself more to ad hoc coalitions of the willing and able than economic affairs. But when divided, Europeans run the risk of being forced into coalitions of the obedient by those much stronger than themselves.

European integration started basically as an economic affair, though with strong political undertones. Economics remains today the backbone of it all. For many years, integration helped to sustain a succession of virtuous circles, which helped strongly growing national economies while also bolstering the essentially permissive consensus of European citizens about further integration. It was very good as long as it lasted. For more than ten years now, the performance of most West European economies has been very disappointing, certainly in comparison with the performance of the US economy even after

216

the bursting of the stock exchange bubble. The transition to EMU may have contributed to this disappointing performance through restrictive macroeconomic policies, although this remains a controversial argument among the *cognoscenti*.

The prospects do not look much better at the time of writing. Were the EU to go through another period of low (perhaps even negative) growth, coupled with high (or higher) rates of unemployment, this would most likely have wider political consequences, including the way popular attitudes evolve towards the EU and the euro in particular. Love of Europe has always had a strong pecuniary dimension. Is the ECB (and its fledgling political counterpart) mature enough, for example, to handle a prolonged recession and/or a major readjustment upwards in the exchange rate between the euro and the dollar that could eliminate one of the few remaining factors making for economic growth in Europe? We may soon find out.

The global economic environment is, of course, not entirely something that European policy-makers can shape according to their wishes. Having just conceded the obvious, we may safely add that the eurozone (not to mention the sum of all EU economies) is big enough not to have to take the rest of the world as given. This assumes that member states act in a coordinated fashion, thus turning the EU into something more than the sum of its national parts. Macroeconomic management and the external dimension of EMU will therefore be crucial. They have not so far received their due amount of attention.

Many tools of economic policy are, of course, still in the hands of national governments. The big challenge for the near future will be whether they succeed, individually and collectively, in reconciling international competitiveness and internal structural reforms with the kind of politically stable and compassionate society that Western Europeans created in the aftermath of the Second World War. They need to handle with great care the problem of losers in times of rapid change and growing uncertainty. The new package should indeed include effective social safety nets and some of the means to enable people to adjust to the new economic environment. In trying to reform social and welfare policies, European countries will, however, continue facing an extremely difficult task as those with more secure jobs and/or accumulated generous pension rights ferociously resist change. In this respect, some countries will be more successful than others. There is both competition and solidarity in the European system.

Europe is crowded, rich, and ageing. It is mostly surrounded by countries with much poorer and younger populations, countries with high birth rates, weak political institutions, and uncertain economic prospects: an explosive combination indeed. The poor are at the gates. Some are already climbing over them. Immigration policy has become an integral part of foreign policy—and also enlargement policy. European governments, separately and (more so with time) jointly, continue to experience great difficulties in reconciling economic interests with social and political constraints; and immigration has unequal effects on their societies—there is no point in pretending otherwise. Some will be tempted to look for a scapegoat in Brussels, while there is no certainty at all that a common policy would also be effective in dealing with the problem. As the EU expands further to the east, an increasing number of those young and worse-off will be turned into privileged citizens of the Union, although after long transitional periods intended to placate the fears of those already in. Immigration will remain a hot political issue, and much will depend on how the economic situation develops.

The other big and largely unpredictable force for change may come from national political systems and European citizens in general. The permissive consensus for regional integration has weakened; nationalist forces, mostly on the right of the political spectrum, have grown in many European countries, while the democratic deficit of the Union has, if anything, become wider and more troublesome. European integration so far has not been successful in mobilizing citizens, except for a small, but still highly influential, minority. Up to the time of writing, this was confirmed in popular responses (or lack of them) to the workings of the Convention. In simple terms, the European integration project looks politically dull.

☆ A Political Europe

This book argues that European integration affects in many different ways the everyday lives of citizens of the old continent, from the big issues of money and security to the micro world of regulation. It has helped to make Europeans more open to ideas and cultures other than their local or national ones; it has helped to make them richer and, in some respects, also safer. Last but not least, it has helped to build a peaceful and democratic continent, with the exception of a few remaining trouble spots on the outer periphery of the Union. Regional integration has served Europeans well—some, of course, more than others. However, as memories of the distant and uglier past of Europe begin to fade, the Union comes up against new and difficult challenges.

It is extremely easy to develop gloomy scenarios for the future. Internal political gridlock, foreign policy impotence, economic weakness, and unfavourable demographics could gradually lead to irrelevance and the undoing of many of the achievements of the past. History teaches us that there is little, if anything, that can be safely considered irreversible in human affairs. True, European integration has already survived several tests of time, but there are new and difficult ones ahead. And there is, indeed, very much at stake.

Integration has been mostly the product of an elite conspiracy, with good intentions and pretty remarkable results. A small number of individuals have played a decisive role in it. But the elitist character of European integration also helps to explain the dearth of public debate on the broad issues related to European integration, except in those countries where sizeable minorities of Eurosceptics challenge the official truth. Admittedly, many issues dealt with by European institutions do not lend themselves to passionate public debate. Economic regulation, for example, is hardly the subject to mobilize citizens. The arcane language often used by professional Europeans does not help matters either. Even EMU did not generate much debate in the majority of member countries. Being the product of intergovernmental negotiations, it enjoyed consensual support from most mainstream political parties, which had also earlier endorsed the precepts of the new economic orthodoxy. More Europe was supposed to be good for the economy, and also for peace and security. And the minority who objected spoke mainly in terms of less Europe.

The elitist character of European integration has been rapidly reaching its limits. Although political leadership may continue to play an important role, especially on the big issues, the European project needs to become more democratic and hence more explicitly political. It also needs a new vision that is more meaningful to the younger generations of Europeans. The integration project often looks old and tired; and so do the large majority of those in charge of it. Of course, common institutions should become more transparent and accountable, while political parties and civil society strengthen their cooperation across national borders. For example, the indirect election of the head of the European executive (a direct election would arguably still be premature) would clearly help in the development of transnational political parties with common platforms on issues that can be no longer handled effectively within national boundaries. But it will not be sufficient by itself to mobilize European citizens, and most notably the young.

Different conceptions about the kind of Europe, and the kind of society, we want to live in are usually hidden behind the question of more or less integration.

Let us try to decode the political contents of some of the main items on the European agenda today. The reform of the Stability and Growth Pact as well as the new powers to be granted eventually to the Euro Group are about different perceptions of macroeconomic policy and the management of the new single currency, including sensitive trade-offs between stability and growth. Also lurking are different ideas about whether democracy should be let inside the sanctuary of money and finance. The reform of the CAP and the Structural Funds in the context of a more efficient and equitable EU budget is largely about the scale and nature of redistribution across boundaries as well as the new, poorer members' prospects for modernization. It is also, of course, about efficiency in the use of scarce resources. The protection of the environment cannot be confined within national boundaries, and there are difficult trade-offs associated with it.

Much of the discussion about taxation and social standards is about free riders and about what constitutes fair competition among different economic systems. As long as member states want to preserve a high degree of autonomy and diversity, they need to agree on rules governing cross-border exchange. The alternative would be to leave it entirely to the market, but this is hardly a politically innocent proposition. What it often boils down to is the extent to which voters or markets should be allowed to decide on the optimum level of regulation or taxation. Who said that democracy and markets always make a happy couple?

There are also important choices to be made with respect to enlargement and foreign policy. The admission of new members, for example, raises awkward questions about criteria for admission, which in turn spill over into existential questions about identity as well as the definition and mission of Europe. The dispatch of policemen, soldiers, and all kinds of advisers to the Balkans and elsewhere, carrying with them large bags of aid, is about the stabilization and reconstruction role that those more fortunate Europeans who crossed the Rubicon many years ago, leaving behind their baggage of chauvinism and intolerance, want to undertake in that troubled part of the continent, knowing full well that instability and crime easily cross frontiers.

Last but not least, the continued attempts at developing a common European policy on the Middle East conflict, poverty in Africa, or climate change stem from the belief (or illusion) that Europeans have some values and interests in common which sometimes may differ from those held by Americans and others. It is, of course, true that the transatlantic community remains extremely valuable and needs to be safeguarded against external threats or implosion. It is equally true, however, that the unilateralist arrogance, backed up by military might, that is so often exhibited by representatives of the new American right has broader implications for transatlantic relations.

Weak European institutions could just about handle an imperfect internal market, performing at best the regulatory function. They certainly could not manage a single currency, nor could they perform effectively the role of nation- and state- building in Europe's troubled neighbourhood or act as catalyst for political change and economic development in the young democracies to the east. Market fundamentalism often masquerades as the defence of sovereignty, while insularity prefers to speak the language of national autonomy. But, surely, this is not all. It would be unfair and misleading to try to reduce any kind of opposition to further concrete policies and measures for integration just to narrow-minded nationalism. Common policies are not desirable per se; they need to be justified in concrete terms and politically legitimized.

There are many different fault lines on the political map of Europe: between big and small countries, strong and weak states, advocates of integration and advocates of independence, rich and poor. Luckily, they overlap; otherwise, the divisions would have been more rigid. One of the arguments put forward in this book is that the nature of the European political system—predominantly intergovernmental—tends to put the emphasis on inter-country divisions at the expense of anything else; and this no longer adequately reflects the real effects of integration on a wide range of issues. Thus, political debate becomes distorted, and there is precious little of it on issues which can no longer be dealt with effectively at the national level. A more political Europe would increasingly recognize that there is at least one more fault line, cutting across the others, which bears close resemblance to the fault line found inside member countries: that between left and right, old and new. And this would change the terms of the debate.

But what if Europeans are not yet ready for democracy at the European level? What if they are not yet ready for federalism of one kind or another? For example, EMU could in the end prove to be a big mistake if politics cannot catch up with the integration of markets and economic policies. Suppose all this turns out to be true: is anybody prepared to calculate the costs of going back, in terms of the single currency or other major achievements of European integration? This is precisely where the political animal parts company with the ivory tower academic.

Trying to reconcile democracy with growing international interdependence is a problem that goes beyond the boundaries of Europe. It is, in fact, one of the key issues in the whole debate on globalization. The Europeans stand a much better chance of dealing effectively with this problem, given their long history of close cooperation founded mostly on common rules and institutions and the outright rejection of hegemonic power. Nowadays, the descendants of those who invented sovereignty and the nation-state are being called upon to devise new forms of supranational democracy in order to match the kind of policy integration already achieved. And they will need novel ideas, since there is not much around to copy or simply learn from. What is at stake is the solidity of the regional construction, and peace as well as democracy in Europe.

There are key democratic choices to be made about trade-offs between efficiency, equity, and stability; productivity and a cleaner environment; integration and diversity; rule by experts and elected representatives in the management of the internal market and the single currency; the degree and kind of solidarity across boundaries; the geographical limits of Europe's fledgling common identity; the export of peace and stability to the near abroad and beyond; and the defence of common values and interests in a world where the ascendancy of markets and the highly unequal distribution of political power increasingly challenge those features that still make Europe distinct from other regions of the world.

Europeans will surely not agree among themselves on the choices they make on these and many other issues. This is, after all, the essence of democracy. But they need to become more aware of those issues and the choices they imply. They need a European public space in which to debate what they want to do together and how. Choices will become starker in a more political Europe. We have long pretended that inter-country divisions were the only ones that really counted and that the choice was essentially between more or less Europe. It is time to move on, building on a politically mature Europe. 'What kind of Europe?' now becomes the key question.

Select Bibliography

Chapter 1. What Kind of Europe?

Writing on Europe, and European integration in particular, has been a popular pastime for authors from different academic disciplines and occupations, covering a very wide range from the general and abstract to the pedantic. The bibliographical references given below are therefore only an indicative list chosen from an extremely rich literature.

For a fascinating history of Europe, from the ice age to the cold war, see Norman Davies, *A History of Europe* (Oxford: Oxford University Press, 1996). For an extremely well-written study of the twentieth century, see Mark Mazower, *Dark Continent* (London: Allen Lane, 1998); and for a comprehensive history of ideas about Europe and European identity, see Anthony Pagden (ed.), *The Idea of Europe: From Antiquity to the European Union* (Cambridge: Cambridge University Press, 2002).

On federalism, the literature is rich in number but of highly uneven quality. One of the better works is Dusan Sidjanski, *The Federal Future of Europe: From the European Community to the European Union* (Ann Arbor: The University of Michigan Press, 2000).

There are many introductory books on European integration. Among the better ones are John Pinder, *The Building of the European Union*, 3rd edn (Oxford: Oxford University Press, 1998); and Desmond Dinan, *Ever Closer Union: An Introduction to European Integration* (Basingstoke: Macmillan, 1999). See also the special fortieth anniversary issue of the *Journal of Common Market Studies*, 40/4 (2002), one of the leading journals in the field.

Larry Siedentop, *Democracy in Europe* (London: Allen Lane, 2000) offers a fresh look by an outsider, arguing that the process of integration poses a serious threat to democracy in Europe. The reader may also want to consult the web site of the European Convention for the current debate on the future of Europe, although trying to separate the wheat from the chaff may prove to be an extremely time-consuming exercise: <http://www.european-convention.eu.int>.

Two French authors provide a tentative political answer to the question 'What kind of Europe?': see Pascal Lamy and Jean Pisani-Ferry, *The Europe We Want* (London: Arch Press, 2002).

Donald Puchala is the author of the highly perceptive article 'Of Blind Men, Elephants and International Integration', *Journal of Common Market Studies*, 10/3 (1972), which points out the difficulties and risks of going for the overall picture as opposed to narrow specialization. It could have served as a warning to the author of this book.

Chapter 2. The Gap Between Politics and Economics—Or, Perception and Reality

For a political economy study of European integration, see Loukas Tsoukalis, *The New European Economy Revisited* (Oxford: Oxford University Press, 1997). See also Jacques Pelkmans, *European Integration: Methods and Economic Analysis*, 2nd edn (Harlow: Pearson, 2001), and Wilhelm Molle, *The Economics of European Integration: Theory, Practice, Policy*, 4th edn (London: Ashgate, 2001).

For the earlier history, see Alan Milward, *The Reconstruction of Western Europe 1945–51* (London: Methuen, 1984), and Nicholas Craft and Gianni Toniolo (eds), *Economic Growth in Europe Since 1945* (Cambridge: Cambridge University Press, 1996).

Two comprehensive and highly informative books on the European political system and EU decision-making are Helen Wallace and William Wallace (eds), *Policy-Making in the European Union*, 4th edn (Oxford: Oxford University Press, 2000), and Simon Hix, *The Political System of the European Union* (Basingstoke: Macmillan, 1999). For a study of the effects of integration on national political systems, see Klaus Goetz and Simon Hix (eds), *Europeanised Politics? European Integration and National Political Systems* (London: Frank Cass, 2001), and Yves Mény, Pierre Muller, and Jean-Louis Quermonne (eds), *Adjusting to Europe: The Impact of the European Union on National Institutions and Policies* (London: Routledge, 1996).

For a sophisticated application of political theory to European integration, see Andrew Moravscik, *The Choice for Europe: Social Purpose and State Power from Messina to Maastricht* (Ithaca: Cornell University Press, 1998); and for a critical approach from a social democratic perspective, see Fritz Scharpf, *Governing in Europe: Effective and Democratic?* (Oxford: Oxford University Press, 1999). Joseph Weiler has written extensively on the link between law and politics in European integration; a collection of essays can be found in Joseph Weiler, *The Constitution of Europe* (Cambridge: Cambridge University Press, 1999).

The 'democratic deficit' of the EU has attracted a great deal of attention. Representative examples of works in this area are Jack Hayward (ed.), *The Crisis of Representation in Europe* (London: Frank Cass, 1995) and Andrew Moravscik (2002), 'In defence of the "Democratic Deficit": Reassessing Legitimacy in the European Union', *Journal of Common Market Studies*, 40/4 (2002). See also Siedentop, *Democracy in Europe*.

The reader may also consult the website on the findings of *Eurobarometer* surveys of public opinion: <http://europa.eu.int/comm/public_opinion/>.

Chapter 3. Winners and Losers . . .

A classic on the relationship between the state and the market in Europe is Karl Polanyi, *The Great Transformation* (Boston: Beacon Press, 1957). See also Andrew Shonfield, *Modern Capitalism* (Oxford: Oxford University Press, 1965). Some of the references mentioned above are also relevant here, such as Crafts and Toniolo,

Economic Growth in Europe Since 1945; Tsoukalis, *The New European Economy Revisited*; and Moravscik, *The Choice for Europe*.

For the *ex ante* study of the effects of the internal market, see Commission of the EC, 'The Economics of 1992', *European Economy*, No. 35 (March 1988); and for the popular version, Paolo Cecchini, *The European Challenge: 1992* (Aldershot: Wildhouse, 1988). For the *ex post* study, see European Commission, 'Economic Evaluation of the Single Market', *European Economy*, Reports and Studies No. 4 (Luxembourg: Office for Official Publications of the European Communities, 1996); and European Commission, *The Single Market Review* (London: Kogan Page, 1996).

For centre–periphery theories, see Dudley Seers and Constantine Vaitsos (eds), *Integration and Unequal Development: The Experience of the EEC* (New York: St Martin's Press, 1980). Two good examples of subsequent works on Europeanization and modernization effects on the periphery are José-Maria Maravall, *Regimes, Politics and Markets* (Oxford: Oxford University Press, 1997); and George Pagoulatos, *Greece's New Political Economy: State, Finance and Growth from Postwar to EMU* (Basingstoke: Palgrave, 2003).

On economic inequalities, the reader may consult Amartya Sen, *On Economic Inequality* (Oxford: Clarendon Press, 1997); Daniel Cohen, Thomas Piketty, and Gilles Saint-Paul, *The Economics of Rising Inequalities* (Oxford: Oxford University Press, 2002); Michael Forster and Mark Pearson, 'Income Distribution and Poverty in the OECD Area: Trends and Driving Forces', *OECD Economic Studies* (Paris: OECD, 2002).

For the distributional effects of EU policies, see Ronald Hall, Alasdair Smith, and Loukas Tsoukalis (eds), *Competitiveness and Cohesion in EU Policies* (Oxford: Oxford University Press, 2001). Among official EU publications, the reader may consult the first and second cohesion reports of the European Commission: European Commission, *First Report on Economic and Social Cohesion* (Luxembourg: Office for Official Publications of the European Communities, 1996); and European Commission, *Unity, Solidarity and Diversity for Europe, its People and its Territory—Second Report on Economic and Social Cohesion*, vols 1 and 2 (Luxembourg: Office for Official Publications of the European Communities, 2001); and the regular reports on *The Social Situation in the European Union*. A critical study of the effects of EU regional policies can be found in Michele Boldrin and Fabio Canova, 'Inequality and Convergence in Europe's Regions: Reconsidering European Regional Policies', *Economic Policy*, 16/32 (2001).

Chapter 4. . . . and the Rest of the World: Americans and Others

On the common commercial policy and external trade of the EU, see H. Paemen and A. Bensch, *From the GATT to the WTO: The European Community in the Uruguay Round* (Leuven: Leuven University Press, 1995); and I. Macleod, I. D. Hendry, and S. Hyett, *The External Relations of the European Communities* (Oxford: Clarendon Press, 1996).

A good introductory book to the new world trading system is Bernard Hoekman and Michel Kostecki, *The Political Economy of the World Trading System: The WTO and Beyond*, 2nd edn (Oxford: Oxford University Press, 2001). Financial services deserve separate study: see, for example, Geoffrey Underhill (ed.), *The New World Order in International Finance* (New York: St Martin's Press, 1997).

Relations with the privileged partners and the subject of regionalism are discussed in M. Lister, *The European Union and the South* (London: Routledge, 1997); Martin Holland, *The European Union and the Third World* (Basingstoke: Palgrave, 2002); and Richard Pomfret, *The Economics of Regional Trading Arrangements* (Oxford: Oxford University Press, 2001). On EU external aid, see the Commission annual reports in <http://europa.eu.int/comm/europeaid/reports/index_en.htm>

For an informative historical survey of the CFSP, see Anthony Forster and William Wallace, in Wallace and Wallace, *Policy-Making in the European Union*. For a critical approach, emphasizing the gap between expectations and capabilities, see Christopher Hill, 'The Capability–Expectations Gap, Or Conceptualising Europe's International Role', *Journal of Common Market Studies*, 31/3 (1993); and also Stanley Hoffmann, 'Towards a Common European Foreign and Security Policy?', *Journal of Common Market Studies*, 38/2 (2000). The transatlantic dimension of the CFSP is also dealt with below in Chapter 7.

For a collective work on the prospects of a European defence policy, see François Heisbourg *et al.*, *European Defence: Making It Work*, Chaillot Papers No.2 (Paris: Institute for Security Studies, 2000); and Gilles Andréani, Charles Bertram, and Charles Grant, *Europe's Military Revolution* (London: Centre for European Reform, 2001).

On recent developments in home and justice affairs, see Jörg Monar, 'The Dynamics of Justice and Home Affairs: Laboratories, Driving Factors and Costs', *Journal of Common Market Studies*, 39/4 (2001).

Robert Cooper was the first to refer to EU states as postmodern states; see Robert Cooper, *The Postmodern State and the World Order* (London: Demos and Foreign Policy Centre, 1996).

Chapter 5. Economic Governance and Policy Choices

For an interesting recent book on persisting different models of capitalism in Europe and their comparative advantages, see Peter Hall and David Soskice (eds), *Varieties of Capitalism* (Oxford: Oxford University Press, 2001); and Vivien Schmidt, *The Futures of European Capitalism* (Oxford: Oxford University Press, 2002). Michel Albert wrote a widely read book on the subject in 1991: *Capitalisme contre capitalisme* (Paris: Le Seuil, 1991); for the English translation, *Capitalism against Capitalism* (London: Whurr, 1993). For the old classics, see Polanyi, *The Great Transformation* and Shonfield, *Modern Capitalism*.

One of the best books on European regulation has been written by Giandomenico Majone, *Regulating Europe* (London: Routledge, 1996). The Centre for Economic Policy Research, *Making Sense of Subsidiarity: How Much Centralization for Europe?* (London: CEPR, 1993) remains one of the most enlightening works on the subject, seen from an economic perspective.

For a rather agnostic conclusion on the effects of the internal market, see Paul Geroski and Klaus Peter Gugler, *Corporate Growth Convergence in Europe*, CEPR Discussion Paper 2838 (London: CEPR, June 2001). The European Commission publishes a regular scoreboard concerning the implementation of internal market measures by member countries. See <http://europa.eu.int/comm/internal_market/en/update/score>

Gallons of ink have been spilled on the reform of the CAP, so far with limited effect. Among the better examples, going in the direction of a rural policy, is the article by Louis Pascal Mahé and François Ortalo-Magné, 'Five Proposals for a European Model of the Countryside', *Economic Policy*, April, 28 (1999); and, for the longer version, *Politique Agricole: Un Modèle Européen* (Paris: Presses de Sciences Po, 2001). See also Elmar Rieger in Wallace and Wallace, *Policy-Making in the European Union.*

Michelle Cini and Lee McGowan, *Competition Policy in the European Union* (Basingstoke: Macmillan, 1998) is a general introductory book on the subject. For a more specialized study of the application of merger legislation, see Edurne Navarro and Andres Font, *Merger Control in the EU* (Oxford: Oxford University Press, 2002).

On financial services, the reader may consult Geoffrey Underhill, *The New World Order in International Finance* for broad and mostly critical coverage of the main issues. In a similar vein, and written in a more provocative style, see Susan Strange, *Mad Money* (Manchester: Manchester University Press, 1998). The annual reports of the Bank for International Settlements (BIS) contain rich information and analysis of the main developments in the international financial system; an official view, although hardly complacent <http://www.bis.org>. The very interesting 2001 report of the Group of Ten, *Report on Consolidation in the Financial Sector*, can be found on the same site. For developments in the EU, one may consult <http://europa.eu.int/comm/internal_market/en/ finances/actionplan/>

Gøsta Esping-Andersen, *Three Worlds of Welfare Capitalism* (Princeton: Princeton University Press, 1990), has written the standard book on different models of welfare state in Europe. For more recent works on the challenges of reform, see also Martin Rhodes and Yves Mény (eds), *The Future of European Welfare: A New Social Contract?* (London: Macmillan, 1998); G. Bertola, T. Boeri, and G. Nicoletti (eds), *Welfare and Employment in a United Europe* (Cambridge: MIT Press, 2001); and Gøsta Esping-Andersen *et al., Why We Need a New Welfare State* (Oxford: Oxford University Press, 2002). A recent work on immigration in Europe is Tito Boeri, Gordon Hanson, and Barry McCormick, *Immigration Policy and the Welfare System* (Oxford: Oxford University Press, 2002).

On tax harmonization, see Ruding Committee, *Report of the Committee of Independent Experts on Company Taxation* (Brussels: European Commission, 1992); and Sijbren Cnossen (ed.), *Taxing Capital in the European Union: Issues and Options for Reform* (Oxford: Oxford University Press, 2000). Clear and informative accounts of the EU budgetary process and the operation of Structural Funds can be found in the chapters by Brigid Laffan and Michael Shackleton, and David Allen respectively in the book edited by Wallace and Wallace, *Policy-Making in the European Union.*

Chapter 6. EMU: A Unifying Factor

There is a rich and rapidly growing literature on EMU with contributions from both academics and practitioners. EMU offers a real-world laboratory for economists and other social scientists to test their theories, and many of them have risen to the challenge. As the big day approached, there was growing recognition of the fact that that this was no mere economic project for which traditional economic theories would suffice. This has been reflected in the more recent literature on the subject.

For the history of European monetary integration, see Loukas Tsoukalis, *The Politics and Economics of European Monetary Integration* (London: Allen & Unwin, 1977); Peter Ludlow, *The Making of the European Monetary System* (London: Butterworths, 1982); Tommaso Padoa-Schioppa, *The Road to Monetary Union: The Emperor, the Kings, and the Genies* (Oxford: Clarendon Press, 1994); and Kenneth Dyson and Kevin Featherstone, *The Road to Maastricht* (Oxford: Oxford University Press, 1999).

For a comprehensive study of the economics of EMU, see Paul de Grauwe, *Economics of Monetary Union*, 4th edn (Oxford: Oxford University Press, 2000). See also Daniel Gros and Niels Thygesen, *European Monetary Integration*, 2nd edn (Oxford: Oxford University Press, 1998); and the special issue of the *Oxford Review of Economic Policy*, 14/3 (1998), especially the articles by Christopher Allsopp and David Vines, and Barry Eichengreen.

For an in-depth political economy approach to EMU, the reader may consult Kenneth Dyson, *Elusive Union: The Process of Economic and Monetary Union in Europe* (Oxford: Oxford University Press, 2000); also Jeffry Frieden, Daniel Gros, and Erik Jones (eds), *The New Political Economy of EMU* (Oxford: Rowman & Littlefield, 1998); Kenneth Dyson (ed.), *European States and the Euro: Europeanization, Variation, and Convergence* (Oxford: Oxford University Press, 2002); and the book edited by Colin Crouch, *After the Euro* (Oxford: Oxford University Press, 2000), especially the article by Robert Boyer.

For a catastrophe theory of EMU, see Martin Feldstein, 'EMU and International Conflict', *Foreign Affairs*, 76/4 (1997); on the legitimacy issue, Dermot Hodson and Imelda Maher, 'Economic and Monetary Union: Balancing Credibility and Legitimacy in an Asymmetric Policy-Mix', *Journal of European Public Policy*, 8/3 (2002); and, on policy coordination, Iain Begg (ed.), *Europe: Government and Money* (London: The Federal Trust, 2002).

Two representative works with a critical approach and proposals for reform are: Paul De Grauwe, 'Challenges for Monetary Policy in the Euroland', *Journal of Common Market Studies*, 40/4 (2002); and Jean-Paul Fitoussi and Jérôme Creel, *How to Reform the European Central Bank* (London: Centre for European Reform, 2002). See also *Monitoring the European Central Bank*, a series published by the Centre for Economic Policy Reform (London). Closer to the official view from the ECB is Otmar Issing *et al.*, *Monetary Policy in the Euro Area* (Cambridge: Cambridge University Press, 2001).

The effects on banking are examined in Edward Gardener, Philip Molyneux, and Barry Moore (eds), *Banking in the New Europe: The Impact of the Single European Market Programme and EMU on the Banking Sector* (Basingstoke: Palgrave, 2002).

228

Thomas Friedman has introduced the idea of the 'Golden Straitjacket' in *The Lexus and the Olive Tree* (London: Harper Collins, 2000).

Chapter 7. Extending *Pax Europea*

The subject of further enlargement has been directly linked to the general debate about the future of Europe, since it touches on literally every aspect of European integration. Thus, many of the bibliographical references mentioned above also deal with different aspects of enlargement. The annual reports of the Commission on the whole process, as well as on each candidate country, contain useful material: see <http://europa.eu.int/comm/enlargement/report2002>

For a clear overview of eastern enlargement and the problems raised by it, see Alan Mayhew, *Recreating Europe: The European Union's Policy towards Central and Eastern Europe* (Cambridge: Cambridge University Press, 1998); and Peter Mair and Jan Zielonka (eds), *The Enlarged European Union: Diversity and Adaptation* (London: Frank Cass, 2002).

On transition economies, there is a good though somewhat dated book: Daniel Gros and Alfred Steinherr, *Winds of Change: Economic Transition in Central and Eastern Europe* (Harlow: Longman, 1995). See also the annual reports of the European Bank for Reconstruction and Development (EBRD) <http://www.ebrd.org/pubs/index/htm> as well as the World Bank reports <http://www.worldbank.org>, including most notably, World Bank, *Transition: The First Ten Years* (Washington, DC: World Bank, 2002). A good case study of the communist legacy in transition countries can be found in Abby Innes, *Czechoslovakia: The Short Goodbye* (New Haven and London: Yale University Press, 2001).

Mark Mazower has written a very good short history of *The Balkans* (London: Weidenfeld & Nicholson, 2000). See also Misha Glenny, *The Balkans 1804–1999: Nationalism, War and the Great Powers* (London: Granta, 1999). On the role of the EU in the region and the prospects for membership, see Wim van Meurs and Alexandros Yannis, *The European Union and the Balkans: From Stabilisation Process to Southeastern Enlargement*, Hellenic Foundation for European and Foreign Policy/Centrum für angewandte Politikforschung (Gütersloh: Bertelsmann Foundation, 2002). See also the excellent article by Ivan Krastev on the absolute despair of electorates in Balkan countries: 'The Balkans: Democracy Without Choices', *Journal of Democracy*, 13/3 (2002).

A recent book on Turkey is Brian Beeley (ed.), *Turkish Transformation* (London: Eothen, 2002). See also Heinz Kramer, *A Changing Turkey: The Challenge to Europe and the United States* (Washington, DC: Brookings Institution Press, 2000).

On the Cyprus problem and EU accession, see Michael Emerson and Nathalie Tocci, *Cyprus as Lighthouse of the East Mediterranean: Shaping Reunification and EU Accession Together* (Brussels, CEPS, 2002); and Thomas Diez (ed.), *The European Union and the Cyprus Conflict* (Manchester: Manchester University Press, 2002).

229

SELECT BIBLIOGRAPHY

On EU-Russia relations, see Dmitriy Danilov and Stephan De Spiegeleire, *From Decoupling to Recoupling: A New Security Relationship Between Russia and Western Europe?*, Chaillot Papers No. 31 (Paris: Institute for Security Studies, 1998); and Michael Emerson *et al., The Elephant and the Bear: European Union, Russia and their Near Abroads*, CEPS Working Paper (Brussels: CEPS, 2001). The effects of enlargement on the Union's near abroad to the east are discussed in Stephen White, Ian McAllister, and Margot Light, 'Enlargement and the New Outsiders', *Journal of Common Market Studies*, 40/1 (2002).

The link between globalization and European integration has been discussed extensively. Some of the better works on the subject include: Henryk Kierzkowski (ed.), *Europe and Globalization* (Basingstoke: Palgrave, 2002); and François Bourguignon *et al., Making Sense of Globalization*, CEPR Policy Paper No.8 (London: CEPR, 2002). For a critical approach to globalization from a historical perspective, see Harold James, *The End of Globalization: Lessons from the Great Depression* (Cambridge: Harvard University Press, 2001); also Joseph Stiglitz and Pierre-Alain Muet (eds), *Governance, Equity, and Global Markets* (Oxford: Oxford University Press, 2001); and for fundamental differences between US and European perspectives, see Stanley Hoffmann, 'Clash of Globalizations', *Foreign Affairs*, 81/4 (2002).

After the arrival of George Bush Jr to power, and even more so after the events of 11 September 2001, much has been written on the growing divergence between US and European policies and the reasons for it, the use of 'hard' and 'soft' power in today's world, and the unilateral tendencies of the strong in contrast to the internationalism of the weak. Some of the more interesting studies are: Joseph Nye Jr, *The Paradox of American Power* (Oxford: Oxford University Press, 2002); David Calleo, *Rethinking Europe's Future* (Princeton: The Century Foundation, 2001); and, a very different approach, Henry Kissinger, *Does America Need a Foreign Policy?* (New York: Simon & Schuster, 2001). Two short and cogently argued pieces of work are: Robert Kagan, 'Power and Weakness', *Policy Review*, No.113 (2002); and Pierre Hassner, *The United States: The Empire of Force or the Force of the Empire?*, Chaillot Papers No. 54 (Paris: Institute for Security Studies, 2002).

Chapter 8. What Is At Stake?

There have been several attempts to develop scenarios for the future development of the enlarged EU, usually with an element of voluntarism included. For a piece of official wisdom, one may consult European Commission, *Scenarios Europe 2010: Five Possible Futures for Europe* (Brussels: European Commission, Forward Studies Unit, 1999). For a short and cogently argued piece, see Charles Grant, *EU 2010: An Optimistic Vision of the Future* (London: Centre for European Reform, 2000).

The ongoing debate on the future of Europe can be followed on the web site of the European Convention <http://www.european-convention.eu.int>. The web sites of the rotating presidencies of the Council usually also contain interesting information. On issues of governance and democracy in the EU, see also European Commission, *Enhancing Democracy: A White Paper on Governance in the European Union* (Brussels: European Commission, 2001).

On the continuing relevance or otherwise of the left–right division in contemporary European politics, a very good book is by Norberto Bobbio, *Left and Right*, translated from Italian (Cambridge: Polity Press, 1996). See also Anthony Giddens, *The Third Way: The Renewal of Social Democracy* (Cambridge: Polity Press, 1998). On left versus right and EU politics, the reader may also consult the website <http://www.eustudies.org/LeftRightForum.htm> for an interesting ongoing debate among academics.

Siedentop, *Democracy in Europe*, has developed the argument that Europe is not yet ready for federalism, although this may be the right goal. For a more constructive approach, emphasizing the need for strengthening of the popular pillar of European democracy, see Yves Mény, '*De la démocratie en Europe*: Old Concepts and New Challenges', *Journal of Common Market Studies*, 41/1 (2003).

Figures and Table

Figures

Table

Abbreviations

ACP	African, Caribbean, and Pacific countries
CAP	common agricultural policy
CFSP	common foreign and security policy
CIS	Commonwealth of Independent States
DM	Deutschmark
EC	European Community
ECB	European Central Bank
ECJ	European Court of Justice
ECOFIN	Council of Economics and Finance Ministers
ECSC	European Coal and Steel Community
EEA	European Economic Area
EEC	European Economic Community
EFTA	European Free Trade Area
EIB	European Investment Bank
ELDR	European Liberal, Democrat, and Reform Party
EMS	European Monetary System
EMU	Economic and Monetary Union
EP	European Parliament
EPP-ED	European People's Party and European Democrats
ERDF	European Regional Development Fund
ERM	Exchange Rate Mechanism
ESC	Economic and Social Committee
ESDP	European security and defence policy
ESF	European Social Fund
EU	European Union
Euratom	European Atomic Energy Community
Europol	European Police Office
FDI	foreign direct investment
GATT	General Agreement on Tariffs and Trade
IMF	International Monetary Fund
MEP	Member of the European Parliament
NAFTA	North American Free Trade Agreement
NATO	North Atlantic Treaty Organization

NTB   non-tariff barrier
OECD   Organization for Economic Cooperation and Development
OEEC   Organization for European Economic Cooperation
PES   Party of European Socialists
PPS   purchasing power standards
QMV   qualified majority voting
SEA   Single European Act
VAT   value added tax
WEU   Western European Union
WTO   World Trade Organization

Index